Natalie Kertes Weaver's *Christian Thought and Practice*, revised edition, is the best introductory textbook of Christian theology that meets the needs of today's diverse theological classroom. Weaver provides depth for students who have previous personal familiarity with Christian thought and life, while providing numerous pathways to support students for whom Christianity, or religion in general, is new territory. It meets the needs of "cradle Catholics" and religious "nones" alike. The revised edition's streamlined chapters and thorough glossary further increase its value for a theology classroom in which nothing can be assumed except the diversity of our students' questions. Weaver's primer gives students the signposts they need to begin their intellectual journeys and gives professors a roadmap to help a classroom of unique seekers explore Christianity together.

—Brian Flanagan, Marymount University
Arlington, VA

From the Bible to bioethics, in *Christian Thought and Practice*, Natalie Kertes Weaver offers an engaging tour of discovery through the historical highlights, key debates, and current issues of Christian theology. This is an inclusive, accessible text written by a teacher who knows her students!

—Edward P. Hahnenberg, PhD
Author of *Theology for Ministry* and other titles

In *Christian Thought and Practice*, Natalie Kertes Weaver provides undergraduate students with an excellent introduction to Christian theology and ecclesial life. It is ecumenically sensitive and pedagogically astute. It is concise but comprehensive. It strikes a fine balance between the descriptive and the normative styles. The questions for reflection at the end of each chapter, the tables, glossary, and other helps for the student make this book very student friendly. Only a master teacher could pack so much into such a small volume! As a professor who is always seeking but rarely finding the perfect introductory theology textbook, reading *Christian Thought and Practice* gave me a "eureka" ("I found it!") sensation. I recommend Weaver's book highly.

—Ron Highfield, Professor of Religion, Pepperdine University

This clear and comprehensive "primer" is an ideal text for an "Introduction to Christianity" course. But it is far more than that. In *Christian Thought and Practice*, Natalie Kertes Weaver provides a readable guide to anyone seeking a balanced description of the history, beliefs, and practices of Christianity. Written by an accomplished teacher, it presumes no background knowledge on the part of the reader, but only a willingness to understand how Christianity today came to be what it is—in all its diversity. A remarkable achievement.

—Terrence W. Tilley, Fordham University

Author Acknowledgments

Teaching and writing about Christian theology is a magnificent challenge and opportunity. I am profoundly grateful to have many and varied conversation partners who help to advance my own understanding of the Christian faith tradition. I am particularly thankful for the authors referred to in the resource sections of this book, whose excellence and scholarship have contributed so much to my own thinking and teaching. Their models and insights have been invaluable in the development of this book. Even more, my personal experience as a Catholic Christian, educator, and writer is bolstered and enhanced by the rich dialogue I am privileged to share with my colleagues and students at Ursuline College. I would also like to offer a special word of recognition for this book's outstanding development and copyeditor, Paul Peterson. Paul contributed both his keen editorial skills to this project as well as generous insight on content and image selection. Paul was a true collaborator and facilitator for this project, for whom I have the deepest gratitude.

Publisher Acknowledgments

Thank you to the following individuals who reviewed this work in progress:

John Allard, *Providence College, Providence, Rhode Island*

Brian P. Flanagan, *Marymount University, Arlington, Virginia*

Patrick Flanagan, *St. John's University, Queens, New York*

Joseph Kelly, *John Carroll University, University Heights, Ohio*

Matthew A. Shadle, *Loras College, Dubuque, Iowa*

Christian Thought and Practice

A PRIMER, REVISED EDITION

NATALIE KERTES WEAVER

Created by the publishing team of Anselm Academic.

Cover image: Galleria degli Uffizi, Florence, Italy / Bridgeman Images

Printed in the United States of America

7069

ISBN 978-1-59982-712-4

DEDICATION

In memory of William Michael Weaver, PhD
You were a marvel, and I miss you.

Contents

Author's Introduction to Teachers and Students

Thank you for choosing *Christian Thought and Practice: A Primer, Revised Edition* for your introduction to Christian theology. I would like to share a few words about why I wrote this book and how I think it can serve the college classroom and reader.

As a teacher, I have encountered many students over the past ten years who are undertaking the study of Christian thought for the first time. I have used many different books, some of which are excellent and are referenced in this book as suggested supplemental reading. With so many good resources out there, one might ask why we need another introduction to Christian thought. My answer derives from my teaching experience.

Today's classrooms are populated with a diverse student body. In my own classes, I find students of all ages, ethnicities, abilities, and aptitudes, as well as a range of religious backgrounds and beliefs. Although I am Roman Catholic and teach at a Catholic institution, my students include Catholic, Orthodox, and Protestant Christians, as well as Muslims, Buddhists, Hindus, and adherents of other non-Christian religions. I also frequently encounter students with little or no religious background, as well as students who participate in a religious tradition but have had little opportunity to study their religion formally or academically. Some students are taking theology classes because they have a genuine interest in the subject, while others are simply fulfilling an academic requirement. I have many local students from Cleveland, Ohio, as well as students from South America, Africa, Canada, and Europe. I have military veterans, industry workers looking for career changes, parents both single and married, senior citizens taking classes as lifelong learners, Catholic sisters, religious studies majors and majors from other academic disciplines, student athletes, first generation as well as legacy college students, transfer students who are just becoming acclimated to a new institution, and native students finishing out their college careers. Some students have had twelve years of Catholic education and are concerned that a theology course will be just another catechism class like the ones they had in high school. Other students are worried because they have never taken a religious studies class before. Still others are worried because they are not Christian or Catholic or religious at all. Students also have varied facility with social media, technology in the classroom, and web-based research skills.

With so many diverse backgrounds and interests in the classroom, teachers and students face multiple challenges. Teachers need to facilitate inclusive discussions and choose proper materials that avoid assumptions about what students might think or how they might have been previously taught. Students need resources that are accessible, engaging, and informative. Teachers need to attempt to level the classroom through the cultivation of a working vocabulary of terms and ideas, so students of all backgrounds can proceed together in their work and conversation as a class. Students need texts that provide foundational tools as well as sophisticated and interesting concepts for investigation and discussion. Teachers and students must ultimately collaborate to achieve maximal learning outcomes, knowing that many students will not choose professional specializations in Christian theology or religious studies.

In teaching Christian theology, I have struggled to find materials that speak to my diverse students at an introductory level with sufficient breadth. Often books that claim to be introductions simply exceed in scope or depth the register of nonspecialist readers. This book, by contrast, was developed as a genuine introduction for all readers interested in Christian thought, whether Christian or non-Christian. It presupposes no theological background, so it is appropriate even for those who have had no prior study of Christian thought or religion. Although this book presents a thorough and broad architecture of Christian thought and practice, it does not inundate the reader with references, historical case studies, or tangential discussions. Moreover, this book endeavors to be ecumenical in tone and friendly to a broad range of Christian communions as well as other, non-Christian groups.

The reader will find in this book an orderly discussion of topics, beginning in chapter 1 with an introduction to the term *theology* and a survey of ideas that will surface in any theological investigation.

Building on the first chapter, chapters 2 and 3 then explore the classical foundations of Christian theology, equipping readers with basic information about Christian uses of the Bible, tradition, reason, and experience. Because these foundations of Christian theology are always encountered contextually, chapter 4 turns to a discussion of key periods in Christian history. Following an established sensitivity to historical context, chapter 5 discusses mainline Christian doctrines. Recognizing that doctrine may vary among Christians of different creeds, chapter 6 explores the history, variety, and differences among major Christian worship communities. Chapters 7, 8, and 9 deal topically with Christian worship and practice, Christian relationships with non-Christian religions, and Christian relationships with secular society. These chapters aim at understanding Christian belief and practice in the world at varying levels of interaction with Christians, other religions, and civil society at large. Chapter 10, on contemporary spirituality and Christian thought, deals with issues involving popular culture, diversity, environmental issues, and liberation movements. Finally, chapter 11, on global Christianity, discusses Christian missions, colonialism and postcolonialism, and Christianity in various parts of the world. The chapters may be read sequentially, individually, or in whatever order best complements the reader's needs. Each chapter concludes with discussion questions and references for additional reading and research. There is also a glossary to help readers with unfamiliar vocabulary.

I hope this book will prove useful in a number of ways. For example, this book may be used as the following:

- The principal textbook for a course on Christian thought. In a traditional 15-week course, students will benefit from reading a chapter or two from this text every other week, interspersed by reading primary source materials and exemplars for each of the chapter's themes.
- One among several principal textbooks to provide content on Christian thought in a comparative religions course
- A leveling tool, a refresher, or a reference guide in intermediate or advanced theology courses, where knowledge of basic Christian terms, beliefs, practices, varieties, and historical periods are presupposed

- A complement to any advanced study of Christian history, the Bible, ethics, ecclesiology, or philosophy

The study of Christian thought and practice is as important today as ever. For the past two millennia, Christian thinkers have contributed to the political, legal, economic, philosophical, architectural, musical, visual, and literary dimensions of Western culture. Such contributions continue today as Christian people participate in policy, advocacy, education, healthcare, and more within an ever-broadening world context. Christian thought underlies many broadly held assumptions and norms, and dialogues with questions of religious pluralism, religious conflict, politics, public policy, medical ethics, legal practice, social sciences, natural history, physics, astronomy, and more. Christianity continues to inform the faith of more than two billion people worldwide. Readers will find a solid foundational understanding of Christian thought and practice beneficial for any line of work and any discipline of study.

First Things First
Beginning Christian Theology

What to Expect

This chapter introduces theology by discussing the following key areas:

- Terms Used in the Study of Religion
- A Functional Understanding of Christian Theology
- Facets of Christian Theology
- Types of Theology
- Audiences and Practitioners of Christian Thought

Terms Used in the Study of Religion

The study of religions may be approached from a number of perspectives. As one of the world's many religions, Christianity may also be studied from many points of view. Sociologists could study Christian practice and belief as sociological phenomena. Historians could study Christianity's multimillennial development from its place of origin to its present-day expressions throughout the world. Those working in literature or the visual arts could study Christian expression, development, and practice by investigating how Christians present their beliefs in text, story, and image. All these different approaches are useful and ultimately necessary to understand any religious tradition in the fullness of its breadth and depth.

Some approaches to the study of religion take religious beliefs as the starting point. That is, they accept the teachings of a religious system as true and valid foundations for one's worldview. One could call these approaches "confessional" because here religious beliefs are assumed. Other approaches to the study of religion may be comparative, as when one places two or more traditions in dialogue with one another and searches for similarities and differences in their rituals, holidays, ideas, and so on. Yet other approaches to the study of religion may directly challenge religious belief systems with questions of philosophical and scientific plausibility, viability, and accuracy. Such approaches might be called secular or skeptical.

It is helpful to clarify some basic terms before we begin this study of Christian thought and belief: *religion, belief, faith,* and *spirituality.*

Religion refers to the collective values, experiences, practices, and beliefs of a community. Such things may be precisely articulated and defined, for example, in books of sacred writings, in ritualized behaviors, and in organizational institutions that train ministers and perform functions such as worship services, wedding ceremonies, social outreach initiatives, funerals, and so on. Collective values, experiences, practices, and beliefs, however, may be much more loosely defined. In fact, they may seem more like operating philosophies or worldviews, as is the case with many traditions of indigenous peoples, such as Native Americans, who make no distinction between the sacred and the mundane. To some extent, "religion" is a scholarly construction, but such a construction is helpful when we try to define and understand what a community thinks and believes. Common features of religions include: sacred or holy books; special places of worship; ritual behaviors that mark seasons; celebration of historical or mythical events, and momentous passages in the human life cycle; myths of origin and destiny; experiences of divine revelation; special musical or performative behaviors and traditions; and a special class of leaders such as clergy, shamans, or priests. Religions may have some, all, or other features than those noted here.

Belief denotes a mindset that something is true, especially something that can neither be confirmed nor proven false. People may believe many things that have no overt connection to religion. For example, I may believe that someone took something from my gym locker or that I set my keys on the nightstand; these are beliefs precisely because (let's assume) I cannot confirm whether I am right or not. Religious beliefs are similar in that they are the statements, events, or revelations that people of a religious community hold to be true. A commonly held set of beliefs is one of the defining characteristics of a religious community. Religions sometimes formalize their beliefs in written documents, such as creeds, or through recited formulas and prayers.

Faith refers to a person's attitude or disposition toward a set of beliefs. If I am open to, accepting of, or committed to a belief or worldview, then I have faith in it. In common parlance, a faithful person is someone who is trusted, loyal, and steadfast. In a religious sense, a faithful person is loyal and steadfast to the tradition's belief that she or he holds true. Similarly, a whole body of believers may collectively be referred to as "the faithful." Sometimes "faith" is also used to refer to the total set of beliefs that a religion holds to be true, such as in the phrase "the Catholic faith."

Spirituality is a term that people often contrast with religion, as in the phrase, "I am spiritual but not religious." In this sense, people are describing an individualized, subjective, or independent sense of inspiration, or connection to the natural world, or awareness of holiness or divinity. However, spirituality is also part of religions, many of which teach unique theories and practices for prayer, meditation, attaining special insight, and practices meant to facilitate intimate communion with God. One aspect of the study of religion is the exploration of its spiritual traditions, which, while related, may be unique from its beliefs, ritual practices, and so on.

A Functional Understanding of Christian Theology

A simple definition of *Christian theology* might be "the systematic study of Christian beliefs." Other definitions might begin with *theology*'s Greek origin: *theologia* means "God-talk," so theology may be thought of as "talk about God." One example of such God-talk is the following biblical description of how and why one ought to relate to

God: "Fear of the LORD is the beginning of knowledge" (Proverbs 1:7). Saint Anselm in the eleventh century classically defined theology as "*fides quaerens intellectum,*" usually translated as "faith seeking understanding." Anselm's definition suggests that theological study is inherently confessional because it assumes Christian beliefs to be valid foundations for one's worldview even while it hopes to understand and make sense of those truths.

In order to understand the function of theology—to comprehend what theology does—an analogy is helpful. A student in my class reported that she had had a bad car accident, which she survived with only a bloody nose. She said, "I am not a very religious person, but I could have died in that accident. The fact that I survived uninjured made me think there is a God. I have been much more religious ever since." This student was theologizing about her accident as she grappled with the meaning it held for her life. She reevaluated her priorities in light of the belief that God had a purpose for her.

Many of us have had similar dramatic moments that subsequently reshaped our sense of meaning and purpose. Groups as well as individuals respond to such experiences in this way. Sometimes, when a whole community has a shared experience of great import, they take that experience as evidence of a divine hand at work in their lives. One sees this phenomenon in the literature that Christians hold sacred, namely the Bible (also called *sacred scripture*). For example, the New Testament reports that followers of Jesus experienced appearances of Christ after his death. Though it is difficult from a historical point of view to say exactly what their experience entailed, the New Testament confirms that these followers believed they had experienced post-Resurrection appearances of Jesus. Their common belief in the Risen Christ became the foundation of their shared identity as a community.

Stories about a people's defining experiences are powerful; witness, for example, the continuing effect of stories of the American Revolution and the civil rights movement for American children today. When such stories have a theological meaning, they often become the core of religion, underlying a religion's sacred rituals, books, calendars, holidays, and prayers. For Christians, the story of Jesus of Nazareth—a first-century Galilean Jew executed under the rule of the Roman governor Pontius Pilate—became the core of their religious beliefs. The story of Jesus, first shared orally, later became the subject of the New Testament of the Bible and the glue that held together an array of culturally, religiously, linguistically, and ethnically diverse people of the first-century Roman Empire.

At the beginning of the Christian era, there were no Christian church buildings or administrative offices, there was not yet a Bible,[1] and there was no formal system of beliefs about who Jesus was or why his life was so important. At the time, believers had only an experience that transformed their notion of life's purpose and meaning, coupled with faith that Jesus was responsible for that transformation.

Theologians in the beginning centuries of Christian history (often called the patristic era) interpreted this experience of transformation and articulated its meaning. An early function of Christian theology

The earliest known representation of Jesus is this fresco from the Dura-Europos church in Syria depicting Jesus healing a paralytic (see Mark 2:1–12); it dates to roughly two hundred years after his death. No reliable record of Jesus' appearance exists.

was to develop clear statements of faith, called *creeds* (derived from the Latin word *credo*, meaning "I believe"), and to begin to define basic Christian doctrine. These early theologians had to look to the foundations, which were the developing books of the Bible, the experiences of the community, their own reasoning and logic, and the emerging tradition. As they sorted through these materials, they developed in councils (or church meetings) creeds that stated what Christians actually believed. Over time the work of these theologians

---

1. Jesus' first followers, who were Jews, accepted the Hebrew Bible as sacred scripture, but the distinctively Christian writings that would become the New Testament took several generations after Jesus' death to produce.

became part of the tradition of faith, which later generations would consider foundations to be interpreted and evaluated in light of their own contemporary experience.

Theology is always situated in a particular historical and geographical context. Different questions and challenges engage the community of believers in every era. As a result, theologians are continually challenged to make sense of the faith anew. Influential twentieth-century theologians have thus suggested that theology is best understood by its function as a mediator or interpreter between tradition and culture. Theology serves as the translator and interpreter of the sources of the tradition (such as the Bible or works of earlier theologians) for the broader public, ensuring that the faith is accountable and meaningful to people's present-day experience. By way of example, theologians today must address a range of bioethical issues related to new reproductive technologies that did not exist even twenty years ago. As another example, theologians who investigate "church" as an area of study are tasked with considering whether, how, or to what degree online forums may legitimately constitute church communities.

Facets of Christian Theology

If the function of theology is to interpret or mediate between the tradition and its present-day context, then one must ask what aspects of the tradition theology interprets. Christian thought deals with a range of concerns, spanning the general, fundamental, universal questions of human purpose and meaning (Why am I here? Does life have a purpose? What happens to me when I die?) to the particular questions that arise specifically out of Christian history (Who is Jesus? What is his relationship to God? How should the Church be structured?). Theology attempts to interpret, study, and integrate systematically the sources of Christian thought and belief both with the questions that arise generally out of the human condition and specifically about the human condition as it is lived in light of Christian revelation. As such, Christian thinkers (especially those who work as professional theologians, teachers, and ministers) will explore many facets of Christian belief, which may be likened to the many surfaces of a cut diamond reflecting light in different directions. Christian thought then represents the continuous historical effort (1) to understand and make internal sense of the sources of Christian tradition while (2) understanding and applying those sources meaningfully to ongoing human situations. Specialized subdivisions of theology address Christian source material as well as its applications to living communities.

Christian Sources

In the Christian belief system, there are four traditional sources for Christian thought: the Bible, tradition, reason, and experience.

The *Bible* refers to the writings that Christians believe are holy and inspired by God. The idea that God reveals Godself is called revelation. Most Christians believe that God reveals Godself throughout the books of the Bible, but their understanding of how the Bible constitutes revelation can vary. Possible meanings include the literal word of God, the unfolding of God's actions in history, personal insight or inspiration, and the record of God's direct self-disclosure. Those who study the Bible attempt to understand many things about it, including what the text actually says, how to understand the claim that it is God's revelation, how Christians should best interpret the Bible, and how it should direct the lives of Christians today.

Tradition refers to the collected writings, practices, artifacts, and wisdom that have been handed down by Christians from one era to the next since the time of the Bible. The Bible itself may be thought of as part of the tradition. Some people will distinguish between *T*radition and *t*radition, with the former referring to official or authoritative components that all or most hold to be binding or true (such as the belief that Jesus was the Son of God) and the latter referring to local or temporary components that are not shared by all (such as eating lamb on Easter). While all Christian denominations have their traditions, some denominations (e.g., Baptists and Pentecostals) are reluctant to assign to tradition any formal role in theology. For those denominations that do formally recognize some elements of tradition as a source of theology (e.g., the Roman Catholic Church), these major elements of Christian tradition include doctrines and church teachings.

Doctrines refer to the specific Christian beliefs or teachings that theologians study and sometimes help to develop. Examples of Christian doctrine include that Jesus is God *incarnated* (Latin for "enfleshed") in human life, that God is three in one, and that Jesus was born of the Virgin Mary. Many key beliefs of Christian faith are complex. For example, Christians typically proclaim that Jesus' death saves humanity from sin. This statement raises many questions. Why did Jesus die? Was it necessary, or did it just happen? What is sin? Why do human beings need to be saved from sin, and what does salvation look like? What is the scope of salvation: is it for everyone, or just Christians, or just very good Christians?

Church teaching in the form of documents and the written resources of the tradition (in addition to the Bible) are one way that doctrines and teachings are preserved and passed down from one generation to the next. Examples of such written documents include letters and treatises by notable Christian thinkers and leaders, papers and records of church councils and synods throughout the ages, statements of the faith called *creeds*, and biblical commentaries. Though a doctrine may not change, the way it is communicated or described may change over time due to cultural contexts. For example, while Christians had always maintained that God creates the world, the way they phrase that assertion has had to change in order to acknowledge the claims of evolutionary theory: some Christians attempt to assert God's role as Creator by refuting evolution, while others find ways of affirming both evolution and God's creative activity.

Reason refers to the rational thought, inquiry, and intellect that human beings use to investigate the surrounding world. In Christian thought, reason is also considered a source for understanding God, on account of the beliefs that God created humanity with rational faculties, that God created a world that can disclose things about its Creator, and that the world can be studied and understood in part if not entirely. Christians use reason in particular in science and philosophy in order to complement and expand upon the revealed truths they hold sacred. *Philosophy* refers to the ancient discipline that investigates epistemology (the study of the nature of knowledge), metaphysics (the study of the nature of the world), and morality (how people should act). Philosophy and theology are closely related, so much so that philosophy has been called the "handmaid of theology." Theology and philosophy are both interested in ultimate truth, but they use different foundations. Philosophy relies on human reason alone, while Christian thought uses reason (including the insights drawn from philosophy and the sciences), the Bible, and Christian doctrine to develop a coherent worldview.

Experience is the broadest source for Christian thought and practice. All knowledge is located in human "knowers"; *people* think about mathematics, perform scientific experiments, theorize about the purpose of literature, and so on. Even the most abstract ideas need human beings to think them.

Christian thought is no different in this way from science and other types of human knowing. It, too, derives from human ability and experience. Although Christians believe that God reveals, it is human beings who receive that revelation within the context of ordinary human life, contingent on personal and social contexts. Christians are interested in the same world that scientists study. For example, Christians, like environmental scientists, might be interested in the problem of pollution in urban settings, but their approach to it would be informed by assumptions specific to the theological discipline. So theologians might see the problem of pollution as a justice issue, as a violation of God's creation, or as an issue of human dignity. In a sense, theology might be thought of as the work of ordinary people reflecting on ordinary experiences made extraordinary by the insights the experiences reveal about human beings, their world, and the meaning and purpose of life.

Because experience is inherently democratic, all Christian people can bring their experiences to the table to add to collective wisdom derived from Christian life. In past eras, Christian thought was dominated by an elite class of religious professionals, such as theologians and priests; some would say it still is. Today, however, an important corrective to this tendency is the incorporation of a broader spectrum of voices. The experiences of women and traditionally marginalized or underrepresented populations now present rich new opportunities for thinking, experiencing, revisioning, and applying Christian faith.

A Note on Theological Method

All academic disciplines use methods of inquiry, and theology is no different. Careful attention to method is key to doing theology well. Thinking about method reminds theologians that they are making choices about what to study, what to attend to, and what temporarily to set aside. An awareness of method also reminds theologians that they are not value-neutral observers making objective interpretations about the material they are studying. People in the United States in the twenty-first century, for example, largely assume that women and men should be treated equally under the law and in most or all areas of society. This assumption affects how theologians today view women in the Bible or in historical theology. By contrast, people in fifteenth-century Europe did not assume gender equality, so their readings of the Bible or doctrine would have been different. Being aware of method means understanding that one's approach to theology is itself an ethical judgment about oneself as an interpreter and about what one thinks is necessary and important about theology. Theologians may employ many methods, but every method involves a choice (even if unconscious) about how to engage the material being studied.

Types of Theology

In a sense, it is more proper to speak of Christian *theologies* than of a single Christian theology. The type of theology that one does reflects the specific function that theology serves in its role as interpreter and mediator between the traditions and the living communities of Christian people. It will also shape the method one uses for practicing theology and the foundations a theologian prioritizes. Some of the most important theologies people do today include biblical criticism, systematic theology, historical theology, moral theology, pastoral theology, liberation theology, natural theology, liturgical studies and sacramental theology, and mystical theology.

Biblical Criticism.[2] This deals with scholarly study and analysis of the Bible. This fundamental study involves many areas of specialization. Some scholars study the Bible at close range, considering such fine aspects as the condition and reliability of ancient manuscripts, the biblical languages of the Old and New Testaments, the literary forms used in ancient cultures, the historical context of the Bible, philosophical approaches to biblical translation and interpretation, biblical archaeology, and more. Other scholars study the Bible for its merit as a persuasive or rhetorical book, its doctrinal themes and teachings, its teachings about the nature of the church, and its teachings about Christian moral conduct. The basic assumption of biblical criticism is that the Bible must be well understood (and what we cannot understand must be acknowledged) if it is to be a useful foundation for the rest of Christian faith.

Systematic Theology. This is the study of the interconnections among theological doctrines and sources. The aim of systematic theology is twofold: to articulate the inherent reasonability of Christian theology and to present the whole system of teachings in a reasonable and clear way for educational purposes. Systematic theologians debate how best to structure the presentation of ideas. For example, some would begin with the notion of revelation in scripture, while others would begin with the doctrine of God. In any event, systematic theology aims to assemble the pieces of Christian faith into a coherent whole, as one would fit the pieces of a puzzle together to make a complete picture. Some contemporary theologians prefer the term *constructive theology* to describe the integrative study of doctrines and sources.

Historical Theology. This is the study of how historical eras and contexts affect the development and articulation of beliefs. Because theology is always done within a specific time and place for a specific community of people, theology and its context of origin are indelibly related. In the early Christian era, for example, Christians struggled to negotiate cultural differences between Jewish followers of Jesus

---

2. Note that "criticism" in this context means simply a detailed, disciplined study, as in the phrase "literary criticism."

and converts to Christianity from "pagan" religions. Jewish law forbade Jews from eating with non-Jews, which raised questions over whether both groups could celebrate Christian communion (sometimes called the Eucharist, the Last Supper, or the Lord's Supper) together. Although this particular issue matters little to modern Christians, they continue to have questions about who can celebrate communion together. The concern today is not one of pagan or Jew but rather of different Christian groups. Especially since the time of the Protestant Reformation, Christians have separated themselves into different denominations, many of which will not celebrate the ritual meal together. Theological reflection on this issue from both the early Christian era and the modern setting will reflect the concerns of their respective historical contexts. Study of historical theology is also central in sorting out how and why some ideas came to be considered orthodox (correct), while others were determined to be heresy (unorthodox, corrupt, or incorrect).

Moral Theology and Ethics. Both philosophy and theology are interested in understanding not only what is right and wrong (ethics) but also how people should act based on what they believe to be right (morality). Christian moral theology investigates the question of right action with respect to its faith-based commitments. For example, while one might bring many considerations to the question of medical ethics, many Christian moral theologians will begin with the belief that God creates all human beings with inalienable dignity and purpose. Christians who begin with this premise are guided by the moral principle of dignity of life. The study of both morality and ethics straddles many facets of society. Christian investigation of ethical questions and moral living will be guided by a faith-based understanding of the meaning, purpose, and value of human life.

Pastoral Theology. This is concerned with the social application of theological statements. This theology ensures that Christian faith is not limited to orthodoxy (i.e., thinking right thoughts) but also extends to orthopraxy (i.e., doing right things). Pastoral theology would note that it is one thing to worry over the proper form and meaning of the Lord's Supper and another to make sure that the people in one's local community actually have supper. Pastoral theology strives to bridge the academic and applied dimensions of Christian faith.

Liberation Theology. This refers to numerous twentieth- and twenty-first-century theologies that take a strong interest in the political implications of Christian faith as a force for social liberation. Emerging from the abject poverty of Central and South America in the 1960s, liberation theology pointed out that the Bible reveals a God who is concerned about the plight of the poor. Contemporaneous with Latin American liberation theology was the black theology movement in the United States, which brought out the religious dimension of the civil rights movement. Beginning with these expressions, today's liberation theologies evaluate the condition of all manner of poverty and oppression. These include a wide range of social, political, economic, racial, and gender oppressions. Feminist, Hispanic, African American, womanist, *mujerista* (which blends feminist, Latin American liberation, and cultural theologies), third-world, and LBGTQ+ (lesbian, bisexual, gay, transgender, and questioning) theologies are all expressions of liberation theologies seeking justice, inclusion, and voice for their constituencies.

Natural Theology. This considers how God may be found in nature, without the benefit of such special revelation as the Bible. Natural theology looks at things like beauty, design, order, and causality in the natural world and evaluates whether and how these aspects suggest a Creator. Modern cosmology and natural theology today engage in dialogue about the origin, destiny, value, and meaning of the natural world.

Liturgical Studies and Sacramental Theology. These disciplines focus on the study of Christian communal worship and prayer. They examine the structure of worship services, the effectiveness of language used in prayer and creed, the style and placement of the music and art that is incorporated in Christian worship, the preparation of children and adults for full and active participation in the Christian community, and the architectural design and layout of spaces of worship. Sacramental theology specifically studies the most sacred rituals in Christian life, for example, the key rite of entrance into the Christian community known as *baptism* (that is, the immersion or sprinkling of the initiate with water in the name of the Father, Son, and Holy Spirit). Liturgy and sacraments are studied not as ends in themselves, but because they have a reciprocal relationship with other branches of theology. For example, the way God is addressed in prayer, sung about in hymns, and depicted in art all draw upon a particular understanding of God and, in turn, help the worshippers to form their understanding of God. This interrelationship is summed up in the Latin phrase, *lex orandi, lex credendi*: "the law of praying is the law of believing."

Mystical Theology. This focuses on the subjective experience of encountering God, attempting to put into words experiences that transcend definition. Just as people attempt to describe the experience of falling in love, even as they realize that words cannot truly describe the experience, so also does mystical theology attempt to describe the conditions and the experience of falling in love with God, being touched by God in prayer and contemplation, or having a direct encounter with God. Mystical theology might thus be thought of as the study of Christian spirituality, prayer, and contemplative practice.

The Audiences and Practitioners of Christian Thought

One popular model suggests that there are three principal and sometimes overlapping audiences for theology: the church, the academy, and the public.[3]

Church refers to the collective body of Christians (as opposed to church buildings or denominations, such as Catholics or Lutherans). The church is the primary location of Christian theology because it is Christian beliefs that are being considered, usually by Christian believers, writers, theologians, and ministers. For example, non-Christians may want to know what Christian theologians are saying about the death penalty or euthanasia. It will be Christians themselves, though, who look to the Bible, church teaching, theologians, and the wisdom of their own experiences for guidance on how to apply Christian beliefs and understandings to such questions.

---

3. David Tracy, *The Analogical Imagination: Christian Theology and the Culture of Pluralism* (New York, Crossroad Publishing Company, 1981).

In theological terms, a church is a congregation of Christians, not the building in which they meet. In this photo, a congregation in Idaho celebrates baptism, the key rite of entrance into the Christian community, in a river.

The term *academy* refers to colleges and universities where theology is a discipline of scholarly research and teaching. Since the Middle Ages, theology has been an important part of university curricula. Theology departments of universities need to meet the same standards and requirements as other disciplines. These standards and requirements might be established through licensure boards, criteria for publishing, national organizations, or other criteria. By making standards and requirements shared and public, research, teaching, and publication are made accountable and preserve integrity of method and discourse. Students of theology must enter into intelligent and integrative dialogue with other disciplines. Theologians cannot well advance their discussions of, for example, natural theology if they are ignorant of biology, physics, or chemistry.

Public refers to the fact that Christian thinkers have a responsibility to understand the world at large and to attempt to hold a dialogue with it as much as possible—although some Christian groups attempt to remain sectarian (detached from the world). Apart from this dialogue, Christian theology would bury its head in the sand,

and this would be a failure to perform its basic function as mediator and interpreter between the religious tradition and society. In addition, if Christian thinking is not public and open, it tends to become cultlike and unaccountable, and risks exploiting the people who take direction from it. Being accountable to the public is a safeguard against untenable and detached ideas. It is also the way theology can engage and even persuade the public about its constructive and prosocial beliefs, values, and works.

Conclusion

Twentieth-century Brazilian Roman Catholic theologians Leonardo and Clodovis Boff said of theology, "All who believe want to understand something of their faith. As soon as you think about faith, you are already doing theology. So all Christians are in a sense theologians, and become more so the more they think about their faith."[4]

All people who think about their faith and try to understand what it means for their life are doing theology on some level. Professional theologians think, speak, and write about faith all the time. Ministers and pastoral workers may use theology to help shape their workplace ethics or their client care. Clergy may use theology to help them write poignant and timely sermons. Stay-at-home moms and dads may use theology to help them get through rough days with noisy kids and piles of laundry.

Although it can be highly academic and refined, theology is ultimately the Christian endeavor to make sense of the beliefs that the faith proclaims. People do theology across all levels of personal interest and professional practice. Theology may be done by highly educated scholars, but it is also the domain of average people attempting to think meaningfully and seriously about what they believe and how those beliefs should shape their lives.

---

4. Leonardo and Clodovis Boff, *Introducing Liberation Theology* (Maryknoll, NY: Orbis, 1987), 16.

Questions for Discussion and Review

1. How would you describe theology to a child?
2. Give an example of theologizing.
3. What are the poignant moments in life—joyful or tragic—that might prompt a person to think about God?
4. Describe the function of theology as mediator and interpreter. Give an example of a current event or situation that could benefit from the mediation of theology.
5. What is the relationship between faith and reason?
6. What is theological method? Is it important? Explain.
7. Give an example of how historical and geographical context can influence theology.
8. Is every religious person a theologian? Explain.
9. Describe and compare two types of theology considered in this chapter.
10. Why is it important for theology to have a public character?

Resources

Books

Boff, Leonardo and Clodovis. *Introducing Liberation Theology*. Maryknoll, NY: Orbis, 1987.

Bultmann, Rudolph. *What Is Theology?* Minneapolis: Fortress, 2000.

Ford, David. *Theology: A Very Short Introduction*. New York: Oxford University Press, 2000.

Lonergan, Bernard. *Method in Theology*. 2nd ed. Toronto: University of Toronto Press, Scholarly Publishing Division, 1990.

McGrath, Alister E. *Christian Theology: An Introduction*. 5th ed. Oxford, UK: Wiley-Blackwell, 2011.

Ormerod, Neil. *Introducing Contemporary Theologies: The What and the Who of Theology Today*. Maryknoll, NY: Orbis, 2002.

Tracy, David. *Blessed Rage for Order: The New Pluralism in Theology*. Chicago: University of Chicago Press, 1996.

Websites

The Christian Century, "Theology," at *www.christiancentury.org/theology*.

The Master's Seminary, "Theology IV, Lecture 1," at *www.theological resources.org/the-masters-seminary/30-theology-iv*. Lectures on theological topics from an evangelical Christian perspective.

New Advent, "Dogmatic Theology," at *www.newadvent.org/cathen /14580a.htm*.

N. T. Wright "How Paul Invented Christian Theology," at *www .youtube.com/watch?v=WkcjFHYIugY*.

CHAPTER 2

A Scriptural Foundation for Christian Theology

What to Expect

This chapter introduces the Bible as the principal foundation of Christian theology. It will discuss:

- Scripture – Getting Started
- Old Testament
- New Testament
- Contemporary Biblical Scholarship

Scripture: Getting Started

For Christians, Scripture, or the Bible, refers to the collected books of the Old Testament and New Testament that Christians recognize as having divine authority for thought and worship. This collection of books comprises what is known as the biblical canon. Although there are other, related books called *Apocrypha* (Greek for "hidden writings") or *pseudepigrapha* ("false writings") that are written by people of the same eras as the authors of the Bible, Christians believe the biblical canon has a special authority and is different in essence from all other written works. This authority comes from the Christian belief that the Bible uniquely contains God's revelation.

What is revelation and how is it manifested in the Bible? These questions do not have quick and easy answers, and investigation into the nature of revelation is itself a major aspect of systematic theology and biblical studies. For the purposes of this discussion, however, revelation may be understood as God's self-disclosure to people, revealing what God is like and how people should act in light of their knowledge of God.

Why do people need to be told about God? The Christian tradition asserts that God is present in nature and thus naturally accessible on some level by human reason; human beings cannot know the full truth about God, however, apart from God's willing it and intentionally making it so. By way of analogy, consider that one learns only part of the truth about someone by reading his résumé or looking at her artwork. To know others fully, they must disclose themselves personally. Christian faith holds that this is precisely how God encounters people, and thus how people experience God.

The Bible developed over time as people orally transmitted and eventually wrote down descriptions of revelatory experiences, insights, and encounters that they deemed sufficiently definitive or authoritative to merit preservation for the good of the present and future community. As these writings became broadly distributed and celebrated, they came to be seen as part of the experience of divine revelation (as opposed to merely a record of revelation). Moreover, as these writings were read aloud and shared in the context of Christian worship, the proclamation of and preaching on the writings came to be seen as aspects of divine revelation. Today revelation in the Bible can be thought of as having at least three layers:

- the original revelatory experiences
- the text or written record of revelation experiences
- the oral reading or preaching of the written text

Who had these revelatory experiences, insights, and encounters that became the Bible? They were the early Israelites and the first followers of Jesus. These two groups, respectively, composed, edited, and transmitted the books of the Old and New Testaments.

Divine Inspiration

The issue of divine inspiration is closely related to the discussion of revelation in the Bible. Christians often speak of the Bible as "the word of God." The phrase *the word of God* and the idea of divine inspiration can both be interpreted in many different ways. The phrase could refer quite literally to God's words, and divine inspiration could refer to the intellectual or mechanical process by which people receive God's words. The word of God could also refer to the mind of God or the wisdom of God. Christians often refer to Jesus himself as the Word of God because they understand him to be fully God and also fully human in the very constitution of his being; that is, he is God Incarnate.

Divine inspiration applies not only to the word of God. Christians have also used the idea of divine inspiration to explain the internal disposition or awareness within human beings that enables people to read, hear, and understand the word of God in the Bible. Divine inspiration has been used to explain how people can translate the Bible from one language to another. In a looser sense, divine inspiration may be used to explain the process by which a person creatively yet accurately preaches on the Bible, theologizes about it, or teaches the faith. Many churches, moreover, claim that they are led by the divine inspiration of the Holy Spirit in their actions, teachings, and leadership structures.

The key concept behind the idea of divine inspiration is that when a person or a text or a teaching is believed to originate in God, it has a unique authority over Christians. The roots of the word *inspire* are the prefix *in-* and the Latin verb *spirare* ("to breathe"). Literally, inspiration is a "breathing into." In Christian understanding, something that is inspired is "breathed into" by God.

Old Testament

The Old Testament is a compilation of books, the core of which is the Hebrew Bible. The Protestant Old Testament consists of only the thirty-nine books of the Hebrew Bible,[1] originally written in Hebrew and Aramaic. Catholics and Orthodox accept additional books, including some that were originally written in Greek, making a total of forty-six books for the Catholic Old Testament and some forty-eight for the Orthodox. The books of the Old Testament date from about 1000 to 100 BCE and were written by the ancient Israelites. The Old Testament is identified by several names, including the Hebrew Bible, the First Testament, and the Tanakh.[2] Modern Jews and Christians regard these books as sacred, although both groups identify the collections by different names.

By the beginning of the Christian era, a Greek translation of the Hebrew scriptures (known as the *Septuagint*) circulated widely. In the third and second centuries BCE, a large community of Jews living in the Greek-speaking city of Alexandria, in Egypt, had begun to lose their facility in the Hebrew language; the Septuagint is believed to have been translated by them. The resultant collection included several books that would be excluded from the Hebrew Bible (see table, p. 35–36). Some Christian groups, including the Catholic Church, call these books the *deuterocanon*, meaning "second canon." At least some of these books were originally written in Greek. Though absent from the Hebrew Bible, Christians accepted them as canonical, and they remained part of the Christian Bible until the Protestant Reformation in the sixteenth century. Protestant Reformers eliminated the deuterocanonical books from their versions of the Old Testament so as to match the Hebrew canon, but Roman Catholic and Orthodox Christians retained them. Despite differences in how they arrange and number these books, today Jews and Christians see the Old Testament/Tanakh as God's revelation.

The major divisions of law, history, prophets, and writings suggest the basic content of these writings. The books of law, which Christians call the *Pentateuch* (Greek for "five books"), explain the origin of God's covenant (or binding relationship) with the Israelites and delineate the religious, priestly, and social obligations that the

---

1. This reflects the Christian numbering of these texts. Traditionally, Jews divide the books differently, resulting in a total of twenty-four books.

2. "Tanakh" is an acronym formed from the three divisions of the Hebrew Bible: T*orah* ("law" or "instruction"), N*evi'im* ("prophets"), and K*ethuvim* ("writings"): TNK.

Canons of the Old Testament

(Hebrew Scriptures)

Jewish	Protestant	Roman Catholic	Orthodox
Torah (Law)	Pentateuch	Pentateuch	Pentateuch
Genesis	Genesis	Genesis	Genesis
Exodus	Exodus	Exodus	Exodus
Leviticus	Leviticus	Leviticus	Leviticus
Numbers	Numbers	Numbers	Numbers
Deuteronomy	Deuteronomy	Deuteronomy	Deuteronomy
Nevi'im (Prophets)	**Historical Books**	**Historical Books**	**Historical Books**
Former Prophets	Joshua	Joshua	Joshua
Joshua	Judges	Judges	Judges
Judges	Ruth	Ruth	Ruth
1 and 2 Samuel	1 and 2 Samuel	1 and 2 Samuel	1–4 Kingdoms (same
1 and 2 Kings	1 and 2 Kings	1 and 2 Kings	as 1 and 2 Samuel
Later Prophets	1 and 2 Chronicles	1 and 2 Chronicles	and 1 and 2 Kings)
Isaiah	Ezra	Ezra	1 and 2 Chronicles
Jeremiah	Nehemiah	Nehemiah	1 Esdras
Ezekiel	Esther (short	Tobit	2 Esdras (same as
Hosea	version)	Judith	Ezra and Nehemiah)
Joel		Esther (long version)	Judith
Amos		1 and 2 Maccabees	Tobit
Obadiah			Esther (long version)
Jonah			1, 2 and 3 Maccabees
Micah			4 Maccabees (as an
Nahum			appendix, if included)
Habakkuk			
Zephaniah	**Wisdom Books**	**Wisdom Books**	**Wisdom Books**
Haggai	Job	Job	Job
Zechariah	Psalms	Psalms	Psalms (includes
Malachi	Proverbs	Proverbs	Psalm 151)
	Ecclesiastes	Ecclesiastes	Proverbs
Kethuvim (Writings)	Song of Solomon	Song of Solomon	Ecclesiastes
Psalms		Wisdom	Song of Solomon
Proverbs		Sirach (Ecclesiasticus)	Wisdom
Job			Sirach (Ecclesiasticus)
Song of Solomon			Prayer of Manasseh
Ruth			
Lamentations	**Prophets**	**Prophets**	**Prophets**
Ecclesiastes	Isaiah	Isaiah	Isaiah
Esther	Jeremiah	Jeremiah	Jeremiah
Daniel	Lamentations	Lamentations	Lamentations
Ezra	Ezekiel	Baruch	Baruch
Nehemiah	Daniel (short	Ezekiel	Ezekiel
1 and 2 Chronicles	version)	Daniel (long version)	Daniel (long version)
	Hosea	Hosea	Hosea
	Joel	Joel	Joel
	Amos	Amos	Amos
	Obadiah	Obadiah	Obadiah
	Jonah	Jonah	Jonah
	Micah	Micah	Micah
	Nahum	Nahum	Nahum
	Habakkuk	Habakkuk	Habakkuk
	Zephaniah	Zephaniah	Zephaniah
	Haggai	Haggai	Haggai
	Zechariah	Zechariah	Zechariah
	Malachi	Malachi	Malachi

Canons of the Old Testament *(continued)*

Jewish	Protestant	Roman Catholic	Orthodox
24–39 Books (Some collections treat the following as single books: Samuel, Kings, the twelve Minor Prophets, Chronicles, Ezra-Nehemiah.)	**39 Books** (Protestant canon follows the Hebrew canon.)	**46 Books** (Roman Catholic canon follows the Septuagint, which includes seven books not in the Hebrew canon.)	**48–49 Books** (Orthodox canon follows an expanded version of the Septuagint.)

© 2014 ANSELM ACADEMIC

covenant entailed. The books of history present the major events and persons associated with the rise, duration, fall, and restoration of the Kingdom of Israel. The books of the prophets record the words and deeds of Israel's spiritual conscience, whose principal role was to evaluate the religious integrity of the kingdom and its leaders. The books of writings are spiritual reflections on what it means to live a proper life in relationship to God and people.

These books are an important foundation for Christian theology because the earliest Christian writers clearly regarded them as inspired scripture. Moreover, the Israelite culture and history they record formed the context from which Jesus and the first Christians emerged. Indeed, the various groups of Jewish leaders mentioned in the New Testament make little sense apart from their history, presented in the Hebrew literature. Perhaps most important, the effect that the life of Jesus had on his followers is best understood in light of the tumultuous history to which the Old Testament bears witness.

Time Line of the Hebrew Bible

2000–1800 BCE	Period of patriarchs and matriarchs (founders of twelve tribes of Israel)
1500–1250	Life in Egypt up through the time of the Exodus
1250–1020	Settlement in Canaan (also called Palestine)
1020–930	United monarchy under kings Saul, David, and Solomon

Time Line of the Hebrew Bible *(continued)*	
930–586	Divided monarchy, with Israel (northern kingdom) falling to Assyria in 722 and Judah (southern kingdom) falling to Babylon in 586
586–539	Babylonian exile (many Israelites deported to Babylon) and the destruction of Jerusalem
539–425	Return of Israelites from Babylonia to Palestine and birth of Judaism under Ezra and Nehemiah
333–175	Conquest of Palestine by Alexander the Great, and subsequent domination by Hellenistic empires: the Ptolemaic Kingdom of Egypt, and the Seleucid Empire of Persia
174–64	Persecution of Judeans by Antiochus IV Epiphanes (of the Seleucid Empire), Jewish revolt against Seleucid control, and the establishment of an independent Jewish state under the Hasmoneon Dynasty
63 BCE through the beginning of the common era	Conquest of Palestine by Roman general Pompey, and the onset of Roman domination of Judea, including (after 44 BCE) the era of the Herodian Dynasty, which was in power at the time of Jesus

© 2014 ANSELM ACADEMIC

New Testament

The New Testament is a compilation of twenty-seven books, dating from roughly 50–120 CE and authored in Greek by early Christians. The New Testament is also called the Second Testament or the Christian Scriptures. These books deal with the life of Jesus, the birth of the Christian church, and the beliefs and practices of the first Christian communities. The New Testament books represent at least four major genres (or types of literature): gospels (the four Gospels), history (the Acts of the Apostles),[3] letters (the Epistles), and apocalyptic literature.

Matthew, Mark, Luke, and John are the four Gospels of the New Testament. Mark, the earliest, was probably written sometime

---

3. Scholars continue to debate the genre of the Acts of the Apostles, but many feel that it best fits the category of history (as that genre was understood in ancient times).

© The Board of Trinity College, Dublin, Ireland / Bridgeman Images

Christian tradition has long taken the four "living creatures" of Revelation 4:6–7, shown here in the ninth-century Book of Kells, as symbols of the four Gospels. The fourfold symbolism tacitly acknowledges that each Gospel presents its own, unique interpretation of Jesus.

between 66 and 74 CE. Matthew and Luke were likely written between 80 and 90 CE. John is usually dated ca. 100 CE. These four books were written anonymously, but Christian custom attributes them to the persons whose names are now appended to these books. The Gospels are the only four books of the Bible that focus on the acts and teachings of Jesus. Culminating in the story of Jesus' death and Resurrection, the Gospels were written to spread the "good news" (the literal meaning of *gospel*) about Jesus. Even though they do not satisfy the criteria of modern biography, they are the best sources Christians have today for learning about Jesus' life and its effect on his followers.

The Acts of the Apostles was written by the author of the Gospel of Luke and functions as its sequel. While the Gospel of Luke deals with the life of Jesus, Acts focuses on the rise of the church after Jesus' ascension into heaven. Appropriately named, the book is an account of the acts of the first Christians, especially Peter and Paul, as they spread their new faith throughout the Roman Empire. Many consider this work the first church history.

The Epistles are the letters of the New Testament, dating from about 50 CE to the mid-second century. These letters were written to advise and encourage the emergent Christian communities. Without benefit of established organizational structures, official doctrines, or leadership models, the first Christians were tasked with developing all three. Through the circulation of letters, the primitive Christian communities (separated by geography,

The Canon of the New Testament

Protestant, Roman Catholic, and Orthodox

Gospels	1 Corinthians	**Catholic Epistles**
Matthew	2 Corinthians	Hebrews
Mark	Galatians	James
Luke	Colossians	1 Peter
John	Ephesians	2 Peter
	Philippians	1 John
Acts of the Apostles	1 Thessalonians	2 John
	2 Thessalonians	3 John
Pauline Epistles	1 Timothy	Jude
(Letters)	2 Timothy	
Romans	Titus	**The Apocalypse**
	Philemon	**(Revelation)**

27 Books

language, and long silences) were able to build consensus on matters of leadership, morals, practices, and core beliefs. Of the twenty-one letters, thirteen are attributed to the Apostle Paul, who was instrumental in spreading Christianity through his missionary activities in the middle of the first century. Many early Christians believed that a fourteenth letter (the Epistle to the Hebrews) was also authored by Paul, even though the letter itself makes no such claim. Of the thirteen letters attributed to Paul, most scholars conclude that seven were actually authored by him (Romans, 1 and 2 Corinthians, Galatians, Philippians, 1 Thessalonians, and Philemon), whereas some or all of the other six (Ephesians, Colossians, 2 Thessalonians, 1 and 2 Timothy, and Titus) are probably pseudonymous, written by others in Paul's name. The remaining seven of the twenty-one New Testament letters are attributed to important leaders of the early Christian movement, namely Peter (two letters), John (three letters), James (one letter), and Jude (one letter), but scholars doubt that these individuals actually authored the letters that bear their names.

The book of Revelation is the only work in the apocalyptic genre in the New Testament. This final book of the Bible was written by John of Patmos in the late first century CE. Revelation focuses on the end

Studying the New Testament Letters

One difficult aspect of studying the New Testament letters is that they were written much the same way people write letters today. For example, let's say two friends stay in touch by correspondence, and one saves the letters she receives. Years later, a grown child finds her now-deceased mother's saved letters. It would be possible to make sense of some of the content of the letters by attempting to recreate their context, but much would be lost because the reader would have only some of what was written, by only one of the two parties writing, about situations that happened long ago, and about which the reader has only a partial understanding.

The New Testament letters pose similar difficulties. The letters are often situational, dealing with specific questions or circumstances that individuals and churches faced long ago and that the contemporary reader does not fully understand. In addition, some of the original correspondence was lost over time, so only a partial record remains. Further, the true author cannot be known for certain, as authors sometimes borrowed a trusted leader's name (such as Paul's) when writing, in order to be more persuasive with readers of the day. Study of the New Testament letters can feel much like a historical scavenger hunt that leads to fascinating, if not definitive, insight into the beliefs, practices, and struggles of the developing Christian church.

of the present world and the events that will usher in the world to come. This book simultaneously reveals and hides its messages with the use of ambiguous language and imagery. Although its meaning is not entirely clear, Revelation was likely intended to give hope to Christians who experienced persecution under the Roman emperor Domitian (81–96).

The books of the New Testament (see table, page 39 The Canon of the New Testament) reflect upon Jesus' works, life, teachings, sacrifice, and Resurrection, and offer the first articulations of faith in Jesus as the Christ (the Greek equivalent of the Hebrew word *Messiah*; both words mean "anointed"). They also lay the foundations for some churches' leadership structures (such as bishop, priest, and deacon) and offer moral instruction for Christian life. As such, the New Testament offers the essential foundation for Christian theology. Although much of Christian theology is postbiblical (meaning it developed after the writings of the New Testament), no defensible Christian theology can be abiblical (or unconcerned with the Bible as a foundation).

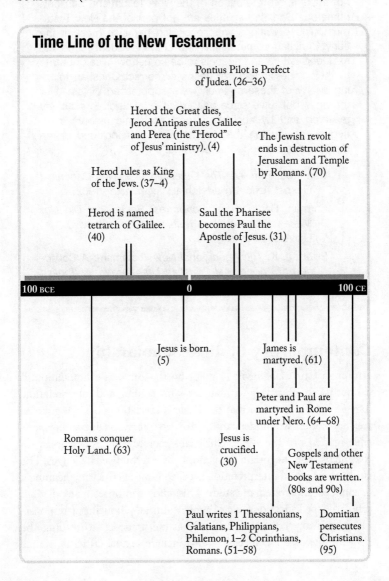

Time Line of the New Testament

Pontius Pilot is Prefect of Judea. (26–36)

Herod the Great dies, Jerod Antipas rules Galilee and Perea (the "Herod" of Jesus' ministry). (4)

The Jewish revolt ends in destruction of Jerusalem and Temple by Romans. (70)

Herod rules as King of the Jews. (37–4)

Saul the Pharisee becomes Paul the Apostle of Jesus. (31)

Herod is named tetrarch of Galilee. (40)

100 BCE   **0**   **100** CE

Jesus is born. (5)

James is martyred. (61)

Peter and Paul are martyred in Rome under Nero. (64–68)

Romans conquer Holy Land. (63)

Jesus is crucified. (30)

Gospels and other New Testament books are written. (80s and 90s)

Paul writes 1 Thessalonians, Galatians, Philippians, Philemon, 1–2 Corinthians, Romans. (51–58)

Domitian persecutes Christians. (95)

Early Christian Apocrypha

Scholars are aware of more than thirty "gospels" that did not make it into the canon of the New Testament. Similarly, numerous Christian epistles are not part of the New Testament. These writings were excluded because most of the early Christian communities and church leaders found the excluded letters and gospels to be somehow false or untrue to their understanding of Jesus or correct Christian thinking. Many of these sources were suppressed or lost over the ages but have since been recovered through scholarly research and by accident. Good academic resources for beginners studying the noncanonical (not included in the Bible) gospels include the following:

Cameron, Ron, ed. *The Other Gospels: Non-Canonical Gospel Texts*. Philadelphia: Westminster, 1982.

Ehrman, Bart D. *Lost Scriptures: Books that Did Not Make It into the New Testament*. New York: Oxford University Press, 2003.

Elliott, J. K. *The Apocryphal New Testament: A Collection of Apocryphal Christian Literature in an English Translation*. Oxford, UK: Clarendon, 2005.

Contemporary Biblical Scholarship

Although Christian theology relies on the Bible as a foundation, it cannot do so effectively without tools for reading and interpretation. The Christian assertion that the Bible is revelation does not guarantee that readers will understand it. To arrive at reasonable and responsible readings of the Bible, Christians require a biblical scholarship that helps them negotiate the panoply of interpretive challenges. The study of scriptural interpretation is called biblical criticism, meaning a disciplined and systematic study. This study comprises many distinct scholarly specializations, all of which aim at producing a responsible, historically conscious, critically astute approach to reading the Bible. Some of these specializations include textual criticism, source

Palestine at the Time of Jesus

© 2009 ANSELM ACADEMIC

Sidon

Damascus

SYRIA

+ Mt. Hermon

Tyre

PHOENICIA

Caesarea Philippi

The Great Sea
(Mediterranean Sea)

GALILEE

Capernaum

Bethsaida

Magdala

Sea of
Galilee

Cana

Mt. Carmel +

Tiberias

Sepphoris

Nazareth

+ Mt. Tabor

DECAPOLIS

Caesarea
Maritima

SAMARIA

Jordan River

Mt. Gerizim +

Sychar

Joppa

Arimathea?

PEREA

Emmaus?

Jericho

Jerusalem

+ Mt. Olives

Bethany

JUDEA

Salt
Sea
(Dead
Sea)

Hebron

0   20   40 miles

0   20   40 kilometers

IDUMEA

criticism, form criticism, historical criticism, redaction criticism, rhetorical criticism, and the study of ancient languages.

Textual Criticism, or manuscript evaluation, is sometimes called "lower criticism" because it is concerned with identifying the original and correct readings of the biblical texts and is therefore a necessary prelude to other forms of biblical criticism. Before the printing press, people wrote by hand on fragile materials like parchment and papyrus. These materials were subject to decay over time, so they had to be copied (by hand), and eventually those copies had to be copied (by hand), and so on; inevitably, mistakes arose in this process, so that no two surviving New Testament manuscripts now agree completely. This raises a question: what was the original reading of a given text? Before biblical books can be read and interpreted today, the original readings of the text must first be determined by careful study and comparison of the surviving manuscripts.

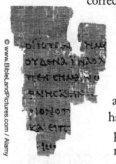

© www.BibleLandPictures.com / Alamy

P52, dated to ca. 125, is the oldest known New Testament manuscript.

Source criticism assumes that earlier written documents underlie the present form of many parts of the Bible. This theory resulted from the detection of at least four authors behind the present version of the Pentateuch (the first five books of the Old Testament), long believed by many to have been authored by Moses alone. When scholars studied these books carefully, they noticed things like different names for God, unique phrasing or emphases repeated at different points in the text, varying names for prominent geographical locations, and repetition of stories with slight differences. As researchers extracted, for example, all the passages that referred to God as *Yahweh* as opposed to *Elohim*, they discovered a whole perspective that was interwoven with other perspectives to create the version of the books that exists today. Source criticism is akin to searching for the bibliography behind the present biblical text. When scholars can reconstruct the sources that comprise a biblical text, they are able to understand the different contexts and concerns of individual biblical authors.

Form criticism assumes that there are also oral and unwritten sources behind the present-day text. The effort to find specific sources, as described above, can be highly conjectural. For example, with regard to the sources underlying the Pentateuch, the dominant theory is the Four Document Hypothesis, associated with the work of Julius Wellhausen in the late nineteenth century. It is hotly debated at present, not because scholars doubt that there were multiple authors of the Pentateuch, but because they disagree on exactly how many there were, what material came from which source, and when and where the various sources originated. Form criticism avoids the excesses and conjectural aspects of source criticism by focusing instead on the original meaning of individual units of the text. First a selection of text is isolated and defined, and then the purpose and effect that the biblical material would have had on its original audiences is considered.

For example, form critics might examine the law code in the book of Exodus by asking who its audience was and how the book functioned in the ancient world, as opposed to asking what written sources contributed to its development. By such methods, researchers are able to arrive at responsible interpretations of challenging content.

Historical criticism considers the historical context of biblical writings. Scholars using this approach actively imagine and enter into the world of the text. They attempt to unveil sociopolitical realities that surrounded the writing of the Bible in order to distinguish between essential biblical content and inessential remnants of historical contingencies. Researchers also study historical context in order to assess what is likely or unlikely to have actually occurred.

For example, researchers studying the letters called the Pastoral Epistles (1 and 2 Timothy, Titus) argue that although these letters are attributed to Paul, they were probably written by others in Paul's name, at a later date. One indication is the concern these letters exhibit regarding women's participation in the emergent church. This does not appear to have been a problem during Paul's lifetime; in his undisputed letters, he acknowledges quite a few women by name who were active in ministry in his churches, and expresses appreciation for them. The attitude of the Pastoral Letters on this issue better fits the context of the late first or early second century, when the churches began to question the validity of women participating in ministry. These and other clues place the letters' time of composition at the end of the first century, well after Paul's death in the late sixties. Presumably the author(s) used Paul's name as a tool to gain credibility for the letters.

Redaction criticism investigates the historical editing of texts. Frequently, material is recounted in several places in the Bible, with minor differences and emphases. Thematic or tonal inconsistencies in biblical texts can suggest that a number of documents were compiled and edited together to produce the text in its present form. By using redaction criticism, scholars can interpret why the same stories make multiple appearances in the Bible, why their authors interpret and relay them differently, and why there are inconsistencies in tone or theme.

For example, scholars studying Paul's correspondence with the church in Corinth (in 1 and 2 Corinthians) have been able to reconstruct a likely scenario about when Paul visited the church there, what happened during his visits to Corinth, and what specific issues occasioned his writing. Through scholarly re-creation of the historical context, researchers have been able to posit a plausible explanation for the radical difference in tone noticed respectively in chapters 1–9 and 10–13 of 2 Corinthians. These two sets of chapters were probably from two separate letters, later edited together to form the letter we now have.

Rhetorical criticism studies the effect of the texts as a whole. Scholars using this approach read the Bible, or segments of the Bible, as works of literature. By using rhetorical criticism, scholars are able to assess the cultural effect and value of the Bible from era to era.

For example, the book of Jonah in the Old Testament is a narrative tale about a prophet of Israel, sent to the enemy city of Nineveh to preach God's word. Jonah resists carrying out God's order because he does not want the enemy people of Nineveh to be saved. Jonah disobeys God by attempting to flee in the direction opposite to Nineveh, but while he is onboard his escape ship, his treachery is revealed. The sailors, fearing for their safety, toss him overboard, where Jonah is rescued in the belly of a large fish (the famed "whale"). Where does the fish take him? To Nineveh!

Often people ask historical questions of this story: How can a man live inside a whale's stomach? Was there really a man named Jonah that had this incredible experience? Rhetorical criticism, by contrast, is interested in why such a story is in the Bible in the first place. What did its original readers learn from it? Scholars argue that this book was written in the 400s BCE, after the time the Israelite people had been exiled from the land of Israel in Palestine. The experience of exile and foreign occupation created in the Jewish people a fierce need to protect and preserve their cultural uniqueness. This need, however, was commonly acted out as intolerance of religious and ethnic differences. By placing the text of Jonah in its historical situation, modern readers can derive a richer awareness of the story's meaning for its original, Israelite audience. It was a comedic portrayal of an unruly prophet and a serious commentary on the universality of God's message that reaches even to one's enemies. Through rhetorical criticism, readers today can appreciate the story as the morality play that it was intended to be.

Study of ancient languages enables scholars to read the Bible in its original languages, which are Hebrew, Aramaic, and Greek. Many scholars also study Latin and Syriac because of important early translations of the Bible into those languages; Latin is also studied because many of the early church fathers quoted and commented upon the Bible in that language.

Translating the Bible

The study of different translations of the Bible offers important help for the vast majority of Christians, who cannot read the Bible in the original languages. Different word choices, phrasings, and so forth from one version to another alert the reader to the possible range of meaning in the passage being translated. Some translators attempt literal (or word-for-word equivalency) translations, while others attempt "dynamic equivalency" (or idea-for-idea) renditions. Today there are dozens of different modern English translations of the Bible, produced and approved by various Christian communities. Learning the philosophies behind different translations and comparing modern versions of the Bible with one another are valuable strategies that expand the contemporary reader's sense of the original text.

Conclusion

The Bible is the principal foundation for Christian faith. It is the primary document that tells us about the life of Jesus as well as the first Christian communities. It represents, moreover, the collection of writings that Christians in the postbiblical era deemed authoritative for the developing Christian tradition. Christians believe that the Bible is an inspired, sacred text (although they disagree about what inspiration specifically means). The Bible also represents a core source for Christian thought about the applications of faith in worship, community responsibility, and moral behavior. As such, Christians today regard the Bible as a source of inestimable value for thinking about and negotiating the life of faith.

At the same time, Christians encounter challenges in applying the Bible to today's life. Since the Bible was written in a very different time and context, the biblical authors could not anticipate every situation that Christians would face in the future. Contemporary technologies, for example, that enable us to manipulate human genetics, raise moral questions about which the Bible can give only general guidance. There are also sometimes ambiguities in the Bible itself over issues that today pose difficulties for some Christian communities, such as legitimate grounds for divorce or the role of women in ministries and leadership. While Christian communities typically seek out biblical instruction in discerning right practice and thought, they also rely on other sources for making the best sense of the Christian faith in every new context. These sources include tradition, reason, and experience, to be discussed in the next chapter.

Questions for Discussion and Review

1. Differentiate between the Old and New Testaments.
2. Name and describe types of scholarly criticism of the Bible.
3. How are the books of the Old and New Testaments respectively grouped?
4. What are some of the contemporary issues that do not receive specific mention in the Bible? How might Christians nevertheless seek biblical instruction on such matters?

5. What are some of the ways in which Christians might understand revelation and inspiration?

6. Why are scholarly tools necessary for responsible biblical interpretation?

Resources

Books

Boadt, Lawrence. *Reading the Old Testament: An Introduction.* 2nd ed. New York: Paulist Press, 2012.

Carson, D. A., and Douglas J. Moo. *Introducing the New Testament: A Short Guide to Its History and Message.* Grand Rapids, MI: Zondervan, 2010.

Ehrman, Bart D. *Lost Scriptures: Books that Did Not Make It into the New Testament.* New York: Oxford University Press, 2003.

Harrington, Daniel. *How Do Catholics Read the Bible?* Lanham, MD: Rowman & Littlefield Publishers, 2005.

Websites

Biblos; "Online Parallel Bible," at *www.biblecc.com*. Multiple translations available for comparison.

Michael D. Marlowe. "Bible Research: Internet Resources for Students of Scripture," at *www.bible-researcher.com/index.html*.

United States Conference of Catholic Bishops, *New American Bible*, rev. ed., online at *www.usccb.org/bible/*.

Films

The Bible's Buried Secrets: Beyond Fact or Fiction. PBS. New York, NY: Films Media Group, 2009.

In the Beginning. BBC Worldwide Ltd. New York, NY: Films Media Group, 2013.

CHAPTER 3

Tradition, Reason, and Experience as Foundations of Christian Theology

What to Expect

This chapter explores the three classic nonbiblical foundations of Christian theology: tradition, reason, and experience. The following topics are discussed:

- Foundations for Christian Thought and Practice
- Tradition: Biblical, Extrabiblical, Informal
- Reason: Christian Revelation and Reason in Dialogue
- Experience: Hermeneutical Circle of Praxis and Theory

What Are Foundations for Christian Thought and Practice?

While Christian communities commonly recognize the Bible as the primary foundation for Christian faith, many identify important and necessary additional sources for shaping Christian belief and applying it in life. Such additional foundations for Christian faith can be crucial to a community's belief system, since many contemporary questions are not explicitly or unambiguously addressed in the Bible. Changing social contexts, new technologies, and discoveries in the sciences raise questions for people in each generation that demand thoughtful attention. For example, a discovery in physics that changes the paradigm (or model) for how we think and talk about the cosmos from a scientific perspective challenges the faith community to engage the new paradigm meaningfully. Questions remain, however, about how such additional foundations are to be utilized. Does human knowing, fueled by reason, inquiry, and observation, function as a place of revelation comparable to the Bible? What should Christians do when the Bible and modern science conflict? Is reason to be trusted? When should Christians defer to tradition, and when should they innovate? On what basis are they to make such decisions?

In the effort to engage the world in a relevant and rational fashion, Christians have historically identified, next to the Bible, three additional foundations for faith: tradition, reason, and experience. It should be noted that not all Christian communities acknowledge supplementary foundations for theology, and among those that do, there is debate over their relative importance. Catholics, for example, understand tradition as being equivalent to the Bible as a source for theology. By contrast, most Protestant denominations allow only a secondary role to tradition, and some (e.g., Baptists and Evangelicals) frequently assert that tradition as such should not play any formal role in theology. It is thus necessary to caution against over-generalization. A careful study of any specific Christian denomination or community (see chapter 5) will take note of the sources that community accepts as reliable for belief and practice.

One could argue that tradition, reason, and experience are important aspects of all human knowing. *Tradition* connects us with our predecessors and provides a past context for understanding not only what we do but also why we do it. *Reason* is the faculty of human knowing that enables us, among other things, to dialogue with one another according to externally and mutually agreed upon criteria for the adequacy of our claims, comments, and conclusions. In other words, the application of reason helps to free us from uncritical subjectivity, opinion, and bias. *Experience* is the means by which we determine whether what we have heard and received is true and is the location of empirical knowing (as opposed to theoretical or speculative knowing). Consequently, each of these three foundations for human knowing intersects with the human capacity for theological understanding, even while not all Christians agree on the extent to which they should inform theology.

Tradition

The Christian concept of church fundamentally refers to the collective body of Christian people. If all church buildings collapsed or governments prohibited people from worshipping in them, Christians could still *be* church with one another, provided they were true to their common faith. Great geographic distances, language barriers, cultures, customs, and even historical epochs may separate Christians; they are still considered the church as long as they are connected by their authentic faith.

How do Christians determine what should or should not be believed? For many Christians the answer is, at least in part, tradition. The word *tradition* derives from the Latin root *tradere* meaning "to hand down." Tradition is not a mystical way of blocking innovation. Much as family traditions are handed down, preserved, and shaped from one generation to the next (think of recipes, family heirlooms, and stories told at the holidays), so too does the faith tradition bear the fingerprints of history, embodying how people have long held and preserved their most sacred notions, relics, and texts.

While more will be said about Protestant and Catholic differences in chapter 5, it is useful to note here that one of the rallying cries of the Protestant Reformation of the sixteenth century was "*sola scriptura*" ("by scripture alone"), meaning that only scripture—and not tradition—served as the valid basis for theology. Most of the Protestant denominations that resulted from the movement continue to see little or no value in tradition; rather, tradition is often seen as a collection of accretions that tend to obscure the pure gospel message of the Apostles.[1]

---

1. Here again, it should be noted that the various Protestant churches differ significantly on this topic. Some, for example, the Anglican communion (the Episcopal Church, in the United States), see great value in tradition, although not according it the authority it holds within the Catholic Church.

Catholics maintain tradition is authoritative,[2] and this belief stems from the Catholic ecclesial (or church) organizational structure. Catholic Christians affirm the magisterial (or teaching) authority of the ordained leadership regarding formal past teachings (usually written) by the popes and church councils. This tradition is recognized as instructive for how persons are to interpret scripture and the doctrines of the faith as well as basic principles of moral behavior. Thus, for Catholics, scripture and tradition are not at odds with each other; rather, they go hand in hand in order to insure legitimate interpretation and practice. Since Protestants reject the authority of the church hierarchy, they see no reason to assume a priori that an interpretation of scripture coming from an official ecclesial office is better than an interpretation of scripture coming from any well-informed, well-meaning individual Christian.

In the early Christian era, tradition was just beginning to form. Because the Christian faith did not have thousands of years of precedents to call on in its first centuries, early Christians often found themselves embroiled in great debates about what they should believe and how they should state those beliefs. When disputes arose, people often claimed that their position was the traditional or original point of view. To defend their positions, they would cite passages from the Bible or letters written by other prominent Christians whose religious authority was considered beyond reproach. By claiming that certain beliefs were more ancient or widely held than others, Christian leaders and teachers established which were authentic. By the fifth century, theologians began to define the parameters of the faith as that which is believed everywhere, always, and by everyone; today, these criteria are called universality, antiquity, and consensus, respectively.

What actually comprises tradition for Christians, and what role does it play for them? Some argue that Christian tradition refers exclusively to the Bible and its history of interpretation. Others hold that tradition may also include other elements, such as doctrinal statements, liturgical (or worship) practices, and even oral or informal

---

2. Tradition also plays a large role in Eastern Orthodox theology, but primarily in regard to the importance attached to the writings of the Church Fathers rather than to pronouncements from church authorities.

Christian beliefs and practices. Still others hold that the Bible alone is authoritative, rejecting the authority of any other aspect of Christianity, including past interpretations of the Bible.

Traditions Flowing from the Bible

Christians of the first several centuries spoke of tradition as it applied to biblical interpretation. When controversies arose, there were as yet no other widely acknowledged sources of authority, so people turned to the Bible. Over time, traditional ways of interpreting the Bible (especially problematic passages) were so often repeated they became the default position of the Christian community. For example, the Song of Songs is a wedding song that speaks poetically about the joys of marital lovemaking. Because of its sexual content, it would likely have been eliminated from the canon of the Bible had there not been a long tradition of interpreting the poem as an allegory for the love between God and his people. An allegorical interpretive tradition of this book of the Bible thus emerged and became the lens through which later generations typically interpreted the meaning of Song of Songs.

In the first few centuries of the church, beliefs were identified as legitimate (or orthodox) if they conformed to the interpretive traditions that emerged over the same period. Beliefs that were inconsistent with the interpretive traditions were considered false (or heretical). In many denominations, consistency with the tradition of interpretation on the meaning of the Bible, dating back to the beginning of the Christian era, is considered a mark of authentic Christian faith even today. By contrast, if someone derives a newfangled meaning from the Bible (as cult leaders sometimes do), many Christian communities are likely to deem the interpretation problematic because it stands in opposition to the traditional interpretation of the Bible.

Extrabiblical Tradition

From the beginning of the Christian movement, Christian thinkers grappled with an array of questions that the Bible did not clearly or definitively address. An early example is the developing doctrine of the Trinity in the third and fourth centuries. The Bible speaks of Father, Son, and Spirit, but it does not explain in a clearly formulated doctrine what is the relationship among them. The Bible likewise speaks of the "Word" (Jesus) becoming "flesh," but it does not explain what is the relationship between Jesus' human and divine natures. As Christian thinkers attempted to distinguish appropriate from inappropriate ways of thinking about God, they developed a large body of writings, including treatises, argumentative papers and letters, and position papers formed by councils of church leaders. These and other writings about an array of topics and issues accumulated over time and eventually became a second source for later generations' thinking about the Christian faith tradition.

To use a current example, the Bible does not comment on whether a married couple may use reproductive technologies such as in vitro fertilization to conceive a child, or whether the couple has the right to determine their child's gender. Because the Bible remains silent on an ever-growing number of questions, some Christians look to church authorities to articulate the appropriate Christian response to such issues. As various churches produce official documents and dogmas (or official teachings), members of those churches look to these materials as another source of authority that complements the revelation of the Bible.

Informal Tradition

Some Christians will distinguish between Tradition, with a capital T, and tradition, with a lowercase t. This is a useful, if imprecise, way of acknowledging that some elements of Christian tradition carry more weight than others. For example, the writings of the early church fathers, such as Augustine or Athanasius, are more often sources for contemporary Christian thought than the obscure poetry of anonymous medieval monks. Formal church services tend to perpetuate practices that have endured for most of Christianity's two-thousand-year history, while homespun practices such as making Advent wreaths with one's children come in and out of vogue. Many Christians feel that essential elements of the Christian tradition manifest a self-evident authority. Other elements of the tradition are more obviously matters of taste and aesthetics and hence lack authority even while they remain sources of the tradition. Such elements might include the following:

- worship styles
- vestments (religious garments)
- spiritual and devotional practices, such as going on pilgrimage, fasting, or meditating

Worship style reflects and reinforces theology. In many Protestant churches, worship space focuses on the pulpit, reflecting the importance attached to preaching in the Protestant tradition.

In some denominations, church authorities largely determine the content of the authoritative Christian tradition, but in the end, the *sensus fidelium* ("the sense of the faithful") has the last word. The church is the people, and what the people deem authentic in each era is ultimately what comprises the Christian faith for every generation.

Reason

In a fundamental sense, human reason must be a source or foundation for Christian theology. Through reason, people are able to acquire knowledge and form conclusions, judgments, or inferences. Christian faith thus assumes that reason is necessary to the theological task, but there are questions about the role and extent of its use. Emerging from the Christian claim that God reveals Godself, the questions of reason in theology become as follows: What is the relationship between reason and revelation? Is reason sufficient? Is revelation sufficient? What is the relationship between Christianity and science?

What Is the Relationship between Reason and Revelation?

Theology has classically incorporated the tools of reason (such as logical deduction, proofs for validity, postulates, and conclusions) into its systematic thinking. In this sense, reason may be understood as a tool that theology uses to unpack the content it receives from God's revelation. For example, theologians ask questions such as, If God is all powerful and all merciful, why does God allow people to suffer? This question reflects what at first glance appears to be an illogical Christian claim that God is both powerful and merciful and yet God allows people to suffer. Christians would use rational argumentation, in this instance, to attempt to demonstrate logically that God's power and mercy can exist simultaneously with human suffering. The basic relationship between reason and revelation is functional, with reason acting as a tool, or a "handmaid," for explicating the mysteries of Christian faith.

Is Reason Sufficient?

Another perspective is that whatever people need to know is available to them through their philosophical investigation and observation of nature. In this perspective, religious faith may complement what is known by reason, but is not necessary. Moreover, religious faith can never trump reason, because reason serves as the judge of religious claims. This position characterized the Enlightenment, an eighteenth-century intellectual movement in Europe and America, which believed reason to be omnicompetent (totally capable) in discerning truth. Enlightenment thinkers were highly critical of Christian truth claims and accepted Christian theology only to the extent that it could be deemed rational. Seemingly irrational claims, such as the belief in miracles or Jesus' Resurrection from the dead, were dismissed as superstitious. Rationally tenable claims, such as Jesus' teachings in the Sermon on the Mount (a famous section of the Gospel of Matthew), were maintained. Here the relationship between revelation and reason is one of critique, with reason judging what is religiously admissible. Reason, in this sense, can marginalize or even negate revealed truth, and as such can be seen as inimical to faith.

Is Revelation Sufficient?

Yet another perspective is that revelation, and not reason, has the final say in matters of human knowing. Although privileging reason is attractive, reason itself does not speak to all aspects of human thought. Dimensions of knowing that are affective (pertaining to the emotions or sentiment) seem to defy reason's ability to describe or contain. To the extent that theology as interpreter of revelation deals with affective dimensions and responses of knowing, including beauty, love, and friendship, it supersedes reason. Christians often speak of the mysteries of their faith, by which they refer to aspects beyond rational description. In these instances, revelation is more abundant than reason. The relationship between revelation and reason is one of transcendence, with revelation simultaneously encompassing and surpassing all that is rationally knowable.

The dialogue between Christianity and philosophy is as old as Christian history. It represents Christian theology's practice of looking toward reason as a source for its own discernment of truth. Although there is no absolute consensus on the relationship between Christian theology and philosophy, their inevitable dialogue demonstrates the timeless foundation of reason for the theological enterprise.

Reason Informing Biblical Interpretation

As discussed in the previous chapter, people can meaningfully read the Bible in many different ways: for inspiration, for consolation, for knowledge of God, for wisdom, and so on. However, reading the Bible well requires an understanding of the nature of the texts. Just as one would be disappointed if one looked to the phone book for poetic inspiration or to a comic book for directions on installing a new dishwasher, so too people may become frustrated if they read the Bible without understanding the nature of what they are reading.

Reason Informing Biblical Interpretation (continued)

Trying to read the Bible as if it provides a natural history of the world is a common mistake. In particular, people make this error when reading the books of the Old Testament, especially the creation stories in Genesis. Though some books of the Bible do refer to the geopolitical history of the kingdoms of Judah and Israel, the Old Testament mostly relates the story of the covenant relationship between the people of Israel and God. This love story is told in fables, poems, liturgies, songs, and myths. Even the historical aspects are told and retold in various lights, depending on what was happening at the time of their final recording.

It is highly unlikely that the human writers of the Bible thought they were recording a natural history of the earth. But if not that, how might the creation stories function in the Bible? Biblical writings on the origins of life do two things: they attribute the totality of life and the cosmos to the work of a single, powerful Creator, and they retain an awe and mystery about the Creator's work, suggesting that human beings have a restricted capacity to understand it. In other words, the creation stories affirm God as the Creator and call human beings to recognize their humility before the Creator. The creation stories in Genesis are complemented in the book of Job and its depiction of God's incomprehensible mastery over nature. A profound insight of this text is that human knowledge is insufficient to grasp the full power and mystery of God. Thus these biblical stories use the language of poetry and myth, literary forms well suited to communicate the inexplicable.

Early Christian interpreters of the Bible did not have a problem recognizing poetry and myth; they felt no need to interpret these stories as a natural history of the earth in order to appreciate their truth. They recognized that the biblical writers were far more concerned with providing spiritual illumination than historical accuracy. Tensions or contradictions in the text were seen as opportunities to delve further into the layers of revelation and as invitations to find truth beyond the superficial accounts of past events.

What Is the Relationship between Christianity and Science?

Occasionally purely fideistic (faith-based) expressions of Christian thought have outweighed rational (reason-based) approaches. The overwhelming consensus in Christianity, however, is that people are encouraged to use reason to explore and understand the world. Christian thinkers—from the earliest writers to contemporary theologians—have looked to a reason-based understanding of the world to enhance their knowledge of God.

Using reason to complement faith rests on two underlying tenets of a Christian worldview. The first tenet is that God created freely. The belief that God created the world suggests the world is a place where people can come to know God. In other words, the world is not random, mechanical, or arbitrary, but rather the intentioned and loving work of a free Creator. As such, the world is like an artist's canvas or a school where God's character reveals itself. Reason is rightly employed to study the world because studying the world is an aspect of studying God. Consequently, reason-based inquiry may lead to surprising new revelations about the world. The world is not "given" or utterly predictable but is a place of discovery. Moreover, human reason itself is a component of God's creation, a blessing and gift to the human species. Indeed, reason is in part what makes humans bearers of the image of God.

The second tenet is that God created human beings to be free. Human freedom acts in dialogue with the freedom by which God created the world. When something is free, its outcome is not pre-ordained. It is not bound by necessity or obligation but is open to new possibilities, new discoveries, and new developments. The whole basis of scientific investigation, invention, human technology, and so on presumes a fundamental freedom. Using freedom to engage the world creatively is a unique vocation of the human species, one that requires the full exercise of reason.

Christian thought and science both seek to understand the world. While theology primarily concerns making sense of faith claims, the world that Christians try to understand from a faith perspective is the same one that scientists try to understand from a perspective of inquiry and observation. This sameness of the world

Evolution: A Question of Science and Faith

Imagine that today you learned you had inherited $10 million. That knowledge would change your sense of everything. The same thing happens as major new discoveries about the universe reframe how it is understood. The discovery that Earth revolved around the sun was one such moment. Before Galileo confirmed the Copernican heliocentric theory of the solar system in the seventeenth century, people believed the sun revolved around Earth. Because many people believed humans to be the greatest creatures on Earth, it followed that these people believed humans to be literally the center of the universe. The discovery that Earth is only one of many planets that revolve around the sun seemed to diminish this sense of human importance. Such an alteration in thinking is called a paradigm shift, which, although both immediate and dramatic, can take decades or centuries to be fully accepted.

In 1859 Charles Darwin published the book *On the Origin of Species*, in which he theorized that life on Earth evolves by the adaptation of species to environmental conditions. Darwin's theory relativized human importance, relegating human beings to the status of other creatures. Many Christian communities found ways of incorporating Darwin's theory into their understanding of how God interacts with the world, but others, especially in the United States, saw the theory as a threat to their understanding of the creation of humans and their special purpose in salvation. In response, they claimed that "true" Christians must read the Bible as a literal record of natural history and reject the findings of modern science. This approach was embraced by the rising "Fundamentalist" movement of the early twentieth century, which insisted that several tenets of Christian faith must be understood as absolutely factual, including the virgin birth of Jesus, the Resurrection of Jesus, and the literal, word-for-word truth of the Bible.

Today many people still wrestle with the paradigm shift brought by the theory of evolution. Many Christians accept

Evolution: A Question of Science and Faith (continued)

the theory of evolution by understanding evolution as part of God's creative process and under God's direction. Other Christians doubt evolution because it is a "theory"—which reflects some confusion about modern science.

Watson Davis/Smithsonian Institution Archives

Clarence Darrow defends John Scopes at his trial in 1925 for violating a Tennessee law that prohibited teaching evolution in public schools. John Washington Butler, the law's author, feared that teaching evolution would cause children to lose their faith in God.

A theory is a principle or postulate used to explain or interpret a phenomenon. When scientists test and retest a theory using the best tools of observation available, they arrive at evidence-based facts. Facts are considered true until proven false or called into question by new theories or new tools of observation. The process of developing a theory, testing it, confirming the tests, and theorizing anew as circumstances warrant is called the scientific method. The facts deduced by scientific method can be thought of as best-case interpretations of phenomena. Science is more properly understood as a method than a series of facts about the world, and the same method that is used to arrive at one set of facts can be used to revise those facts when new tools of observation or discoveries allow.

Evolution: A Question of Science and Faith (continued)

Science, then, is not simply about facts that people either accept or do not accept as true. Essentially, science is a way to engage the world to understand its nature and how it functions. The methods of science need not conflict with other methods of human knowing. Even if not directly employed, science can nevertheless enhance other methods that are used. In a fundamental sense, all people who study the world methodically are scientists.

---

we study invites several possible relationships between theology and science. These include complementary or integrative dialogue, discreet or unrelated dialogue, conflicting or contradictory dialogue, and dialectical and revisionist dialogue.

Complementary or Integrative Dialogue. Natural science and Christianity may engage each other by sharing their findings in an effort to complement each other. Some people argue that theology describes the meaning and value of the world, whereas science describes the physics and structure of the world. Natural scientists ask one set of questions, and theologians ask another, but the questions concern the same world. Both sets of answers are useful in arriving at a rich understanding of the world.

Discreet or Unrelated Dialogue. Science and Christianity may claim that each investigates something unrelated to the study of the other. Revelation is the subject matter of theology. The natural world is the subject matter of science (e.g., biology or physics), which is independent of revelation from God. In this model, science and theology need not battle each other—or even engage each other—because their respective objects of investigation are independent.

Conflicting or Contradictory Dialogue. Natural science and Christianity may engage each other in conflict. Proponents on either side may conclude that science and Christianity offer conflicting, mutually exclusive understandings of the same phenomena. This can lead people to feel that they must choose between science and religion.

Dialectical and Revisionist Dialogue. A constructive approach to conflicts between science and theology is dialectical and revisionist dialogue. In this context, "dialectical" refers to an engaged conversation, driven by logical discussion, between competing perspectives. Each perspective helps to enlarge, inform, and correct the other; new insight emerges from willingness to revise scientific theory and religious understanding to best accommodate all available information.

Experience

Theology is rooted in human experience. On some level theology cannot be detached from human experience, because doing theology is itself a human endeavor. However, good theology must self-consciously pay attention to lived experience as a source and judge of truth if it wants to remain authentic, relevant, and vital to people's lives. Experience, in Christian understanding, may be thought of as a source and a gauge for truth, as an interpretive framework, and as establishing a hermeneutical circle of theory and praxis.[3]

A Source of Truth

How is lived experience a source of truth? One could argue that experience carries truth within itself, almost as a type of revelation. Often truth gleaned from experience is more powerful than truth learned in a book or a classroom. In fifth-grade health class, for example, children can learn about human reproduction, and in eighth-grade home economics, children can simulate the experience of caring for a baby by carrying around a bag of flour for a day. Such lessons, however useful, cannot really prepare people for the experience of parenthood. The experience of parenting teaches patience, forgiveness, leadership, discipline, nutrition, and more in a way that no merely theoretical approach can.

In a similar manner, experience is a touchstone for theology. Christian theology may speak about love, justice, forgiveness, and redemption, but the reality of these truths is borne out by living

---

3. The hermeneutical circle is discussed later in the chapter.

them. Experience is a source that gives rise to insight and also conditions theoretical knowledge with the wisdom of "having been there." Moreover, the recognition that human experience is a foundation for Christian theology enables theology to speak for and out of human experience in general. In other words, Christian theology is not only interested in how Christians believe and behave. It is also interested in human life as a whole.

Are all experiences potentially theologically valuable or revelatory? One could answer either yes or no, depending on how rigidly one separates sacred (divine) from secular (worldly) encounters. By way of illustration, sometimes I will ask students to report on or analyze things that reveal God to them or teach them something about forgiveness, or justice, or other theological themes. Students will often talk about songs they love, beautiful experiences of nature, or relationships they enjoy. What is deeply revelatory to one may not be so for another. In effect, "truths" derived from experience may only be recognized as true by a small group or even an individual. Consequently, "experience" is a conceptually tricky source for deriving universal truths. One must ask, "Whose experience?" and "When?" Such questions often reveal tensions, which are not inherently problematic but which do warn against extrapolating too broadly.

Experience and reason also exist in tension with tradition and scripture. This is because experience and reason are unavoidably involved in our efforts to read and interpret the Bible and the tradition. There is no absolutely "objective" way for people to read, such that they remove their assumptions, biases, and preferences from the interpretive process. Contemporary people always bring their experiences, including knowledge of modern science, to the challenge of interpreting and understanding documents written long ago. Interpreters may have difficulty making sense of past things they may not fully understand. Moreover, rival contemporary readings raise questions: Which interpretation is most adequate? What criteria should be employed in making our determination?

A Gauge for Truth

When theology speaks meaningfully to lived experience, it becomes a vital tool for the application of faith in daily life. On the other hand, when theology makes claims that do not resonate with people's lived experience, it risks being discounted as irrelevant at best and dangerous at worst. Experience serves as a gauge for determining whether religious truth claims are adequate and valid.

For example, throughout most of Christian history, celibate (unmarried and not sexually active) clergymen produced the dominant works of theology. Nevertheless, they discussed marriage, sexuality, and family issues, and their discussions include many negative statements on sexuality and marriage. The writers often saw their celibate lifestyle as superior to married life. Today, theology is more "democratic," both in its views and in the scope of its authors. Married persons reading negative comments from the past about marriage recognize a discontinuity between their lived experience and the words of those who spoke about, but did not experience, marriage. Trusting more in the truth derived from married life, people today widely discount the negative views of the past in favor of contemporary voices that celebrate marriage and family as venerable expressions of Christian living. Across a wide range of theological concerns, experience serves as a gauge to keep theological claims honest and true to people's lives.

An Interpretive Framework

Lived experience, beyond serving as a source and gauge of truth, also relates to Christian theology in the sense that human experience needs to be interpreted. Human experience is often ambiguous. People question the origin, purpose, and destiny of their lives and of collective human experience: What do we know? How do we know it? Why do we exist at all? These perennial questions originate with people reflecting on their experience. Christian theology provides a framework for interpreting experience. Indeed, at base, the purpose of Christian theology is to provide a framework for making sense of human life. Moreover, having a faith-based, interpretive framework for life helps people avoid an exaggerated sense of individualism and the attitude "anything goes as long as I like it," so common in contemporary, industrialized cultures. In this way, experience not only gauges theological adequacy, it also is gauged itself.

The Hermeneutical Circle of Theory and Praxis

This dialogue between theology and experience may be more closely examined as the intersection between theory and praxis. *Theory* describes the theoretical component of theology, for theology could also be loosely described as "religious theories about human life." *Praxis* refers to intentional, reflective action that is driven by theory. For example, one may theorize that she will find more meaning in life by helping others, but it is praxis when she subsequently volunteers at a women's shelter on the basis of her theory.

The relationship between theory and praxis is sometimes called a hermeneutical circle. *Hermeneutics* in this context means "self-conscious interpretation of theory." Frequently used to describe interpretation of the Bible, hermeneutics may also more broadly be understood as an interpretive theological approach that connects theory and reflective action. In the introduction to his work *A Theology of Liberation*, Gustavo Gutierrez argues that theology rises only at sundown.[4] This colorful image communicates the basic point that Christian faith is mostly about lived, day-to-day experience. At sundown, after the day's work, it makes sense to theorize and reflect on the day's lessons and value. The evening reflection may shed new insight on how to act tomorrow. This creates a circular pattern of doing, reflecting, revising action, reflecting further, and so on.

The model of the hermeneutical circle captures the indelible connection between experience and theology. Theology must begin in people's lives and return its reflective insights back to people's lives. Experience is an inescapable source for insight and authenticity in Christian thought.

---

4. Gustavo Guttierrez, *A Theology of Liberation: History, Politics, and Salvation* (Maryknoll, NY: Orbis Books, 1973, 1988).

Conclusion

Christian thought is immersed in history, in the world, and in people's experiences. Christian thought is dialogical and developmental and uses classical sources from its tradition, as well as contemporary insights drawn from nearly every discipline of study and every walk of life. Christian thought begins with the Bible, which must be encountered anew in every generation of believers. As contexts change, Christian people are challenged to make sense of their faith in light of their own personal and social circumstances. In order to do so, Christians rely, with varying degrees, on tradition (both formal and informal), on reason, and on experience (both personal and communal). The foundations of Christian thought considered in this chapter illustrate the interplay and some of the tensions between the past and present, the tradition and lived experience, reason and faith, and the Bible and its interpretation and application.

Questions for Discussion and Review

1. Name and describe the sources or foundations of Christian theology. What are some ways in which they intersect or overlap?
2. Describe some of the differences among Christians in their reliance upon or rejection of nonbiblical sources of faith.
3. Describe the role of tradition in Christian theology. How would you differentiate between formal and informal aspects of this tradition?
4. What are the possible relationship models between reason and revelation in Christian theology? Which model makes the most sense to you, and why?
5. How is experience both a source and a gauge for theological insight?
6. Describe the hermeneutical circle. How does theory inform action, and conversely, how does action inform theory?
7. Can you think of other extrabiblical or nonbiblical sources that could contribute to a Christian's sense or knowledge of God? What are the risks and benefits of drawing on such sources?

Resources

Books

Albl, Martin C. *Reason, Faith, and Tradition: Explorations in Catholic Theology.* Winona, MN: Anselm Academic, 2009, 2015.

Bonsor, Jack A. *Athens and Jerusalem: The Role of Philosophy in Theology.* Eugene, OR: Wipf & Stock, 2003.

Brooke, John Hedley, Russell Re Manning, and Fraser Watts, eds. *The Oxford Handbook of Natural Theology.* Oxford: Oxford University Press, 2013.

Gelpi, Donald. *The Turn to Experience in Contemporary Theology.* Mahwah, NJ: Paulist Press, 1994.

Paley, William. *Natural Theology.* New York: American Tract Society, 1881. Online at *Natural Theology Internet Archive, https://archive. org/details/naturaltheology00pale.*

Sokolowski, Robert. *The God of Faith and Reason: Foundations of Christian Theology.* Washington, DC: Catholic University Press, 1995.

Websites

The Gifford Lectures: Over 100 Years of Lectures on Natural Theology, at *www.giffordlectures.org.*

Films

Harvard Divinity School; "Comparative Natural Theology," at *www .youtube.com/watch?v=Y8uCC-wpjkA.*

NOVA; "Intelligent Design on Trial," at *www.pbs.org/wgbh/nova /evolution/intelligent-design-trial.html.*

CHAPTER 4

Periods in Christian History

What to Expect

This chapter is a basic introduction to the major historical divisions in Christian thought. It discusses the following key periods:[1]

- The Biblical Era, 2000 BCE[2]–100 CE
- The Patristic Era, 100–700
- The Middle Ages, 700–1500
- The Reformation, 1500–1750
- The Modern Era, 1750–Present

The Biblical Era

The biblical era has two major divisions: the Old Testament period[3] and the New Testament period. Together these periods constitute the principal foundation for Christian thought. The main textual

---

1. All dates are approximate.

2. The reader should understand that while the Bible preserves traditions that claim to reach back into this early period, most biblical scholars believe that even the oldest portions of the Bible did not receive their current form until closer to 1000 BCE. Most sections of the Bible are considerably more recent.

3. Of course, the Old Testament period is actually Jewish, not Christian, because it predates Christianity. However, inasmuch as Christian thinking draws upon the Old Testament, an account of the development of Christian thought must begin there.

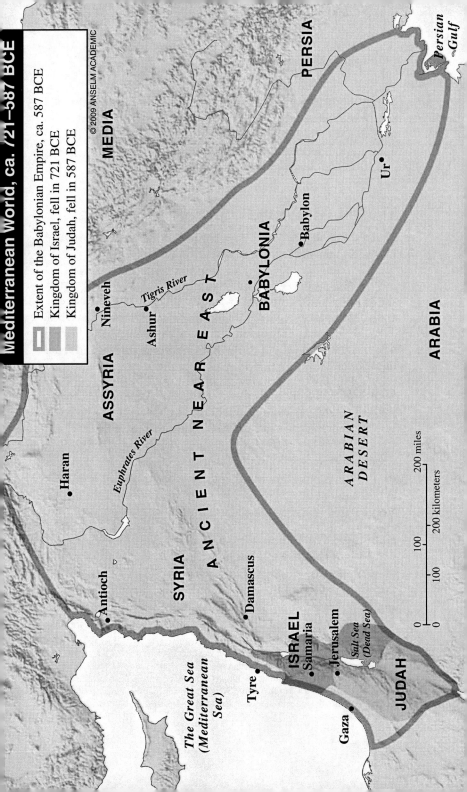

Mediterranean World, ca. 721–587 BCE

Extent of the Babylonian Empire, ca. 587 BCE
Kingdom of Israel, fell in 721 BCE
Kingdom of Judah, fell in 587 BCE

© 2009 ANSELM ACADEMIC

MEDIA

PERSIA

Persian Gulf

ASSYRIA

Nineveh

Ashur

Tigris River

BABYLONIA

Babylon

Ur

ANCIENT NEAR EAST

Haran

Euphrates River

SYRIA

Antioch

Damascus

ISRAEL

Samaria

Jerusalem

Salt Sea (Dead Sea)

JUDAH

Tyre

Gaza

The Great Sea (Mediterranean Sea)

ARABIAN DESERT

ARABIA

200 miles

200 kilometers

0   100   200

0   100   200

materials that come from these periods are the books of the Old and New Testaments. Noncanonical books, as well as materials from neighboring cultures of the ancient Near East, archaeological discoveries, and artifacts are also useful tools for understanding these eras and the biblical writings.

The Old Testament Period[4]

Christians divide the Old Testament period into several important historical moments, as follows (all dates given are BCE):

2000–1500: In the first subdivision of the Old Testament period, the Bible tells of the lives of the great patriarchs, such as Abraham, Isaac, Jacob, and Joseph, and the formation of the tribes of Israel. The Bible depicts the ancient Israelites as seminomadic herders who migrated throughout the Fertile Crescent to pasture and water their flocks.

1500–1250: The Bible describes the ancient Hebrews (later known as the Israelites) as living in Egypt during this period. The numbers of the Israelites increased significantly, they were enslaved and treated harshly by the Egyptian pharaoh, and they were led by God through the prophet Moses to freedom. This last event, known as the Exodus, became the central unifying story for the tribes of Israel in the centuries that followed. The historicity of parts of the biblical account is generally considered questionable.

1250–1020: The biblical account next describes the Israelites as settling into the land of Canaan, where they lived under the rule of tribal leaders, called judges. Archaeological evidence suggests that some, at least, of the groups that later identified themselves as Israelites were native to Canaan, and not freed slaves who migrated there from Egypt, as the Bible asserts. There are also inconsistencies

---

4. The corpus of writings Christians call the Old Testament is in fact the Hebrew Bible—supplemented, in some Christian canons, by a few additional texts. From the Jewish perspective, these writings are emphatically not an "Old Testament," for they do not look forward to a corresponding "New Testament." These foundational texts of Judaism are Christian only in the sense that, at a much later date, Christians too came to accept them as sacred scripture.

between the biblical description of how Canaan was settled (in the books of Joshua and Judges) and what the archaeological record indicates. Some evidence points toward Israelite conquest (as in the book of Joshua), but other evidence suggests a more peaceful, long-term, mutual enculturation between Canaanites and Israelites, punctuated by infighting and tension among tribes (more akin to the account in the book of Judges).

1020–930: The tribes of Israel coalesce as a nation ruled by a king. The biblical record indicates a mixed attitude concerning the risks and benefits of having a king (especially in 1 Samuel). Three kings are said to have reigned over the united Israelite tribes: Saul, David, and Solomon. Among the highlights in the biblical account of this era was the construction of the Temple in Jerusalem during the reign of Solomon.

930–722: The Kingdom of Israel is divided. After the death of Solomon, ten tribes in the north elected an independent king and established independent shrines for worship at the key sites of Dan and Bethel. The Bible indicates that the ten tribes separated from the southern kingdom due to overtaxation and forced labor. The northern tribes concluded that they had no "share" in the kingdom of the south (see 1 Kings chapter 12). The account of the division of the kingdom into the northern kingdom of Israel and the southern kingdom of Judah (replete with the stories of the kings who reigned in each region) may be found in the books of 1 and 2 Kings. The northern kingdom was destroyed by the Assyrians in 722. Israelites were torn from their homes and forcibly relocated, causing the Diaspora (or scattering) of Hebrew persons and culture throughout the ancient Near East (see 2 Kings chapter 17).

930–587: The remaining southern tribes of Judah and Benjamin continued their kingdom of Judah during this period, maintaining a capital in Jerusalem and leadership under the dynasty of David. The kingdom of Judah was destroyed by the Babylonians in 587 (see 2 Kings 25). (See map, Mediterranean World, ca. 721–587 BCE, p. 71.)

587–539: Following the Babylonian conquest of the kingdom of Judah, many poor Israelites remained in the land, under Babylonian control. Most professionals and individuals of high birth were forcibly relocated to Babylon. This event, called the Babylonian exile, constituted a major alteration in Israelite culture, principally because the people lost the land, which they believed God had promised them, and the Temple, which had been the focus of their worship practices. Without their land and Temple, Israelites turned to their oral and written traditions to preserve their culture. Much of the Hebrew Bible was developed during the Exile.

539–425: Babylonian forces that had once conquered Israel were themselves conquered by the Persian king Cyrus the Great. Cyrus allowed those who had been forcibly relocated to Babylon to return to their homelands, under the rule of Persian-approved governors. Many Israelites thus returned to Jerusalem to rebuild the city and restore their culture.

425–333: The Israelites lived under relatively peaceful Persian rule.

333–175: Judea was once again conquered, passing from Persian to Greek control. Under the tactical genius of Alexander the Great, Greek forces overwhelmed Palestine. Toward the end of this period, Greek rule became oppressive for the Jews. Under the cruel rule of Antiochus IV Epiphanes in the second century BCE, Jews suffered brutality, religious oppression, and forced cultural transformations. Jews of this era developed several strategies for preserving their faith and culture, eventually resulting in the emergence of various sects within Judaism, including the Pharisees, Sadducees, and resistance movements (all of whom are mentioned in the New Testament).

175–64: Led by Judas Maccabeus, the Jews revolted and threw off their oppressors. The Maccabean revolt led to a period of Jewish independence and the establishment of the Hasmonean Dynasty. During this era, the final books of the Old Testament were composed. The era between the close of the Old Testament writings and the beginning of the New Testament writings is sometimes called the intertestamental period.

The New Testament Period

The New Testament period is much briefer than the Old Testament period, spanning roughly one hundred and fifty years.[5] It marks not only a change in historical context but also, and perhaps more important, a change in perspective about the meaning of Israel's history and, within the emerging Jesus movement, significant changes in the ethnic and cultural vantage point of the New Testament authors. The events of the life of Jesus occur in Roman-occupied territories, comprising Galilee in the north, Judea in the south, and Samaria in between. Jesus' life spanned roughly 4 BCE to 30 CE, during which time the political situation was highly tumultuous.

The Roman general Pompey had conquered Jerusalem in 63 BCE. Jewish autonomy was seriously curtailed under Roman rule. The Romans appointed Herod (descended from the Jewish Hasmonean Dynasty) as king over Judea. However, Herod remained under Roman control. He reigned from 37 BCE until his death in 4 BCE. After Herod's death, Judea was ruled directly by Roman governors, without mediation from a Roman-appointed Hasmonean king. This was an oppressive situation for the Jews, who resisted Roman rule and revolted sporadically throughout the first century.

A widespread revolt occurred in 66 CE, which ended in the destruction of Jerusalem and its Temple. The Jewish historian Josephus records massive Jewish casualties during this uprising. A Jewish high court, or sanhedrin, reconvened in the city of Javneh in 70 CE. Over the next several decades, Jewish communities stabilized throughout the Roman Empire. Because the Jerusalem Temple and its priests no longer existed, the focus of Jewish religious life shifted to the rabbis, the study of Torah, and the communal gathering in synagogues. Life for Jews and the Jewish offshoot sect that would eventually be called Christianity was perilous throughout the first century and beyond.

The life of Jesus and the birth of the early Christian church occurred in this sometimes violent and always oppressive context of Roman occupation. Much of the apocalyptic (or "end-of-the-world")

---

5. The period begins with the birth of Jesus and closes with the writing of the last of the books of the New Testament.

thinking found in both the teachings of Jesus and the beliefs of the early Christians can be attributed to this context, which was rife with injustice, vulnerability for the occupied people, and hope for deliverance. People could be seized from their homes and forced into labor, women and girls suffered sexual violence at the hands of the Roman military, and people were heavily taxed.

The emerging Christian community and the development of the Christian New Testament must be understood against this violent colonial backdrop. Among the tensions and conflicts underlying the burgeoning Jesus movement were the following issues and questions:

What was the nature of the Messiah? Jews had long hoped for deliverance from occupation and restoration of their kingdom. The prophetic writings from the period during and after the Babylonian exile imagine a free and flourishing Jewish kingdom, in which the northern and southern tribes would be reunited and stronger than ever (for example, see Ezekiel chapter 37). Many Jews expected a Messiah (or anointed king) to be the catalyst and leader of this new golden age. By the time of the New Testament writings, beginning around the middle of the first century CE, followers of the Jesus movement were identifying Jesus by the term *Messiah*. The problem, however, was that the Jewish homelands were still occupied by the Romans, and the Jewish kingdom had not been restored. The issue forced the Jews to question not just whether God would send a Messiah, but what would be the Messiah's role. Was he to be a temporal, political figure who would deliver the Jews from oppressive Roman rule, or was the Messiah an apocalyptic figure who would usher in a new age? In short, was Jesus indeed the Messiah of Jewish ancestral hope? Some Jews said yes, becoming the first Christians; others said no, stringently opposing the first Christians.

What was the relationship between Judaism and the Jesus movement? Jesus and his followers were Jewish, and the original Christians were Jews. This fact led to one of the most challenging issues for the New Testament community. Jewish followers of Jesus and Jewish opponents of Jesus are seen in the New Testament as vying against one another over important claims, including the identity and role of the Messiah, the meaning of past Hebrew prophesies, and the interpretation of Hebrew texts (i.e., the Old Testament writings). There is a sense, moreover, in some of the New Testament writings (for example, the Letter to the Hebrews) that some Christian Jews, who were experiencing hardship and disappointment as they waited to enjoy any benefit from their Christian beliefs, were tempted to revert to a non-Messianic form of Judaism. Furthermore, the Jesus movement quickly began to attract non-Jewish converts. These Gentile converts were interested in the benefits of the Jewish/Christian God but did not want to have to receive circumcision or follow the rigorous Jewish law. As more and more Greeks and Romans became Christians, distance grew between the Jesus movement and its roots in Judaism, putting Christians at even greater pains to prove themselves legitimate heirs to the Jewish heritage.

What was the relationship between Gentiles and the Jesus movement? Initially, the followers of Jesus, being Jews, continued to observe the Jewish law. It appears that many key leaders of the emerging church felt that Gentile converts also needed to follow Torah—that, in effect, in order to become a Christian one needed to become Jewish. Others, envisioning an inclusive community that accepted both Jewish and Gentile believers, asserted that Gentile converts should not be required to follow Torah. This debate permeates the New Testament letters written by Paul—for example, Galatians, where there was disagreement about whether Jewish Christians and non-Jewish Christians could share the Christian ritual meal together, because Jewish law forbade the practice of Jews eating with non-Jews. The "Gentile question" became a huge problem for the early Christian church.

How should the Jesus movement proceed into the future? After the death of Jesus and the first apostles,[6] questions arose about the nature and structure of the Christian community. At the center of the controversy was Paul, an apostle who did not know Jesus in life, but only through a visionary encounter with the Risen Jesus (see Acts chapters 9, 22, and 26). Paul's New Testament letters bear

---

6. Apostles were followers of the Jesus movement who spread the message about Jesus after his death.

witness to conflicts between Paul and other leaders, including some of Jesus' intimates: Peter, James, and John. In the absence of Jesus himself, early leaders of the Jesus movement had to deal with such questions as: Who has the authority to set church policy? How should disputes be settled when they arise? What are the accepted beliefs and practices of the community—and which beliefs and practices are not to be tolerated?

Against a backdrop of political oppression, cultural cross-pollination, and doctrinal development, the emergent Christian community navigated issues of identity, political persecution, civic responsibility, group organization, and future sustainability. These concerns largely directed the historical development of Christian thought in the following centuries.

The Patristic Era

The patristic era (derived from the Latin *pater*, meaning "father"), typically refers to the period between 100 and 700. In this era, Christianity spread from its origins in Palestine throughout much of the Roman Empire. The spread of Christianity included both geographical and ideological expansion, as this once-Jewish movement became thoroughly entrenched in and informed by elements of the broader Greco-Roman culture.

Significant Persons and Places

Christian ideas spread through the missionary efforts of early Christians. The New Testament recounts in some detail, for example, the missionary work of the Apostle Paul.[7] Paul's activities offer insight into the nature of the spread of the early Christian community. Missionaries would go alone or in small groups to a new location, where they would take up work and residency while sharing the "good news" about Jesus. Once a community of believers was established, the missionary would move on to a new location,

---

7. It should be noted, however, that the historical accuracy of the account in the Acts of the Apostles is considered questionable at many points.

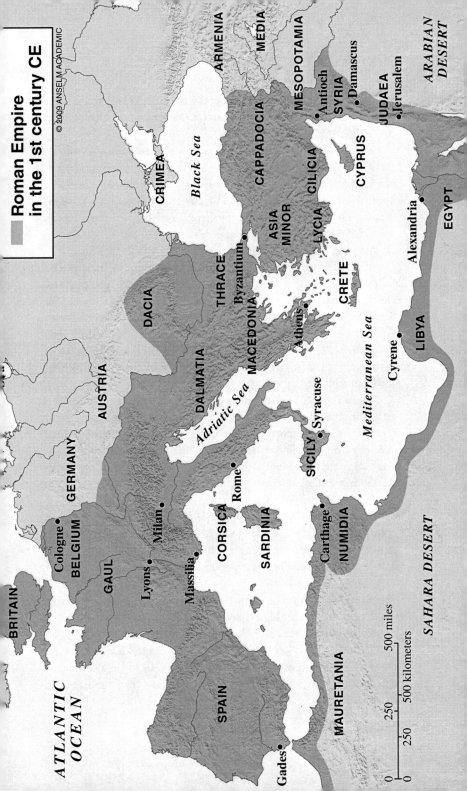

Roman Empire in the 1st century CE

© 2009 ANSELM ACADEMIC

Roman Empire
in the 1st century CE

BRITAIN

ATLANTIC
OCEAN

GERMANY

BELGIUM

Cologne

GAUL

Lyons

Milan

AUSTRIA

DACIA

CRIMEA

Black Sea

ARMENIA

MEDIA

MESOPOTAMIA

Damascus

Antioch

SYRIA

CAPPADOCIA

JUDEA

Jerusalem

ASIA
MINOR

CILICIA

CYPRUS

ARABIAN
DESERT

Massilia

SPAIN

Gades

CORSICA

Rome

SARDINIA

Carthage

NUMIDIA

DALMATIA

THRACE

Byzantium

MACEDONIA

Athens

Adriatic Sea

SICILY

Syracuse

CRETE

LYCIA

Mediterranean Sea

Cyrene

LIBYA

Alexandria

EGYPT

MAURETANIA

SAHARA DESERT

0   250   500 miles

0   250   500 kilometers

staying in touch via letters and occasional visits. The letters of the New Testament represent the correspondence among early Christian communities.

Christian missionaries expanded the reach of the new movement throughout North Africa, the Mediterranean area, and Eastern Europe. A number of hub cities beyond Jerusalem and Rome became important locations for Christian theological development. Among the most important were Antioch (in modern-day Turkey), Alexandria (in modern-day Egypt), and Carthage (in modern-day Algeria).

Antioch was a principal location to which Christians fled following the fall of Jerusalem in 70. Antiochene theology was characterized by its emphasis on the humanity of Jesus and its literal interpretation of the Bible. Major thinkers associated with Antioch include John Chrysostom (ca. 347–407), Basil the Great (ca. 330–379), Gregory of Nyssa (ca. 335–395), and Gregory of Nazianzus (ca. 330–389). The last three are known collectively as the Cappadocian Fathers.

From the city of Alexandria came Alexandrian theology, which served as the foremost rival to the Antiochene approach. Deeply rooted in Greek philosophy, especially that of Plato, Alexandrian theology emphasized the divinity of Christ and the allegorical, or symbolic, interpretation of the Bible. Key thinkers associated with Alexandria include Clement of Alexandria (ca. 150–215), Origen (ca. 185–254), and Athanasius (ca. 293–373).

Carthage was a third city crucial to the developing Christian communities of the patristic era. Located in North Africa, Carthage was an important center for commerce and culture. It was distinctive in its theological approach, in part because Latin was the dominant language of the region, rather than Greek, as in Antioch and Alexandria. A more legalistic approach to developing doctrine and Christian terminology characterized the theology. Key thinkers associated with Carthage include Tertullian (ca. 160–220), Cyprian of Carthage (third century; Cyprian's birth and death dates are unclear), and Augustine of Hippo (354–430), whose influence and range make him one of the most important theologians of the patristic era.

Major Doctrinal Disputes and Developments

The doctrinal conflicts and developments in the patristic era stemmed from numerous root causes. Persecution of Christians under the Romans, for example, left communities divided over what to do with repentant Christians who had renounced their faith under threat of physical torture. Should they be readmitted to Christian worship? If so, ought the community impose penalties on them? In addition, diverse cultures and languages often led devout believers to different conclusions regarding questions of faith. The Hebraic roots of Christian thought differed dramatically from the worldviews expressed in Greco-Roman traditions. In particular, Hebraic thought argued for strict monotheism (one God), whereas pagan religion was polytheistic (multiple gods). Christians came from both backgrounds, and such different starting points led to confusion when Christians asked questions about the relationship of Jesus to God and the Holy Spirit. (Were they one God? Two gods? Three gods?) These and other such factors fueled many heated debates in the patristic era. Because there was no official church teaching and only limited historical precedent, these debates constituted the beginning of the development of Christian doctrine.

Following are some of the principal subjects of these debates:

- the structure of the church, the role of bishops, how authority was to be passed down, and the primacy of the Bishop of Rome (i.e., the pope)
- the selection of books to be included in the New Testament
- the role of tradition versus novel developments and ongoing "revelations" of the Holy Spirit, giving rise to heresies such as Montanism (a belief that new prophets and prophesies were revealed by the Holy Spirit even after the time of Jesus and the close of the New Testament writings) and Gnosticism (a variety of beliefs in elaborate hierarchies of divine beings)
- the nature of Christ, especially the relationship of his humanity to his divinity, which gave rise to the heresies of Nestorianism (the idea that the human and divine natures of Jesus were separate from each other) and Apollinarianism (the belief that Jesus had the mind of God, not a human mind)

- the relationship among the Father, the Son, and the Holy Spirit in the Christian conception of God, especially the Arian heresy (which asserted that the Son of God is a created being, and that he is not divine in the same way that the Father is divine)
- the relationship with Christians who renounced Christ under persecution but wanted to return to the church after the persecution ended, giving rise to the Donatist controversy; Donatists refused to forgive church leaders who had buckled under persecution, thus rejecting the reinstatement of fallen priests and bishops, and denying the validity of sacraments (e.g., baptism) celebrated by such "apostate" priests and bishops
- the role of grace versus free will in human salvation, a debate that gave rise to the Pelagian controversy, in which different factions debated the extent to which the human will has freedom, apart from divine grace, to do good works

Conciliar Outcomes of Doctrinal Debates

The patristic era of Christian thought must be understood against the changing background of Roman political life. Roman emperors throughout the first two centuries after Jesus' death were largely ambivalent about Christians. The Roman leadership was fairly tolerant of the budding Christian population, especially on account of Christians' notable public works and charities. However, Christians were required, with everyone else, to venerate the Roman emperor. When Christians refused on the grounds of religious belief, they risked persecution and even martyrdom. Christians were thus at pains to demonstrate to their rulers that they were good, upstanding citizens. They produced many works of classical apologia (or defenses of Christian practice and belief) on behalf of the Christian faith, a number of which survive today and tell us what life for Christians was once like. Despite these efforts, Christians were often a marginalized and at-risk population from the start of the movement until the beginning of the fourth century.

This situation changed due to the dramatic conversion of Emperor Constantine (ca. 272–337) to the Christian faith. Historians debate whether Constantine's conversion was driven by religious or political motives, but the effect of his conversion was great. In 313 he issued the Edict of Milan, which officially required the toleration of Christianity, making Christianity a legitimate and protected religion in the empire. Christianity became the official religion of the Roman Empire under Emperor Theodosius (379–395) seven decades later. Constantine's effect on this era cannot be overstated, as he reversed the fortunes of Christianity from an oft-persecuted sect to the official religion of the Roman Empire.

This official status led to many changes: Christian holidays became part of the calendar; Christian church buildings were erected; persecution of Christians ended; church worship became formalized, with the incorporation of non-Christian ("pagan") practices; and priests and bishops received special social status. Also, Constantine moved the seat of his empire from Rome to Constantinople (modern Istanbul), which gave rise to later power struggles between the church establishments in Constantinople and Rome. In addition, with the emergent institutionalization of the church came a need to formalize Christian doctrine and settle tense doctrinal disputes. Throughout the third through eighth centuries, Christians met in councils to sort out conflicts of belief, organization, and leadership. Key councils of this era, and the central doctrinal outcomes they arrived at, include the following:

- The Council of Nicaea (325) concluded that Jesus was of the same substance as the Father, and produced the first form of the Nicene Creed. This council also helped to settle the Arian controversy, wherein some argued that Jesus was "created" rather than "eternally begotten."
- The Council of Constantinople (381) taught that Jesus had a human mind, as opposed to Apollinarian theories that held that Jesus' mind was the divine Logos. This council also issued a slightly modified version of the Nicene Creed; this is the form of the Nicene Creed that is used in many churches to this day.
- The Council of Ephesus (431) affirmed that there is only one person in Jesus. This was helpful in dispelling the Nestorian claim that there were two persons (one human and one divine) inhabiting the body of Jesus, and the Apollinarian claim that Christ had no human mind, only the divine mind.

- The First Council of Chalcedon (451) concluded that in Christ there are two unconfused and undivided natures (human and divine) in one divine person, dispelling the Monophysite heresy, which argued that Christ had only a single nature that was either wholly divine or a mixture of human and divine.
- The Second Council of Constantinople (553) reaffirmed the teaching of the First Council of Chalcedon.
- The Third Council of Constantinople (681) taught that just as there is a human and divine nature in Christ, so also is there a human and divine will in Christ. This position refuted Monothelitism, whose proponents argued that Christ had only a divine will and no human will.

The Middle Ages

From the perspective of a history of Christian thought, it is helpful to subdivide the Middle Ages into the Early Middle Ages (700–1000), the High Middle Ages (1000–1300), and the Renaissance or Late Middle Ages (1300–1450). As with most eras, there are no absolute dates for the start and end of the Middle Ages.[8] However, the rough time frames above are useful, because they correspond to changes that occurred in the life of the church.

---

8. Although the Middle Ages is typically said to span roughly 700 to 1500, some will place the opening date of the Middle Ages as early as the year 410, when Rome was sacked by invading Northern European tribes. This signified for many the beginning of the end of the Roman Empire. By the end of the fifth century, the political stability of the Roman Empire had been replaced by the militaristic and feudal systems of these conquering tribes. The introduction of their Germanic culture resulted in what is called the "Germanization" of the church.

Many conquering peoples became Christian, bringing with them new customs and values that influenced Christian practice and belief at the popular level. In a more formal way, churches were influenced because their control shifted from the bishops to the feudal lords. Conflict thus arose over who had the authority to name church clergy and leaders—kings or church leaders? This era classically has been referred to as the Dark Ages because of the fall of the Roman Empire. Many consider the Dark Ages to be the Early Middle Ages (lasting from about 410 to 700). Nevertheless, because much of the patristic literature and conciliar activity were still developing at this time, these years can also easily be categorized as part of the patristic era.

In this scene from the Bayeaux Tapestry, Norman troops carry the papal banner, signifying the pope's blessing of William the Conqueror's invasion of England. The church was a major player in the political and military struggles of the Middle Ages.

Early Middle Ages

Several key developments shaped the landscape of Christian thought in this era. First, the religion of Islam (which started about 622) began to spread throughout North Africa and into Europe, eventually overtaking Constantinople itself. Second, regular fighting among feudal lords resulted in political instability throughout Western Europe. Third, to facilitate stability, garner protection, and gain political power, numerous Christian bishops consecrated or crowned kings, thus claiming for the church the power to determine who would rule. By doing so, they also directed who would be the "legitimate" lord of the land. A dramatic example of this occurred when Pope Leo III crowned Charlemagne as Holy Roman Emperor on Christmas Day in 800. In this role, Charlemagne's job was to spread and protect Christian worship and practice throughout Europe, which he did with great success. This close relationship between the papacy and political rulers, however, proved the cause of much corruption in later generations.

High Middle Ages

By the eleventh century, Christian culture predominated throughout Western Europe. Monastic orders, begun in the patristic era, had become important social institutions and leading centers for the preservation and development of Christian theology. Known for its distinctive, highly ordered style of argumentation, theology of this era is referred to as "medieval" or "scholastic." Among the most important exemplars of scholastic theology is the corpus of Thomas Aquinas (1225–1274). Monastic orders were also important centers for moral reform, especially when the church became too politically inclined or corrupt. Among the most important reformers was Pope Gregory VII (reigned 1073–1085). His "Gregorian reform" spread canon law (or church law) throughout Europe and claimed for the pope the highest spiritual authority.

Bleaker features of this age include the Crusades (ca. 1095–1204), a series of military campaigns in which Christian armies sought to reclaim formerly Christian lands from Islamic rule. Moreover, a long history of conflict over doctrine and authority, exacerbated by the violent behavior in Eastern Europe of the Western crusaders, resulted in the Eastern Schism (sometimes also called the Great Schism or East–West Schism) between the Eastern and Western Christian churches in 1054, discussed below. This split resulted in the Eastern Orthodox Church and the Roman Catholic Church as separate entities. Finally, to stem doctrinal questions and perceived error, the Catholic Church instituted the Inquisition (a church tribunal that investigated matters of faith and doctrine), known for its often brutal treatment of alleged heretics, Jews, Muslims, and persons considered witches.

Renaissance (Late Middle Ages)

This highly transitional period represents the apex of Roman Catholic political power. Key members of the Catholic Church hierarchy came from noble families or were wealthy merchants who had risen to high social status. Remarkable building projects and artistic works inspired by classical Greek and Roman models were commissioned by the popes, and today constitute some of the most valuable treasures held by the Roman Catholic Church. Scholars and theologians produced some of the finest works of theology extant, still consulted as authoritative.

This era also saw the rise of independent, secular schools as centers for learning. Theology in these universities took on a new, speculative character, resulting in fresh debates—and heresies. Political and theological conflicts arose in the Roman Catholic Church in the fourteenth century. Some conflicts stemmed from an increase in financial abuse by the popes and upper clergy. As successive popes demanded more and more financial support from the clergy, the clergy turned to the impoverished laity for money. The popes also experienced a great power struggle with French kings, compounded by the fact that from 1309 to 1377, seven popes resided in Avignon, France, instead of Rome, Italy. When the last of these popes, Gregory XI, left France and returned to Rome, some of the French cardinals were disgruntled. These same cardinals, feeling ill-treated under Gregory's successor, actually elected a second pope to rule from Avignon!

Although this period produced a multidimensional cultural "rebirth" (from which the term *Renaissance* comes), it also brought a time of corruption and excess that proved unsustainable in the following era.

The Reformation

Reformation is the general term used to describe the broad changes in Western Christian church doctrine, practice, and organized leadership that occurred from 1500 to 1750. Sometimes this period is called the Protestant Reformation, a name derived from the "protest" movement of German princes and cities against the edict of the Second Diet of Speyer (1529), which had condemned Martin Luther's views as heretical. Those who protested against this condemnation of Luther came to called "Protestants."

Why was reform of the Roman Catholic Church necessary? To begin, the political situation had worsened; monarchs increasingly resented their subservience to and overtaxation by the church. In addition, there was a growing sense of nationalism throughout

Europe, especially among the peasantry, who also resented the wealth of the church and its clergy while they were left wanting. Furthermore, many monarchs had made arrangements with the pope in which they retained immediate governance of their local churches. Such monarchs began to wonder whether they had any need for papal administration or affiliation.

The Roman Catholic Church had become corrupt in many ways during the Renaissance. Among the problems reformers noted were the selling of indulgences (or a remission of punishments for sin), exploitation of the poor, burdensome pilgrimage requirements, excessive veneration of saints, poor training and moral laxity among the clergy, and the vast financial wealth and landholdings of the church. These problems raised questions about the character and authority of the Bishop of Rome and the hierarchy under his administration. The question of authority was intensified by the fifteenth-century event known as the Western Schism (also called the Papal Schism), in which confusion arose over who of three contenders was the rightful pope following the period of the Avignon papacy.

Another cause underlying the Reformation was humanism. Largely spread by Erasmus of Rotterdam (1469–1536), humanism was an intellectual movement that stressed a return to classical sources. For theology, this meant a return to the patristic literature and, most importantly, to the Bible. Unlike the highly ordered scholastic theology of the previous era, the humanist movement encouraged speculative philosophy and freedom of inquiry, which flourished in the newly founded secular universities. Humanism also encouraged literacy among the general populace. This, coupled with new translations of the Bible into the vernacular (or common language) of the people, gave the average person immediate access to scripture for the first time in Christian history. This trend was furthered by the advent of mass-printing technology, which allowed for rapid, cheap reproduction of texts, pamphlets, and images. All of these factors combined to create a more learned and hence more critically aware citizenry; authoritative knowledge handed down from "on high" was replaced with study and discernment from the grassroots up.

The organizational and doctrinal reform of Christian churches during the Reformation varied greatly. For the purposes of classification, however, several major dimensions of the Reformation are usually noted. These include the following:

- **Mainstream Reformation** refers to the Lutheran and Reformed church movements. The Lutheran Reformation resulted from the efforts of German-born Martin Luther (1483–1546), whose critiques of Roman Catholic doctrine and practice resulted in a break from Roman authority and the institution-alization of a new church. Luther is often credited with starting the Reformation. The "Reformed" tradition is the outgrowth of John Calvin's (1509–1564) second-generation reform efforts. Calvin was a Swiss-born theologian whose systematic approach to theology helped to order and institutionalize Protestant Christian doctrine.

- **Radical Reformation** refers to the reform efforts of a variety of sectarian groups, characterized by their rejection of many mainstream Christian practices. These groups, known variously as the Anabaptists and the "left wing of the Reformation," brought strong critiques to the institutional churches. Their sense of Christian community derived from close readings of the New Testament, and they sought to re-create the New Testament model in their own time. Notably, these groups generally stressed adult baptism (hence, rebaptism or "anabaptism" of those who had been baptized as infants), common ownership of property, and pacifism.

- **Catholic Reformation**, also called the Counter-Reformation, was a movement within the Roman Catholic Church that tried to respond to the criticisms of the Protestant reformers. In this movement, the Catholic Church focused on founding service-oriented religious orders (such as the Ursulines and the Jesuits), cultivating spiritual discipline, educating the clergy, and morally improving the Roman Catholic Church leadership. The most significant move of the Catholic Reformation was the convening of the Council of Trent in 1545, in which the moral, doctrinal, and institutional developments of the Protestants were formally discussed, addressed, and denounced. In addition, the decrees of Trent introduced necessary reforms in the moral, spiritual, clerical, and service dimensions of Roman Catholicism.

Through these reforms, many of the Protestants' grievances were corrected. Nevertheless, the theological and institutional differences between most Protestants and Catholics remained too deep to allow for reconciliation.

The Modern Era

The modern period of Christian history dates loosely from the mid-eighteenth century to the present day. The modern period of Christianity has occurred in a global context, during a time of scientific, cultural, and technological advancement unprecedented in human history. Perhaps the best way to consider the modern period of Christian thought is to simply note the breadth of topics one encounters in its study.

From the eighteenth century on, philosophical movements such as rationalism, empiricism, and the Enlightenment prevailed throughout Western Europe and colonial North America. These movements placed great confidence in human reason: people sought to know the world by reason, without the aid of religious faith, myth, or superstitions from the past. The effect was a shifting of truth from the purview of learned authorities or church teaching to the domain of the free human mind. Key Christian beliefs, for example, in the miracles of Christ or his Resurrection, were thus profoundly challenged in this "Age of Reason" and have remained matters of debate and reflection. Likewise, this era witnessed the rational critique of revelation and divine inspiration in the Bible, resulting in modern biblical criticism. Exemplary of this type of critique of Christian belief is Immanuel Kant's work, *Religion within the Limits of Reason Alone* (1793).

Church authority also shifted dramatically in the modern era. From the time of the Reformation, the Roman Catholic Church lost its monolithic control of the West. Nor did Protestant ecclesial institutions attain the unchallenged power that the Catholic Church wielded at its apex. Especially in colonial North America, church authority was largely relativized by the spirit of independence and reason-based inquiry. This change in authority over time has been enhanced further by a freer academic culture in both secular and church-affiliated universities. This shift is particularly evident in contemporary evangelical and charismatic Christian expressions, which are generally decentralized in their organizational structures. Although church authorities have often been reluctant to cede power, contemporary Christian people are today more likely to be instructed in matters of faith and practice than they are to be coerced or bound by legal or policy structures informed by church authorities.[9]

After the Reformation, religious wars raged throughout Europe in the sixteenth and seventeenth centuries. Following decades of relentless bloodshed, a spirit of tentative religious tolerance and denominationalism (multiple Christian groups coexisting and going by different names) arose by default. The plethora of Christian groups throughout the world today has its origin in this era. At present, international organizations, such as the World Council of Churches (WCC), boast membership of hundreds of different Christian communions attempting both to resolve conflicts with one another and also to collaborate in practical ways for justice-oriented and peacemaking initiatives.

Democratic revolutions, such as the American and French Revolutions, occurred throughout Europe and America in the eighteenth and nineteenth centuries. Where monarchs once reigned with church support, new civil governments and laws emerged, based on Enlightenment principles that elevated the individual and cultivated a sense of common humanity. In the United States and many parts of Europe, the classic "separation of church and state" arose. An excellent example of this is the First Amendment to the Constitution of the United States of America, which states explicitly that the U.S. government can neither institute religion nor prohibit its free expression.

More recently, in the nineteenth century, Western culture underwent radical transformations. Among the most significant developments were industrialization, capitalism, Marxism, and advances in modern science (spurred by Darwin's evolutionary theory). The

---

9. For example, for Roman Catholics, the document *Ex Corde Ecclesiae* (From the Heart of the Church), promulgated by Pope John Paul II in 1990, describes the identity and mission of Catholic colleges and universities and provides norms to help fulfill its vision. This document reveals the more dialogical nature of the relationship between Roman Catholic Church authority and Catholic colleges that is characteristic of the contemporary era.

© Friedrich Stark / Alamy

Modern technology raises new possibilities and new questions. Subscribers to the website Second Life can participate in virtual worship services—but are such services "real"?

twentieth and twenty-first centuries saw unprecedented advances in travel, communication (including the personal computer, the Internet, and social networking), and warfare technology (including nuclear and biological warfare). Contemporary Christian culture is marked by dialogue with ongoing advances in medical technologies, social revolutions such as feminism and the gay rights movement, new forms of media and communication, the intellectual culture of postmodernism, and environmentalism and conservationism.

In the twenty-first century, Christianity is present throughout most of the known world and continues to grow. It is but one of many world religions, however, and a context of religious pluralism is assumed. Christians are represented across the range of academic fields of study, political parties, lifestyles, and professions. Christian faith directs believers' moral behavior in matters ranging from the use of medical technology, participation in war, and development of educational curricula to those as seemingly inconsequential as which (if any) TV programs to watch, companies to invest in, and fashions to wear. Christian thought is as varied as its adherents, and many Christian theologians argue that respecting diverse opinions among

Christians is a foremost ethical and methodological concern. Surveys of contemporary Christian thought, such as David Ford's helpful anthology *The Modern Theologians*,[10] quickly reveal the diverse range of modern Christian belief and practice. Topics considered in Ford's anthology include the following:

- theology in dialogue with the physical, biological, and social sciences
- theology in spiritual practice and pastoral application
- feminism and gender in theology
- black, Latin American, Hispanic, African, and Asian Christian theologies
- Christian theology in dialogue among diverse Christian communities and with non-Christian religions
- theology in dialogue with politics
- theology in dialogue with visual arts, film, and music

In short, one can assume little about the contemporary Christian. Any study of Christian thought today should begin with a discussion of context—social and geographical location. Because there are hundreds of Christian church institutions, many of which have structures of organization at the international level, it may be more appropriate today to speak of "Christianities" than of Christianity.

Conclusion

Christian thought has grown and developed for two thousand years and cannot be understood outside its historical contexts. Christian thought in second-century Antioch differed widely from Christian thought in third-century Alexandria. Thought from both periods differs widely from Christian thought in sixth-century France, and so on. Today, Christian thought can differ tremendously from church to church in the same town. When studying Christian thought, one must attend to historical and contextual questions to arrive at

---

10. David Ford, *The Modern Theologians: An Introduction to Christian Theology since 1918* (Malden, MA: Wiley-Blackwell, 2005).

a responsible and informed grasp of the issues. By exploring key questions, the rationale behind Christian theology and the formal expressions of faith and worship become clear. Some questions to ask when doing theology include the following:

- What is the era?
- What is the geographical location?
- What is the political situation?
- What is the status or quality of life for the average person?
- To what technologies, including medicine, do people have access?
- What is the average level of education?
- How could the economy of the era be described?
- What challenges, issues, or conflicts do people face?
- With what other Christian or non-Christian religious groups does the particular Christian community interact, and what is the nature of that interaction?

Questions for Discussion and Review

1. What are the two major divisions in the biblical era? What are the major differences between them?
2. Describe key aspects of the historical context of the Israelites in the Old Testament.
3. Describe five major challenges that the Christian community faced in the New Testament era.
4. Describe the patristic era and the reasons why development of doctrine was often a contentious process.
5. Name the time periods within the Middle Ages, and identify several important developments in church history associated with each period.
6. Give several reasons why the Reformation occurred. What are the major groupings of Reformation activity?
7. In your opinion, what are the three most influential cultural developments of the modern era that affect Christian thought?

What challenges do you think Christian thinkers must face today?

8. What sorts of questions should one ask when considering Christian thought from a historical point of view?

Resources

Books

Baker, Robert A., and John M. Landers. *A Summary of Christian History*. 3rd ed. Nashville: Broadman and Holman, 2005.

González, Justo. *Church History: An Essential Guide*. Nashville: Abingdon, 1996.

Jones, Timothy Paul. *Christian History Made Easy*. Torrance, CA: Rose, 1999, 2005, 2009.

McGrath, Alister E. *Historical Theology: An Introduction to the History of Christian Thought*. 2nd ed. Oxford, UK: Wiley-Blackwell, 1998, 2012.

Prothero, Stephen. "Christianity." In *God Is Not One: The Eight Rival Religions That Run the World—and Why Their Differences Matter*, 65–100. New York: Harper One, 2010.

Shelley, Bruce L. *Church History in Plain Language*. 3rd ed. Nashville: Thomas Nelson, 2008.

Websites

New Advent, "Ecclesiastical History," at *www.newadvent.org/cathen/07365a.htm*.

Theopedia, "Church History," at *www.theopedia.com/Church_history*.

Films

Frontline. "From Jesus to Christ: The First Christians." PBS, 2009.

Two Thousand Years: The History of Christianity. New York, NY: Films Media Group, 1999.

CHAPTER 5

Christian Doctrines

What to Expect

This chapter provides a basic introduction to major subjects of Christian doctrine, or Christian teaching and belief. The following doctrinal topics are discussed:

- God
- Jesus the Christ
- Holy Spirit
- Trinity
- Church
- Salvation, Sin, and Grace
- Eschatology

What Is Doctrine?

As is typical of faith traditions, Christianity has a system of beliefs that characterize its worldview. Some of these beliefs are termed *doctrines*, deriving from the Latin word *docere*, meaning "to teach." Doctrines are a religious tradition's core beliefs. Christianity has doctrines about God, the church, people, and the world. Doctrines result from a faith experience that becomes formalized and passed down over time. A substantial body of Christian teachings has accumulated over the centuries, but the principle doctrines may be thought of as describing God and God's relationship to people.

Although there is great similarity among many Christian communities, not all Christians share all doctrines or understand them in the same way. This chapter will note a number of the more significant differences.

Is it a problem that Christians disagree in regard to some doctrines? On the one hand, differences in doctrine can be the cause of separation and even conflict among Christians; in this sense, doctrinal differences can be problematic. On the other hand, differences and debate over what to believe, how to express belief, and how to behave as Christian believers have historically been the engine that drove Christians to formulate doctrine. In this sense, doctrinal tensions can be constructive and reflect of the vital and dynamic nature of a living religious community. Such debates continue to this day. Some differences are divisive—for example, attitudes regarding sexual lifestyle, or leadership opportunities for homosexual persons in Christian churches. When two Christian communities disagree, sometimes one community views the disagreement as trivial, while the other views it as crucial.

Organizing Christian Doctrine

Most Christian groups have statements of faith, usually called creeds or confessions, which articulate their specific doctrines. Like the systems of a physical body, Christian doctrines work together, forming a holistic worldview. When well explicated, doctrines ideally have an internal logic or rationale, so that each doctrine complements the others, and together these doctrines form a reasonable whole, providing a persuasive account of human experience, the created world, and the ultimate destiny of all things. When doctrines are taken together, they should present a reasonable worldview. Indeed, one of the main tasks of Christian theology is to provide a worldview that is capable of making sense of Christian beliefs against possible alternative beliefs and perspectives. This integrative approach to Christian doctrine is called "systematic theology."

Because every doctrine is linked with the others, there is an overlapping quality to the study of each individual doctrine. For example, study of the doctrine of God overlaps the study of Jesus and the study of revelation. Deciding where to begin a discussion of individual Christian doctrines is somewhat arbitrary, as is the selection of topics to discuss. This chapter concentrates on doctrines commonly held by most Christians. The discussion will attempt to preserve the classic approach to systematic theology, which treats, in order, God, Jesus, the Holy Spirit, and the church. The pattern derives from the Nicene Creed. Although it might seem logical to begin a discussion of Christian doctrines with the person of Jesus, one must recall that even before people experienced Jesus they had an operating theological framework; they thought about God in ways shaped initially by Hebrew and Gentile religious categories. The early Christians interpreted their experience of Jesus against the backdrop of extant theological worldviews. The doctrine of God, then, is the most reasonable place to begin to explore the Christian worldview.

God

A Christian conception of God begins with the models of God presented in the Bible. The biblical presentation of God is often analogical, meaning that it invokes various images and experiences drawn from

© Ivan Vdovin / Alamy

In this seventeenth-century Russian icon, an enthroned Lady Wisdom is visually more prominent than Jesus.

ordinary life to suggest what God may be like. Images used throughout both the Old and New Testaments, such as "lord" and "king," reflect how the ancient imagination envisioned a powerful God. These images often inform how people think of God even today. Depictions of God as an elderly but powerful male sitting on a throne in the sky (think of such diverse examples as Michelangelo's depiction of God giving life to Adam on the Sistine Chapel Ceiling and Morgan Freeman's portrayal of God in the film *Bruce Almighty*) stem from this biblical imagery, which reflects the patriarchal context of the Bible's origin, in which lords and kings constituted the highest power among human beings.

The Bible presents other images of God, however, such as the mother hen (see Matthew 23:37 and Luke 13:34), the romantic lover (see the Song of Solomon), the Lady Wisdom (see Proverbs 8), a geographical marvel (see Psalm 76:5), or the beloved spouse (see Hosea 2:18). These lesser-known analogies for God help to deconcretize, or break down, the idea that God is actually a man who behaves like a king or a warlord.

Why use analogies? The Christian tradition holds that God is simultaneously knowable and unknowable to the human mind because the human mind is limited. Even what we know by close observation, study, and reflection is subject to revision once more information is obtained or better tools for observation are available. Some aspects of human experience elude our comprehension altogether. As such, one must acknowledge the finite character of what human beings can know about the world.

By contrast, the Christian faith holds that God is infinite. Limited human beings cannot fully grasp that which is limitless, so all pronouncements about God must retain a tentative, metaphorical, or analogical character.

Christians throughout history have processed the biblical images of God through various intellectual traditions. In the first centuries of the Christian era (30–600), this processing largely drew upon Greek philosophy. The interface between philosophical and biblical thoughts regarding divinity resulted in several concepts that helped describe how Christians typically understand God. The Nicene Creed[1] begins: "I believe in one God, the Father almighty, maker of heaven and earth, of all things visible and invisible." This sentence provides a basic outline of the qualities that Christians attribute to God: oneness, omnipotence, and ultimate creativity.

---

1. The Nicene Creed came to its final form at the Council of Constantinople in 381 CE. It is recognized by Roman Catholic, Eastern Orthodox, and many Protestant Christian denominations. The translation quoted in this chapter is from the United States Conference of Catholic Bishops at *www.usccb.org/beliefs-and-teachings /what-we-believe/*.

One and Uniquely Divine. In Christian faith, God is the only being or substance in the universe that is self-sufficient. The being or substance of every other thing in the universe, and the universe itself, is derived from divine self-sufficiency. As such God is one (*monos*, as in *monotheism*) and unique in the absolute qualities of eternality, limitlessness, power, knowledge, being-ness, freedom, and so on. No other divine powers—no other gods—exist.

All-Powerful. Christians understand God as all-powerful (*omnipotent*). Thus God is the foremost cause of the universe. Christians further refine the concept of omnipotence by saying that God can even limit God's own power. An example of such self-limitation would be the laws of nature, which most Christians argue were established by God in creation; once established, they remain fixed, ordinarily beyond God's election to contravene. In the Christian tradition, miracles represent a deliberate but rare action by which God contravenes the natural laws that God has established. Christians believe that God limits divine power so that creation can be free rather than robotic. If God interfered in natural life, even for a good reason (such as to prevent an act of violence or suffering), the parties involved would have their essential freedom revoked. God's choice to limit God's power becomes actually the finest and fullest expression of God's might. Thus omnipotence and self-limitation are twin aspects of the Christian conception of divine power.

All-Knowing. Related to God's omnipotence is the idea that God is *omniscient* (all-knowing)—that God has full knowledge of all that was, is, could have been, and is yet to be. Although this aspect is debated, Christians typically do not believe that God's foreknowledge of events and human choices violates human freedom. Some Christians have argued, for example, that just as a person might be able to anticipate a car accident while looking on from a hilltop at out-of-control cars rushing toward one another, so God's ability to foresee an event does not compromise the freedom of the actors in the event. By extension, any pursuit in life might lead to illness, accident, mistake, or injury (driving a car, going to the beach, hiking through the woods, working as a doctor). If God were to stop people from doing such things because they might end poorly, God would ultimately stop life itself. Many Christians affirm God's providential love and total knowledge of creation, including human beings, from the moment of their inception to death, even while they affirm that God endows human beings with fundamental freedom to pursue life unhindered by divine interference.

Eternal. Christian faith holds that, just as God is infinite (or limitless), God has no beginning and no end. This means also that God does not exist in a particular spacial or temporal location, such that God cannot be here if God happens to be there. While God is always everywhere, God also transcends the categories of space and time as creatures experience them.

Creator. Christians hold that God creates the universe. Although some people read the Genesis creation story literally, many Christians today accept modern scientific understandings of cosmology and evolutionary theory while affirming that God is responsible for cosmological processes and evolution as the providential power and free agent behind all natural events. These Christians view the biblical creation accounts as metaphoric truths about the origin of the universe. Such accounts do not literally describe what happened but speak of the divine intention and power of creation. Related to the idea that God is the Creator are the beliefs that God is personal, free, and good.

Personal. Christianity holds that God has a personal relationship with humanity and all other life. God is understood to be deeply relational and involved in the life of the world. As such, the Bible describes God as a parent, lover, spouse, and protector. Sometimes it even depicts God as angry with, jealous over, or suffering on account of human life, all of which suggest a God who cares personally rather than a God who remains aloof from the concerns of the world. A key indicator of the Christian conception of God as personal is the prayer tradition in Christian spirituality, which holds that God's action can be informed and even directed by the needs, wishes, and hopes of human beings.

Free. Christianity holds that God is free. This means God may choose to act or not to act. God could have chosen not to create, just as God chose to create. By claiming that God is free, Christians suggest that divine life is *agential* rather than merely process or necessity. This means that God is not uncontrollable power, like a spewing volcano, but rather a personal will that acts—by analogy—as a person acts when choosing to do something. God's freedom and God's personal character are thus intertwined in the Christian model.

Good. Christian faith holds that God is good. This goodness defines how Christians understand God's power. Even though God may have total power, God elects to act in a way that is good and loving, just and merciful, toward God's creation. Most Christians do not believe God acts arbitrarily or vindictively, or that God toys with people (as the gods of Greek and Roman mythology did). Rather, Christian faith holds that God is the font of goodness and acts in ways that are essentially good and consistent with—although superior to—human conceptions of goodness.

Jesus the Christ

Although God's revelation in Israel's history precedes Jesus both chronologically and contextually, the key element of revelation, from which all other Christian teaching flows, is Jesus himself. Jesus is the central figure of the Christian faith, so it is important to know something of his historical life, as well as how he is perceived in the Christian faith.

Jesus was a Jewish man who lived from roughly 4 BCE to 30 CE and whose life and teaching form the basis of the Christian faith. Although few people debate the historical existence of Jesus, little is known of his human life. What is known is drawn primarily from the four Gospels in the Bible: Matthew, Mark, Luke, and John.

Details about Jesus' life that many scholars hold as true include the following: Jesus lived in northern Palestine near the Sea of Galilee, where much of his ministry took place. He was likely a skilled tradesman who worked as a carpenter or stonemason. Details in the Gospels suggest that his family observed Jewish laws and customs, such as traveling to Jerusalem for feast days. In his late twenties, Jesus was baptized by John the Baptist, after which he began a short career as an itinerant preacher. His preaching and teaching took the form of parables (short stories with an unexpected moral lesson), proverbial sayings (brief tokens of wisdom), and prophetic actions (such as healing on the Sabbath even though it was considered a violation of Jewish laws, or dining with "unclean" people even though it was a social taboo to do so). His ministry was oriented largely toward people pushed to the margins of society, such as persons with contagious diseases, persons engaged in "unclean" professions, or persons usually considered sinners. The basic content of his message was the advent of the "kingdom of God" or the "kingdom of heaven," for which people needed to prepare by means of repentance from their sinful lives.

Jesus was a charismatic figure with a powerful ability to persuade. He gained a reputation as a healer and an exorcist and drew large crowds as he preached and traveled. He had a close coterie of disciples who traveled with him and were responsible for sharing his message after his death. Scholars debate whether Jesus saw himself as the Son of God or merely as a prophet. What is clear, however, is that local religious and Roman political authorities perceived Jesus as a threat to the standing social order because he challenged their teaching and particularly their treatment of "undesirable" people. This challenge, for example, was manifest in Jesus' violent disruption of commercial activity in the Temple, where people were buying animals for religious sacrifices. While turning over the money-changers' tables, Jesus said that the house of God should not be a location for commerce (see Matthew 21:12–13, Mark 11:15–17, Luke 19:45–46, and John 2:15–16). As a result, during his visit to Jerusalem for the Passover feast, he was charged with political insurrection, arrested, tried, humiliated, and executed. His manner of death was crucifixion, which was death by suffocation while nailed to a cross and physically exposed to the elements. Although the Jewish high court was responsible for Jesus' arrest, his death fell under the jurisdiction of the Roman governor, Pontius Pilate. (Accounts of Jesus' arrest, trial, and execution begin in Matthew 26:47, Mark 14:43, Luke 22:47, and John 18). After his death, Jesus was buried in the tomb of Joseph of Arimathea. At the time of Jesus' death, the Bible records that Jesus' friends denied their relationship with him and fled from his side, perhaps for fear that they too would be executed.

Although the sketch just rendered covers generally accepted details of Jesus' human life, the Christian religion is based largely on claims about Jesus that are made and accepted through faith. For this reason, many scholars differentiate between the Jesus of history and the Jesus of faith. Faith-based claims about the life and significance of Jesus began three days after his death, when some of Jesus' female companions visited his tomb and found it empty (the Gospel accounts vary as to which women visited the tomb). The Bible records that this event was a visitation, whereby an angel told the women not to look for Jesus in his tomb, for he was risen from the dead and would shortly appear to them (Matthew 28:1–10). Accounts of the post-Resurrection appearances of Jesus appear in the Gospels of Matthew, Luke, and John, and in 1 Corinthians (chapter 15). The Resurrection—the Christian pronouncement that Jesus is risen from the dead (aso called the Easter event)—led to the claim that Jesus was the Messiah ("anointed one," Greek: *Christos*) of ancestral hope.

The first phase of the Christian movement, roughly 30–110 CE, commenced with the teaching that Jesus was resurrected and that his followers could also hope for resurrection after death if they lived according to Jesus' teaching and in communion with other Christian people. Jesus had revealed the nature of the kingdom of God, the purpose of human life, and the moral conduct expected of people covenanted to God. By Jesus' revelation of the kingdom of God, people could be saved from both the disappointments of life and the finality of death.

The followers of this new movement began to ask questions about the exact nature of Jesus, who, unlike previous great prophets, was held to be the savior. Christians reasoned that Jesus was indeed a human being, but a human being alone could not accomplish the miracles he performed, nor could a human being of his own power rise from the dead. Thus Christians further concluded that Jesus was also divine. Christian theologians debated the question of his precise nature over the next several centuries (as seen in the discussion of Trinity below). In the fourth century the Nicene Creed captured the results of the debate:

> I believe in one Lord Jesus Christ, the Only Begotten Son of God, born of the Father before all ages. God from God, Light from Light, true God from true God, begotten, not made, consubstantial with the Father, through him all things were made. For us men and for our salvation he came down

from heaven, and by the Holy Spirit was incarnate of the Virgin Mary, and became man. For our sake he was crucified under Pontius Pilate, he suffered death and was buried, and rose again on the third day in accordance with the Scriptures. He ascended into heaven and is seated at the right hand of the Father. He will come again in glory to judge the living and the dead and his kingdom will have no end.[2]

Among the most significant aspects of Jesus' nature that theologians found articulated or implied here are the following claims:

- Jesus revealed that God is Trinitarian, not a simply monotheistic deity.
- Jesus was the Incarnation of the Second Person of the Trinity, whose distinct action as the Son was to become incarnate (or enfleshed). Implied here is that the Father and the Spirit did not experience the human life or death on the cross that Jesus, the Son, experienced.
- Mary, Jesus' mother, conceived Jesus by the power of the Holy Spirit. He did not have a human, biological father.
- Jesus really died, and Jesus really rose from the dead; in other words, his death was not an illusion or an appearance. Implied in this belief is the idea that God understands and experiences death itself through Jesus, even though God never properly died or temporarily went out of existence.
- Through Jesus' Incarnation in human life, death, and Resurrection, humanity is saved from sin and ultimately reconciled with God.

Councils held thereafter would articulate additional beliefs:

- Jesus is fully human and fully divine, having two distinct natures in one person. These natures are not confused or combined but are rather fully intact and co-present.

---

2. The English translation of the Nicene Creed quoted in this chapter is from the Roman Missal, Third Edition, published for use in Catholic liturgies in the United States in 2010.

- The person Jesus incarnated in Mary's body was fully divine and fully human at the time of his conception, and thus it is proper to refer to Mary as the Mother of God.
- Jesus had a fully human will and a fully divine will, distinct yet simultaneously present in one person.
- Because Jesus was fully human and fully divine, as God Incarnate, he is humanity's savior.

Holy Spirit

The Nicene Creed also mentions the Holy Spirit—briefly, almost as an afterthought: "I believe in the Holy Spirit, the Lord, the giver of life, who proceeds from the Father and the Son, who with the Father and the Son is adored and glorified, who has spoken through the prophets."

The major doctrinal issues at the time of the Council of Nicaea concerned the relationship of Jesus to God. The authors arrived at the consensus that the way to explain their relationship as separate persons yet equally one God (and not two gods) was to argue for a relationship of (1) begetting/having been begotten, and therefore (2) of sharing the same substance (to be explained more fully in the next section under "Trinity"). However, the Fathers at this council also were keenly aware of the biblical precedent of God as Holy Spirit, which was also part of the baptismal formula. As such, they included doctrinal language of the Holy Spirit, whom they described as:

- Lord
- Life-giver
- Processing from the Father (the Western church adds, "and the Son")
- Glorified and worshipped with the other two persons of the Trinity
- The source of God's revelation to human beings in the prophets of the Old Testament

Trinity

The Christian conception of a monotheistic God differs from the monothesims of Judaism and Islam in that Christians alone affirm that God is triune, or Trinitarian. *Trinity* refers to the belief that God is three persons in one Godhead (which is the nature of God, especially as existing in three persons). These three persons are usually named Father, Son, and Holy Spirit. The term *person* is itself a difficult concept because it can be overly concretized to suggest something akin to three individual human beings. It is helpful to remember that "person" language has a metaphorical quality as well, and the same idea could be approximated by other terms, such as "aspects" or "modes." "Persons" is used instead of a term like "modes" because it is able to capture a fundamental sense of differentiation between Father, Son, and Holy Spirit. To move away from the exclusive use of male analogies, some contemporary Christians (borrowing from feminist writers such as Elizabeth Johnson and Sallie McFague) will also use other, less androcentric names to suggest the Trinitarian nature of God, such as Creator, Redeemer, and Sustainer, or Mother, Lover, and Friend.

Private Collection / Photo © Bolton Picture Library / Bridgeman Images

Attempts to depict the Trinity artistically generally fail as badly as attempts to explain the Trinity logically. In Christian belief, the doctrine of the Trinity cannot be comprehended by the human mind. It is a mystery that defies human understanding.

Skeptics might argue that the Trinity simply does not make sense. Three do not add up to one; one cannot be three. Christians, in fact, recognize the basic illogicality of the Trinitarian notion of God and thus often refer to the Trinity as a mystery that defies ultimate explanation and understanding.

How did Christians arrive at such a notion of God? The Trinity sprang primarily from belief in Jesus' divinity. In the early Christian period, followers of Jesus' way believed that Jesus was imbued with divine power and presence, but it remained unclear at first how Christians were to understand the nature of this power and presence. The use of different names in the New Testament to describe Jesus suggests that early Christians held an array of understandings of his identity. Such names include Messiah, Son of God, Son of Man, and prophet. Each of these descriptions opened possible ways for thinking about Jesus in relationship to God, but also left questions. Was he a lesser god, a second god, a divine son (such as the Greek figures of Achilles and Hercules), or the one-and-only God come down from heaven?

As Christians tried to define their understanding of Jesus, they were at pains to preserve the oneness of God and the divinity and humanity of Jesus. Christian theologians gradually developed key terms and ideas to try to explain how Jesus could be at once human and divine, as well as how Jesus could be divine without compromising the oneness of God.

Economy. This term derives from *oikonomia*, Greek for "household management." Christian theologians argued that God's household was creation itself, and though God was distinct from creation, God nevertheless was involved in its affairs. The "economic" Trinity explained how God managed creation through different modes of action, such as creating, redeeming, and inspiring. The persons of the Trinity in this model were understood as expressing simultaneous yet distinctive aspects of God's interaction with the world. The Father refers to God's personal creative action, the Son refers to God's personal redemptive action in the life of Jesus, the Spirit to God's personal inspirational action.

Immanent. The economic Trinity is sometimes contrasted with the immanent Trinity, which refers to the inner logic of God's being. Early Christian theologians argued that a Trinitarian model was necessary for understanding God appropriately, because threeness expresses relationality within God's very self. For example, Richard of Saint Victor (twelfth century) noted that in a simple monotheism, one could argue that God is alone. In such isolation, God could be found wanting for companionship or love. For God to be deprived of these things would mean that God experienced a deficit and an imperfection, which would be inconsistent with the notion of an all-powerful and perfect God. In a Trinitarian model, by contrast, God is never alone but is internally relational. This type of argument builds upon that of Augustine of Hippo (fifth century): the Trinity may be understood by the analogy of love, which requires three elements: a lover, a beloved, and the love between them.

Homoousios. This Greek term, which means "same substance," became a key element in explaining the Trinity. The term was incorporated in the creed produced by the Council of Nicaea in 325, the precursor to the Nicene Creed, which many Christians continue to recite even today. In the face of great debate over the nature of the Trinity, the patristic-era Christians who prevailed at the Council of Nicaea argued that God's substance was distinct from the substance of everything else, because God alone in the universe is uncreated. Anything that had God's substance would therefore be God, while anything that did not have God's substance would be something created. In this way, the persons of the Trinity could be understood as distinct in their actions, as well as in their relationships to one another, and yet be one by virtue of their sharing the same divine substance.

Begetting/Begotten/Processing. As Christian theologians argued that the key element that made the persons distinct was their relationships to one another, the Father came to be understood as the one who eternally begets the Son. The Son came to be understood as the one who is eternally begotten of the Father. The Spirit came to be understood as the one who is eternally breathed (or processed) from the Father. Later, Western Christians added that the Spirit proceeds from both the Father *and the Son* (Latin: *filioque*), an assertion that the Eastern churches have never accepted. The emphasis concerning all these relationships is twofold: (1) the relationships are eternal, and (2) the uniqueness of each person of the Trinity lies in the relational distinction and the action associated with that distinction vis-à-vis creation. The Father alone eternally begets the Son; the Son alone is eternally begotten; the Spirit alone eternally proceeds from the Father and the Son. Each person, furthermore, has distinct actions as Father, Son, or Spirit in the economy of salvation (see the discussion of "economic Trinity" above).

Christian councils also identified two categorically flawed ways of understanding the Trinity. These included (1) any approach in which the distinctions between Father, Son, and Spirit are diminished so as to suggest that there is really only one person who acts in three distinct ways (for example, I am a single, individual person who sometimes acts as a teacher, other times as a mother, and other times as a writer), and (2) any approach in which the distinctions are so sharply contrasted as to create three separate deities.

Jesus Is *What*?

The doctrine of God as Trinity and the doctrine of Christ as God are inseparable in Christian theology. Because belief in Jesus is the core of Christianity, one might assume that Christians had a clear theological understanding of him from the beginning. The history of debates and councils from the second through the seventh centuries, however, tells a different story.

Driving one of the most important elements of debate was the question, Was Jesus fully human? The issue here was that if Jesus was fully human, then he could represent humanity in his sacrifice on the cross, expunging humanity's sin. If he was not fully human (like an angel, or a demigod like Achilles), his sacrifice would not effect any change in humanity's fallen state (because it would be effective only for other angels or demigods or the like). Thus Jesus needs to be human in order to save. However, if Jesus was fully human, then how could he be divine at the same time?

Popular solutions in the second century were offered by such groups as the Docetists and the Gnostics. They argued that Jesus only appeared to be human and that his humanity was irrelevant to humanity's salvation. By the beginning of the third century, groups such as the Ebionites emerged, who argued that Jesus was fully human and was only the "adopted" son of God (not God eternally but only becoming so after some point in Jesus' human life). By the fourth century, the question of Jesus' humanity came to a head because of the beliefs of a group known as the Arians. This

Jesus Is *What*? (continued)

group held that Jesus was the greatest of all creatures—not begotten of God as a son but made by God as other creatures are made. The debate was so fierce that the new Christian emperor, Constantine, summoned the bishops to Nicaea in 325 to settle the issue. The dominant position was that the Second Person of the Trinity, incarnate in Jesus, was "born of the Father before all ages, God from God, Light from Light, true God from true God, begotten, not made, consubstantial with the Father."

Even though the Council of Nicaea produced the creed that we have here been considering, which established the relationship between the Father and the Son, it did not settle all questions. For example, in the fourth and fifth centuries, questions arose as to whether Jesus had a human soul as other humans have souls, whether Jesus was really two persons (one human and one divine) existing in one human body, and whether Mary could be called the Mother of God or was just the mother of the human aspect of Jesus. In the seventh century, the question arose again in a slightly different way: Did Jesus have a human will only, a divine will only, or both? Councils met throughout the fourth through the seventh centuries to resolve these questions.

Analogies. To help explain the possibility of three-in-one, Christian theologians have compared the Trinity to a number of ordinary objects experienced in daily life. Some examples include a triangle; a three-leafed clover; the water that flows in a spring, river, and sea; and a tree that has roots, branches, and leaves.

Church

The Nicene Creed states: "I believe in one, holy, catholic, and apostolic Church." These characteristics of the church may be understood as follows:

- One – that there should be unity among Christians
- Holy – that the church should be filled with God's spirit

- Catholic – that the church is universal
- Apostolic – that the church is consistent with or a continuation of the church established by the first followers of Jesus

Through the Creed, the doctrine of the church is thus connected intimately with both the doctrine of Christ's Incarnation and the doctrine of grace. Christians believe that Jesus ascended to heaven forty days after his Resurrection. Upon Jesus' ascension, his physical, earthly presence was lost to humanity. Acts chapter 2 recounts that at Pentecost, fifty days after Easter, Jesus' disciples and followers experienced an outpouring of the Holy Spirit, after which time they understood that their task was to spread the good news about Jesus throughout the world. This event marks the beginning of the Christian church.

As ministers of this new church, Jesus' early followers believed themselves to be empowered by the Holy Spirit to continue Jesus' work in the world, for the redemption of all people. Composed of real human beings inspired by God's Spirit and made holy by Christ's grace, the church, as Christians understand it, is the ongoing, incarnational presence of God in the world.

Christians therefore have used physical and bodily metaphors for describing the nature of the church from its inception. Terms Christians frequently have used from the time of the New Testament until the present day to describe the church include "body of Christ," "people of God," and "brothers and sisters in Christ." Roman Catholics and Orthodox Christians extend bodily references to the church with the claim that during their sacramental worship services (discussed subsequently), the ministers act in the person of Christ, and through them the bread and wine are transformed into the literal body and blood of Christ.

The study of the church is called ecclesiology, from *ekklēsia* (Greek for "congregation" or "assembly"). Different Christian groups espouse different ecclesiologies; there is no single, inclusive sense of how Christians understand themselves as church. The differences among various Christian worship communions will be discussed in the following chapter. Here it is sufficient to note that for all Christians the church is a community of Christian people, as opposed to a building or even an institutional organization. As a community of believers, the church plays a vital role in the way individual Christians experience their faith. The church is also critical to Christians' understanding of the way in which Jesus' grace is made available to them.

Sacraments

Many churches teach that the sacraments are the principle conveyor of grace to Christians. Sacraments are rites or practices in the worship life of the community that Christians believe communicate God's grace to them in a special or unique way. As actions of the church community, sacraments represent the special way that Christian salvation is thought to be communal rather than individualistic. Most Christian communities celebrate at least two sacraments: baptism and the Eucharist (also called the Last Supper, the Lord's Supper, and Holy Communion).

Baptism is a sacrament of initiation; the person is immersed in water (or has water drizzled on the forehead), in the name of the Father, Son, and Holy Spirit. This act signifies the cleansing of sin and entrance into the community. Some groups baptize only adults, while others baptize infants and children (as well as adults) on the basis of the parents' intention to raise the child as a Christian.

The Eucharist is the memorial celebration of the last meal Jesus had with his disciples, during which he instructed them to break bread and drink wine in memory of how his body was broken and his blood was shed on their behalf. Some groups believe that through this ritual reenactment, Jesus' body and blood are really made present, while others believe this ritual is only a symbolic representation of the event.

Other sacraments that Christians (particularly Roman Catholic and Orthodox) may observe include confirmation, holy orders, matrimony, penance and reconciliation, and anointing of the sick. Confirmation is the sacrament of commissioning, in which a baptized Christian is anointed with oil and thereby specially graced to do God's work in the world. Holy orders is the sacrament whereby an individual is ordained into the priesthood. In the sacrament of matrimony,

---

Sacraments (continued)

Christians recognize marriage to be a religious vocation and special occasion of grace. Reconciliation, also called penance, is the sacrament whereby a Christian confesses sin and, through acts of contrition, is restored to a proper relationship with God and the church. In the anointing of the sick (the sacrament of healing), holy oil is administered to a person experiencing physical or psychological disease for the purpose of bringing peace and spiritual healing.

Those Christian groups that affirm the sacraments feel that their material character captures the essence of incarnational theology—that Christ's saving grace is made tangible, even physically present, to Christians through the life of the church. Thus sacraments connect powerfully to the physical "body" images by which Christians understand God's presence in the world through the church.

Salvation, Sin, and Grace

The final sentence of the Nicene Creed speaks to the ordinary human being's participation in God and God's church: "I confess one Baptism for the forgiveness of sins and I look forward to the resurrection of the dead and the life of the world to come. Amen." This simple sentence expresses the entirety of Christian hope, namely, that through baptism, one:

- participates in the life of the church
- experiences forgiveness from earthly transgressions
- anticipates personal resurrection after death
- anticipates new life in the world yet to come

The greatest impact of the fundamental Christian belief that Jesus is the savior of the world is felt in the Christian's hope for forgiveness and life beyond death, for oneself and for all the baptized.

Jesus' short life and violent death would not have occasioned hope and a new religious movement apart from the belief that Jesus saved people in some elemental, essential way. Why did people feel the need to be saved, and how did they think Jesus' life and death provided that salvation? These questions lie at the heart of the theological task called *soteriology* (from *sotēria*, Greek for "salvation"). To fully appreciate what the Christian concept of salvation means, one must understand two other Christian concepts related to the religious study of the human person. This study, properly termed *theological anthropology*, concerns the doctrines of sin and grace.

Sin is the name Christians ascribe to the fundamental brokenness or fallenness in the world. Based on the biblical account of the creation of human beings, Christians hold that humans were created with free will. This means that God intended people to be independent moral agents capable of making decisions about how they live. The Bible indicates, however, that the first human beings abused their freedom by disobeying God. The sin of disobedience stemmed from egotistical self-love, which may be found at the core of all other types of bad actions and vices, including greed, lust, wrath, gluttony, sloth, pride, and so on.

Sin is experienced as original in every human life as a result of our being born into a corporate (or collective) sinful condition at the societal level and as a matter of history. For example, if a parent exposes her children to prejudice or bad habits, her children will experience a sinful condition in the dysfunction of their home in childhood, and they may also be inclined to reproduce those same behaviors as adults. Sin is also experienced as personal in the human life when individuals succumb to egotistical or selfish thoughts and deeds. On account of sin, both personal and corporate, humanity lost its paradisiacal existence and marred its friendship with God.

The broken relationship between humanity and God was beyond humanity's power to repair on its own. God thus aided humanity by becoming incarnate in human life. Christianity understands Jesus as the one, by virtue of his joint human and divine natures, who would be able to repair this rift. As a human being, he was obliged to live in right relationship to God; as God himself, Jesus had the power to overcome human sin and selfishness so as to model and live out a proper human response to God. Through the excellence of his life and also his death, which was offered by Jesus as a free self-sacrifice, human beings gained an advocate and a mediator in the Trinity. Christians believe that after his Resurrection, Jesus ascended to heaven, taking his humanity with him, and now helps human beings through the gift of grace.

Christians believe grace is the special way Jesus extends his unmerited friendship and forgiveness to sinful humanity. Different Christian groups debate how Jesus' grace saves or affects people. Indeed, some of the fiercest historical debates in Christianity center on the question of how Jesus' grace operates in and for human life. A common, though not exclusive, way that Christians explain grace involves Jesus' death. The belief is that Jesus' death atoned for (or made up for) the disordered relationship between God and humanity that resulted from sin. Once sin was repaired, humans could experience deliverance from the consequences of sin (namely, suffering and death) if they followed Christ. Christ gives grace to his followers, who are thereby justified (or sanctified or made righteous) and ultimately saved to eternal life with the Risen Christ. Different ways Christians have understood the operation of grace include the following:

- Grace is imparted internally to the person through the gift of faith, and by faith, people are saved. In this model, faith is like a seed planted in a person, which grows and blossoms throughout life.

- Grace covers a sinner as a cloak covers a body. The person remains internally sinful but is saved by the cover of Christ's righteousness. In this model, a person is inherently unchanged but nevertheless protected by Christ as a winter coat protects from the cold.

- Human beings are given grace internally in their willpower, and by this grace are able to cooperate with God in the performance of good deeds. In this understanding, people over time contribute positively toward their own salvation. An analogy for this model of grace might be an athlete who has been given a gift of speed or agility but has to use and cultivate that gift through practice to become excellent at her sport.

- The grace of Christ comes by way of the moral example he set in his life and death. In this model, people are so moved by Jesus' example as to become morally improved in their own lives. The slogan "What Would Jesus Do?" often seen on bracelets and bumper stickers, captures the essence of this understanding of grace.

Eschatology

For Christians, the final hope of salvation is that they will enjoy resurrected life with Jesus after their mortal lives end. Christians recognize that although they speak of salvation as if it is already occurring or in process, final or ultimate salvation is not yet realized. Christian faith, therefore, has an already-but-not-yet quality to it. This characteristic is properly identified by the term *eschatology*, which means "study of the last things."

All aspects and dimensions of Christian doctrine are somewhat eschatological, or oriented toward a future fullness. For example, the Christian church is in the process of becoming; it is at present imperfect and regularly subject to revision and correction. Similarly, salvation from sin is in process in Christian lives but is not yet complete. The world itself is in process. Though Christians hold that God originated the world and constantly creates and sustains it, the final destiny of the world is still to come. As such, Christians typically hope for a time in which the whole world, indeed the universe itself, will be perfected under the full reign of God's will and goodness. Christians often use the biblical metaphor of a "kingdom of God" for the longed-for future condition in which everything is perfectly ordered under the benevolent rule of God.

Beyond the generally eschatological nature of all Christian doctrine, different Christian communities articulate their expectations for the future with considerable variety. Some of these eschatological doctrines include the following:

The Second Coming of Christ. The belief that the Risen Christ will return to Earth to usher in the final days and events of this present world (also called the *parousia* or *advent*). Elements variously believed to be associated with the second coming include the rapture, a time of tribulation, and a period of peace. Christians debate the anticipated order of events and time frame associated with Jesus' return.

Resurrection and Judgment. Beliefs that Christians will rise from death to face judgment about the moral quality of their lives. Many believe that the physical body will be restored at the time of resurrection, while others believe that each person will be given a "spiritual" body, the nature of which is presently unknowable.

Heaven. The belief that under God's full reign, evil and suffering in every manifestation (including death) will be overcome. Some believe that all persons, indeed all creation, will be restored and perfected after the resurrection. Others believe that only Christians (called the "elect") will experience heaven. Still others believe that only particular, chosen Christians (the "elect within the elect"), will experience heaven. Heaven has frequently been imagined as a physical space, but it is also appropriate to conceive of heaven as a nonspatial state of being in oneness with God.

Hell. The belief that persons who by their own free will ultimately refuse God's offer of salvation and friendship will not ascend to heaven but will experience an afterlife removed from the being and presence of God. Because hell is conceived of as the absence of God's goodness, it is understood to be a torturous existence. As with heaven, however, it is not necessary to think of hell as a physical space rife with fire and pain. Nor is it necessary to think of hell as eternal. Hell can also be conceived of as a shadowlike state of being in total isolation.

Purgatory. The belief that persons who have lived a fine, but imperfect, life will experience a period of cleansing before realizing their final destiny in heaven. Some historical notions of purgatory imagine it as akin to a "waiting room," although contemporary conceptions liken it more to the experience of one's eyes adjusting to the brightness of the sun.

Conclusion

The full range of Christian thought may be discussed from the perspective of any individual doctrine. One could begin a systematic consideration of Christian thought with a discussion of brokenness in the human experience, or creation, or God as revealed in nature, or Jesus. The aim of any treatment of Christian doctrine is to understand how the system of faith comprehensively accounts for human experience of the world in light of Christian revelation. Essential Christian doctrines include God, the Trinity, revelation, Jesus the Christ, salvation, sin, grace, church, sacraments, and eschatology.

Doctrine cannot be overgeneralized. Each Christian communion takes the individual doctrines and systematizes them in its own way. Although different communities share great similarities of belief, they also sometimes exhibit profound differences regarding specific doctrines, nuances in how a doctrine is expressed or understood, worship structure, organizational patterns, recognition of authority, and use of the Bible. This chapter has provided a rudimentary architecture, with accompanying terminology, for thinking about Christian doctrine. More advanced study would focus upon a specific Christian communion.

Questions for Discussion and Review

1. Describe systematic theology: What are its goals? How is it studied? What are its principle divisions?
2. Choose three Christian doctrines discussed in this chapter and describe how they systematically work together.
3. Why is Christian language about God necessarily metaphorical?
4. What terms or metaphors do you think best convey the doctrine of the Trinity? How would you explain this doctrine to a child?
5. How do Christians understand Jesus as both God and human? How do both natures relate to the idea that Jesus is the savior?
6. What is the relationship among salvation, sin, and grace in the Christian understanding of the human person?
7. How does the idea of church relate to the idea of grace?
8. What does it mean to say that a doctrine is "eschatological"? Why are all Christian doctrines eschatological in some way?

Resources

Books

McGuckin, John Anthony. *The Westminster Handbook to Patristic Theology.* Louisville, KY: Westminster John Knox Press, 2004.

Pelikan, Jaroslav. *Credo: Historical and Theological Guide to Creeds and Confessions of Faith in the Christian Tradition.* New Haven, CT: Yale University Press, 2003.

Pelikan, Jaroslav. *The Christian Tradition: A History of the Development of Doctrine.* 5 vols. Chicago: University of Chicago Press, 1975–1991.

Websites

Baylor University; "Primary Source Material in Religion and Politics," at *www.baylor.edu/church_state/index.php?id=36168*.

John Henry Newman. "An Essay on the Development of Christian Doctrine," at *www.newmanreader.org/works/development/index.html*.

Examples of recent Christian statements of faith include:

Presbyterian Church; General Assembly Mission Council; "Brief Statement of Faith," 1983, at *www.presbyterianmission.org /ministries/101/brief-statement-faith/*.

Mennonite Church General Conference; "Brief Statement of Mennonite Doctrine," 1963, at *www.anabaptists.org/history/cof -1963.html*.

Film

Himes, Michael, SJ. *The Mystery of Faith: An Introduction to Catholicism.* Cincinnati, OH: St. Anthony Messenger Press, 1994, 2004.

CHAPTER 6

Diversity in Christian Communities

What to Expect

This chapter is a basic introduction to the major divisions within Christian groups. It will discuss the following:

- Early Christian Diversity
- Eastern Christianity
- Roman Catholic Christianity
- Protestant Groups of the Reformation and Beyond
- The Ecumenical Movement

What Is a Christian Communion?

Christianity is a broad term that encompasses a vast range of beliefs, practices, and historical epochs. Although Christianity began in first-century Palestine, it has spread and changed throughout the world for nearly two thousand years. Even at its inception, Christianity was a diverse phenomenon.

One can infer from the New Testament writings a variety of communities that followed Christ yet maintained slightly different interpretations of his meaning and message. Some early Christians were former pagans; others were Jews. The early Christian communities in Jerusalem, Asia Minor, Rome, Greece, Syria, Persia, and North Africa all reflected their respective cultural and social contexts. Their differences only intensified during the patristic era—prompting efforts to formalize and standardize Christian doctrine.

It would be an error to think that at one time in Christian history all Christians agreed about all aspects of their faith and worship. But it would also be a mistake to conclude that the divisions outweigh the common elements.

Each individual communion shares a set of beliefs, rites (or worship practices), theologies, priesthood or ministerial structures, biblical texts, and more. Shared beliefs in regard to baptism and the Eucharist are especially important. When churches are in full communion with one another, such as the Evangelical Lutheran Church of America and the Episcopal Church, they not only recognize one another as counterparts of a larger whole (something that might be said of many, if not most, mainline Christian churches) but also have a mutual recognition of baptism and sharing of the Eucharist. When groups do not exist in communion, they see other groups as having significant doctrinal error, faulty or different leadership practices and worship structures, and no binding authority over one another. Many churches recognize some elements of other churches as legitimate while taking issue with other aspects.

What characteristics distinguish one communion from another? We could talk about histories, points of doctrinal distinction, notable figures in the tradition, leadership structures, unique worship practices, approaches to reading or interpreting the Bible, service emphases or ministries, attitudes toward ethics questions, or questions of morality and more. Each of these areas provides opportunities for fruitful comparison. It is helpful to ask how and why two traditions view a specific aspect of Christian worship or a specific doctrine (like baptism) as they do. Care must be taken not to overstate differences, creating the illusion that newer denominations start out of nowhere, detached from the larger Christian story. Again, a helpful caveat is to look not only for points of distinction among Christian communions but also for the linkages among them, with special reference to a specific communion's self-understanding. This chapter, after considering diversity among the early Christians, focuses on some of the historical developments that underlay the emergence of the major classifications of Christians today: Eastern, Roman Catholic, and Protestant.

A Note to Students

When researching different Christian communions, it is helpful to keep in mind a list of questions to ask of each group. The following are useful:

- What is the role of tradition in this community, and how does this community tell its own history?
- What are the major events or persons responsible for reform or revival in this specific community?
- How does this communion understand the nature of the church, including its understanding of (or rejection of) sacraments and the role of priests or ministers?
- How does this community worship? Are there distinctive holidays, services, musical preferences, preaching styles, or actions on the part of the congregation?
- What are the roles of women?
- How does the community nurture Christian life (e.g., ministries for children or the elderly, outreach to the poor, or service programming for families and married couples or for single adults)?
- Does this community participate in collaborative projects or dialogues with other Christian communities? What is its rationale for doing so or not doing so?

Early Christian Diversity

The Jesus Movement. The first Christian communities (roughly 30 to 100 CE) lacked the formal structure of an institutionalized religion. These first communities may be termed the "Jesus movement" because they coalesced around people who had known Jesus in the flesh, then around people who had learned the faith from people who had known Jesus, and so on. Most of the initial followers of Jesus would have been Palestinian Jews who had listened to Jesus' teachings and whose understanding of their ancestral religion was subsequently transformed. Even among this group, one could find a variety of approaches to Jewish religion and culture. Three major

Jewish groups can be identified throughout this period: the Pharisees (scribes and strict observers of the law), Sadducees (the priestly class and collaborators with the Roman government), and political revolutionaries, some of whom came to be called "Zealots." Many scholars believe that the majority of early Jewish members of the Jesus movement were drawn from the Pharisees or persons sympathetic to the Pharisees.

Hellenistic and Roman Christianity. From the mid-first century (with the missionary activity of the Apostle Paul) through the early fifth century, the Jesus movement spread in a world of mixed Jewish, Greco-Roman, and other influences. As the movement attracted more and more persons of non-Jewish heritage, it took on a distinctively Hellenistic (Greek) or Roman character. This shift is noticeable in the language that late-first-century Christians began using to describe Jesus, as well as in the nature of the doctrinal debates that flourished in subsequent centuries. A good example is the advance in nonbiblical terminology to describe the Trinity (e.g., *persona*, *substantia*, and *trinitas*) introduced by Tertullian in the early third century. These nonbiblical terms figured prominently in the fourth-century debates about the nature of God as three-in-one. Another fine example is Augustine of Hippo in the fourth and fifth century, who imparted Neoplatonic ideas throughout the corpus of his broadly influential theological writings. This was a period of transition from Christianity's principally Jewish heritage to a movement in active dialogue with Mediterranean culture and philosophy.

Diverse Attitudes toward Women. The Jesus movement transformed social structures. At its inception it appeared to dissolve certain social and class divisions among people, providing new space and status for persons once confined to the margins of religious and social participation. Recorded in the Gospels, Jesus' ministries to the poor, the sick, and the socially "unclean" (prostitutes, tax collectors, menstruant women, and so on) defied conventional boundaries and set the precedent for a more inclusive Christian community. This socially flexible attitude also allowed members of the crafts and merchant classes to take leadership roles that elsewhere would have been reserved for political and financial elites. The early baptismal rule described in Paul's Letter to the Galatians reflects this transformed view of social roles: "For through faith you are all children of God in Christ Jesus. For all of you who were baptized into Christ have clothed yourselves with Christ. There is neither Jew nor Greek, there is neither slave nor free person, there is not male and female; for you are all one in Christ Jesus" (Galatians 3:26–28).

Women, in particular, benefited from the early Jesus movement, because it afforded women more than the normal opportunities of Greco-Roman society. Although scholars debate the degree to which women assumed leadership in the earliest years of the Jesus movement, by the end of the first century (evidenced in the later letters of the New Testament, such as 1 and 2 Timothy), Christians already were divided about the role women should play.

The Role of Women: Then and Now

Women represent roughly half of all Christians, but for most of Christian history, women have not led church communities as pastors, deacons, priests, elders, bishops, or popes. Historically, and in many church communities even today, women do not vote in church councils, are not educated formally in theology or the study of the Bible, and have limited opportunity to participate in the official leadership structures of their churches. More far-reaching, the restriction of women's religious participation both reflects and contributes to biased attitudes toward women more generally. In Christian history, much of the restrictions placed on women drew upon the Bible—or at least particular ways of reading and interpreting the Bible. As the suffragist Elizabeth Cady Stanton observed in her introduction to *The Woman's Bible* in 1895:

> From the inauguration of the movement for women's emancipation the Bible has been used to hold her in the "divinely ordained sphere," prescribed in the Old and New Testaments.

The Role of Women: Then and Now (continued)

The canon and civil law; church and state; priests and legislators; all political parties and religious denominations have alike taught that woman was made after man, of man, and for man, an inferior being, subject to man. Creeds, codes, Scriptures and statutes, are all based on this idea. The fashions, forms, ceremonies and customs of society, church ordinances and discipline all grow out of this idea. . . .

The Bible teaches that woman brought sin and death into the world, that she precipitated the fall of the race, that she was arraigned before the judgment seat of Heaven, tried, condemned and sentenced. Marriage for her was to be a condition of bondage, maternity a period of suffering and anguish, and in silence and subjection, she was to play the role of a dependent on man's bounty for all her material wants, and for all the information she might desire on vital questions of the hour, she was commanded to ask her husband at home. Here is the Bible position of women briefly summed up.[1]

From the nineteenth century until the present day, many Christian theologians have been seeking to understand and improve the role of women in the church. Challenged by critics such as Stanton, Christians have explored a range of theological topics, including what Jesus' attitudes were toward women; what the Bible as a whole says about women; how modern people are to interpret derogatory attitudes toward women found in the Bible and elsewhere throughout the theological tradition; what major Christian thinkers of the past said about women; how much authority one should place on past precedent (for example, the traditional exclusion of women from ministry); how to constructively bring women's voices into the theological conversation today.

---

1. Elizabeth Cady Stanton, *The Woman's Bible: A Classic Feminist Perspective* (Mineola, NY: Dover, 2002), 7.

> **The Role of Women: Then and Now** (continued)
>
> The breadth of contemporary scholarship on the role of women in the Christian faith tradition and churches reveals two critical insights about diversity within Christianity: though often overlooked, women have played a fascinating and creative function in the formation and preservation of Christianity throughout its two-thousand-year history, and Christian men and women in all eras have held an array of ideas about what role women should play. Today the status of women's participation and leadership is one of the more noticeable aspects of diversity among different Christian worship communions, with some fully embracing women in all ministerial capacities and others retaining restrictions on women.[2]

Gnostic Christianities. Divided attitudes toward women often parallel other aspects and emphases of Christian groups' doctrinal development. For example, some varieties of early Christian groups (e.g., Marcionites and Valentinians), believed that Jesus held a special knowledge of the cosmos, to which his followers could gain access. Such groups stressed the spiritual realm and denigrated the material realm. These groups are commonly called gnostics (from *gnōsis*, Greek for "knowledge").

As a result of such emphasis on the spiritual dimension, physical distinctions such as gender, race, and status were even less important to these Christians than to others, and women were often afforded higher status in their circles. Over time, however, other Christians came to oppose their doctrines—and their admission of women to the highest leadership. During the patristic era, the most prominent Christian leaders ultimately labeled gnostic opinions heretical and suppressed them. Consequently, most gnostic doctrines were known only secondhand, through the writings of church fathers who opposed such doctrines, until a library of gnostic texts was unearthed in a 1945 excavation in Nag Hammadi, Egypt.

---

2. For an illuminating history of women in Christianity, consult Rosemary Radford Ruether, *Women and Redemption: A Theological History* (Minneapolis: Augsburg Fortress, 1998).

An Early Christian's View of Gnostics

Irenaeus, a Christian author of the second century, recounts the beliefs of gnostic "heretics" in his work *Against Heresies*. The following excerpt from the first chapter of this work details the elaborate levels of divine hierarchy that typified gnostic systems of belief:

They maintain, then, that in the invisible and ineffable heights above there exists a certain, perfect, pre-existent Aeon, whom they call Proarche, Propator, and Bythus, and describe as being invisible and incomprehensible. Eternal and unbegotten, he remained throughout innumerable cycles of ages in profound serenity and quiescence. There existed along with him Ennoea, whom they also call Charis and Sige. At last this Bythus determined to send forth from himself the beginning of all things, and deposited this production (which he had resolved to bring forth) in his contemporary Sige, even as seed is deposited in the womb. She then, having received this seed, and becoming pregnant, gave birth to Nous, who was both similar and equal to him who had produced him, and was alone capable of comprehending his father's greatness. This Nous they call Monogenes, and Father, and the Beginning of all Things. Along with him was also produced Aletheia; and these four constituted the first and first-begotten Pythagorean Tetrad, which they also denominate the root of all things. For there are first Bythus and Sige, and then Nous and Aletheia. And Monogenes, perceiving for what purpose he had been produced, also himself sent forth Logos and Zoe, after him, and the beginning and fashioning of the entire Pleroma. By the conjunction of Logos and Zoe were brought forth Anthropos and Ecclesia; and thus were formed the first-begotten Ogdoad, the root and substance of all things.[3]

3. Irenaeus, *Against Heresies*, in *Ante-Nicene Fathers*, eds. Alexander Roberts and James Donaldson (Peabody, MA: Hendrickson, 2004), 1: 316–317.

Early Christian Orthodoxy. When Diocletian (ruled from 284 to 305) split the Roman Empire into eastern and western territories to be ruled by two emperors, Christianity began to develop two distinct strains of thought, which would dominate the first millennium of Christian history: Eastern and Western. Eastern Christians generally spoke Greek and their theological traditions stemmed primarily from Alexandria and Antioch. The Greek traditions in the fourth century gained influence under Constantine, the first Christian Roman Emperor. Western Christians typically spoke Latin, and their theological traditions stemmed primarily from Rome and Carthage. They retained a sense of primacy over their Eastern counterparts because, they argued, the Bishop of Rome (the pope) was the universal pastor for all the Christian churches by virtue of his historical lineage descending from Jesus' disciple Peter. However, both Eastern and Western Christians considered themselves apostolic, which means they believed their bishops fulfilled an unbroken succession descendant from the first apostles. Eastern and Western Christians participated in doctrinal debates throughout the patristic era, and each considered the other orthodox (conforming to correct, accepted, or traditional doctrine). When conflict arose, the geographic, linguistic, and cultural differences between Eastern and Western Christians often exceeded real doctrinal disagreement.

Eastern Christianity

The Eastern Christian churches of the patristic era covered a vast range, stretching from the Eastern Mediterranean area through Persia, India, and China, geographically outstripping the Western churches. Eastern churches varied significantly. Some patristic-era churches stood out as unusual in the spectrum of Eastern Christianity; others were doctrinally identical to Western churches but were culturally Eastern.

One prominent early Eastern church was the Church of the East in Sassanid, Persia, which in the early fifth century followed the views of a man named Nestorius. Nestorius held that Jesus' human and divine natures were separate from each other in such a way that there were actually two distinct persons in Jesus. As such, Nestorius argued that Mary could be considered the mother of Jesus but not the mother of God. Nestorius' position was condemned at the Council of Ephesus in 431 and again at Chalcedon in 451, where the majority opinion was that Jesus was one divine person in whom two natures (one human and one divine) coexisted without confusion or change. The anti-Nestorian position became standard in the West. Because the Eastern Church in Sassanid espoused the views of Nestorius, other Christians referred to it as the Nestorian Church. This church still exists.

A number of Eastern churches, unlike the Nestorian Church, developed in doctrinal agreement with the first three ecumenical councils of the patristic era (Council of Nicaea in 325, First Council of Constantinople in 381, and the Council of Ephesus in 431), but rejected the creedal language produced by the councils of the late fifth century and beyond. These churches are known as the Oriental Orthodox churches and have Armenian, Syriac, Coptic, Indian, and Ethiopian varieties. They are in communion with one another and share doctrine but preserve independent leadership structures (that is, they are *autocephalous*, "self-headed"). These churches continue to exist today, maintaining their distinctive ethnic and linguistic heritages.

Another group of churches of the East, the Eastern Orthodox, identify themselves as apostolic and stem from the earliest Christian period. The first such churches were located in Jerusalem, Antioch, Alexandria, and Constantinople and spread throughout Eastern Europe, Russia, and Greece. Roughly fifteen Eastern Orthodox (or simply Orthodox) churches exist today, each with independent organizational structures and authority, specific geographical jurisdiction, cultural uniqueness, and ethnic distinctions. The Orthodox churches are equal to one another but honor the church of the Patriarchate of Constantinople as the "first among equals." The Orthodox churches share a common doctrine rooted in the major ecumenical councils of the patristic era, as well as the belief that they carry the legacy and lineage of the Christian church established by Jesus.

For the first millennium after Christ, the Orthodox churches remained in communion with the Western churches, despite occasional tensions. Contentious issues included: the role and authority of the Roman pope over the Eastern churches, how to determine whether territories were Western or Eastern, the correct language of the Nicene Creed pertaining to the nature of the Trinity, the proper manner of worship in church liturgy, whether priests could marry, and whether churches could have icons for the faithful to venerate. Tensions came to a head in 1054 when the Eastern Patriarch Michael Cerularius and the Roman Pope Leo IX feuded over church practices. The feud escalated, with the heads of both churches mutually excommunicating each other. This event is known as the Eastern Schism (also called the East–West Schism and the Great Schism). Divisions between Eastern and Western Christians worsened during the Crusades of the eleventh through the thirteenth centuries. Since the mid-twentieth century, however, the Eastern Orthodox and Roman Catholic churches have engaged in dialogue aimed at restoring full communion between the two.

Despite the schism, more than twenty Eastern churches remain nonschismatic (or in full communion) with the Western churches and recognize the primacy of the Bishop of Rome. These churches, referred to as the Eastern Catholic Churches, include churches that have always remained in communion with Rome as well as others that have returned to communion from schism.

As a group, Eastern churches encompass a range of worship models or liturgical rites. Some common aspects of Eastern Christianity include observing seven sacraments, allowing men to marry before becoming priests, practicing chrismation (or anointing with sacred oil) immediately after baptism, and emphasizing salvation as divinization of the human.

> The Christians of Saint Thomas make up another Eastern church. Originally situated off the Malabar Coast of India, this community claims to have been founded by the Apostle Thomas in the mid-first century. Geographically insulated for centuries, theirs is one of the oldest Eastern Christian churches.

Roman Catholic Christianity

Roman Catholic Christianity (simply Roman Catholicism), like Eastern Orthodox Christianity, believes itself to be the ongoing presence of the original church established by Jesus and his apostles. Catholics believe that the historical connection of the modern church to the original church is guaranteed by the apostolic succession of bishops, who fulfill an unbroken lineage to the first disciples. The Roman Catholic Church further argues for a continuity of Catholic doctrine from the time of Jesus to the present. This legacy is believed to be guaranteed and carried on by the church leaders through their special teaching authority, called the Magisterium.

Just as the Eastern traditions reflect the cultural influences of the Eastern Roman Empire, so Roman Catholicism reflects the cultural heritage and history of the Western Roman Empire. Until recent times, Catholic worship was conducted in Latin, and Latin is still used for many important documents. The Vatican, housing the pope's residence and the administrative center of the Roman Catholic Church, is located in Vatican City, an independent territory within the city of Rome.

Rome is vital in Roman Catholicism because Catholics believe that the church in Rome was established by Jesus' disciple Peter. Catholic teaching traces to Matthew 16:18–19 the belief that Peter's church in particular has central significance for Christians. In the passage, Jesus says to Peter:

> And so I say to you, you are Peter, and upon this rock I will build my church, and the gates of the netherworld shall not prevail against it. I will give you the keys to the kingdom of heaven. Whatever you bind on earth shall be bound in heaven; and whatever you loose on earth shall be loosed in heaven.

Based on these verses (which are interpreted differently by other Christian churches), Catholics assert that Peter and his apostolic successors have unique authority and responsibility in the Catholic Church. As Bishop of Rome, the pope is heir to this legacy. Although all bishops of the Roman Catholic Church have a collegial (or equal and mutual) relationship to one another, they nevertheless stand under the ultimate authority of the pope, who is considered the universal pastor of the Catholic Church. The pope's doctrinal authority is unique; the First Vatican Council (1870) proclaimed that the pope speaks without error (infallibly) when he speaks on behalf of the Church in matters of faith and morals.

Pope Francis addresses the curia, a body composed of high-ranking administrators of the Catholic Church. Of the many Christian denominations, the Roman Catholic Church has the most elaborate hierarchy.

Catholic churches or parishes are led by local priests, and sometimes lay (or nonordained) administrators, often accompanied by a staff of lay ministers and sometimes deacons (ordained men who may be married). Parishes are organized in regional clusters called dioceses. Bishops lead dioceses and participate in dialogue with one another at the regional and national levels. For example, the U.S. Conference of Catholic Bishops (USCCB) produces materials and instructions (sometimes based on Vatican direction) for Catholics in the United States. Occasionally bishops convene an international ecumenical council, as with the 1962–1965 Second Vatican Council. Through the collegial dialogue of bishops, councils provide guidance to the pope on the direction of the Roman Catholic Church. Most often, however, the pope is counseled by his College of Cardinals, bishops appointed by a pope to a lifetime of special service and advisement. When a pope dies, the College of Cardinals convenes in a conclave to elect a new Bishop of Rome. The overall church leadership structure is referred to as the hierarchy.

The hierarchy is one feature that distinguishes the Roman Catholic Church from other Christian communions. Other characteristics include the observance of seven sacraments, the celibacy of the priesthood, ordained religious orders of men, lay religious orders of men and women, infant baptism, and confirmation during adolescence.[4]

Vatican Council II

In 1959 Pope John XXIII announced an international ecumenical council of bishops. He hoped to deepen the spiritual life of the church, address conditions of the modern world, update the code of canon law, invite separated Christians to renewed unity with the Catholic Church, and further enlighten all Christians. The spirit of the council was characterized by *aggiornamento*, Italian for "bringing up to date." Many of the pope's closest advisers were concerned about the effect such an updating would have on the church. Indeed, the council proved to be the most profound renewal of the Catholic Church in four centuries.

The council was difficult to initiate, organize, and manage due to the logistical challenges of working with thousands of bishops, their aides, and staff. In addition, Pope John XXIII died and was succeeded by Paul VI in 1963, right in the middle of the council. Nevertheless, four sessions, convened from 1962 to 1965, produced a number of major and authoritative documents that reflected and helped bring a renewed sense of the Roman Catholic Church's vigor, vibrancy, engagement, openness, and service in the modern world.

Protestant Groups of the Reformation and Beyond

The Protestant Reformation was a reform movement in Western Europe wherein certain theologians and heads of state rejected key teachings, practices, and the governing authority of the Roman Catholic Church and established independent churches. The Reformation was not a single, consolidated movement with a unified theological agenda. Rather, it was a series of movements in various

---

4. The latter two features, regarding baptism and confirmation, are not the exclusive practice but the norm.

geographic locations, shaped by local political situations, charismatic leaders, and other developments. The theological disagreements between the resultant Protestant groups were often as significant as those between Protestants and Catholics. Principal groupings of Reformation Protestant churches or movements included the following:

Reformation Church	Key Figures	Start Date	Location	Offshoots
Lutheran	Martin Luther	1517	Germany	Pietism movement
Church of England/ Anglican/ Episcopalian	Henry VIII Elizabeth I	1534	England	Society of Friends (Quakers) Baptist Methodist
Anabaptist	Thomas Munzer Nicholas Storch Conrad Grebel Felix Manz George Blaurock	1525	Germany The Netherlands Switzerland England	Mennonite Amish
Calvinist/ Reformed	John Calvin John Knox	1536	Switzerland Scotland	Church of Scotland Presbyterian

Protestant denominations have continued to multiply in the past four centuries, and the numbers are staggering. A study conducted by Gordon-Conwell Theological Seminary estimates that there are over 45,000 Christian denominations in the world today.[5] This number is so large, in part, because of a freedom from organizational

5. See *www.gordonconwell.edu/resources/documents/StatusOfGlobalMission.pdf*.

structure and the impulse to reform, both of which have character-ized Protestant churches since the sixteenth century. Most Protestant churches lack the monolithic leadership controls characteristic of the older Roman Catholic or Eastern Orthodox churches. Moreover, the older churches acted, to varying degrees, in concert with the ancient monarchies of Europe. As monarchies were replaced by democratic governments, an unprecedented religious freedom followed. The democratic impulse in political governance was mirrored by a diversity of new religious communities.

Many Protestant denominations originated in the time of the Reformation, but many others are more recent expressions resulting either from further church schisms or simply from newfound inspirations or movements. The following list of Christian churches that have emerged since the sixteenth century is by no means exhaustive:

Adventists
Amish
Anabaptists
Anglicans[6]
Apostolic Christians
Assemblies of God
Baptists
Brethren
Charismatic Christians
Christian and Missionary Alliance
Christian Science
Church of Christ
Church of God
Church of Jesus Christ of Latter Day Saints
Church of the Nazarene
Congregationalists
Disciples of Christ
Evangelical Christians
Fundamentalist Christians
Holiness Churches
Independent or non-denominational Christian churches
Jehovah's Witnesses
Lutheran Church–Missouri Synod
Mennonites
Methodists
Pentecostal Christians
Pietist Christians
Plymouth Brethren
Presbyterians
Quakers
Shakers
Unitarians
United Church of Christ

6. This refers not to the Church of England but to several conservative offshoots of the Episcopal Church.

Each group has its own structure, statement of faith, practice for ordaining or recognizing leadership, worship models, understandings of scripture, and more. Were one to study any group or denomination on this list, it would become clear that some hold widely shared doctrines, while others are so idiosyncratic that the majority of the other groups would not consider them "Christian." Christian communions debate whether some of these are "churches" or "cults." Such debates reflect the ongoing tension within Christian churches over right doctrine, leadership, spirituality, organization, and practice.

The Pentecostal and Charismatic Movements Today

In the late nineteenth century, the United States witnessed fervent religious revivals among poor and working-class people who felt dissatisfied with the lack of apparent godliness in the mainline churches. The "holiness Christian" movement, in response, aimed at intensifying Christian godliness. Holiness Christians asserted that the New Testament church, chiefly as depicted in the book of Acts and in Paul's letters, prominently featured the Holy Spirit as energizing, inspiring, and guiding Christian worship and practice. Based on this model, holiness Christians began seeking greater personal inspiration, fueled by the "baptism of the Holy Spirit," which they believed was evinced by the manifestation of spiritual gifts (such as those described in 1 Corinthians 12–14).

At the beginning of the twentieth century, key holiness preachers such as Charles Parham (1901) and William Seymour (1906) popularized the notion that baptism by the Holy Spirit was demonstrated through the gift of *glossolalia*, or speaking in tongues, as described in Acts 2:1–4. According to this passage, the eleven apostles of Jesus, having witnessed Jesus' ascension into heaven, reconvened in Jerusalem to await the baptism of the Holy Spirit promised by Jesus in Acts 1:5. The promised outpouring occurred shortly

The Pentecostal and Charismatic Movements Today (continued)

thereafter, on the Jewish Feast of Pentecost, fifty days after Passover (*Pentecost* is Greek for "fifty").

> When the time for Pentecost was fulfilled, they were all in one place together. And suddenly there came from the sky a noise like a strong driving wind, and it filled the entire house in which they were. Then there appeared to them tongues as of fire, which parted and came to rest on each one of them. And they were all filled with the holy Spirit and began to speak in different tongues, as the Spirit enabled them to proclaim. (Acts 2:1–4)

Parham and Seymour quickly spread the message of baptism by the Holy Spirit and speaking in tongues in their new "Pentecostal" movement through missions, churches, and camp meetings. Their preaching and message spread throughout the United States and other parts of the world during the twentieth century. As of today, there are nearly six hundred million Pentecostal Christians of various denominations, composing one of the largest Christian groups worldwide.

From the middle of the twentieth century until today, the success of the Pentecostal churches has been an inspiration to nearly every mainline Christian denomination. Though they do not all seek the gift of glossolalia, churches globally are adopting and preaching a more vital sense of the presence and role of the Holy Spirit in the life of their communities. The term *charismatic* (from *charisma*, Greek for "gift") describes this modern movement.

Charismatic Christians may belong to any denomination or they may be independent, nondenominational Christians. They share a common sense that the Holy Spirit is active, present, and propelling Christians into more energetic and vigorous applications of their faith throughout the world. Together, the Charismatic and Pentecostal movements are arguably the most transformative development in Christianity in the past century.

Ecumenical Movement

One might ask how the various Christian groups understand one another and why they do not unite as one Christian church, particularly since the New Testament urges Christian unity.

The ecumenical movement, aimed at restoring Christian unity, developed in the twentieth century. Churches participating in ecumenical efforts are driven by a sense that human beings often err, especially at the institutional level. Among the greatest of errors is the historical separation of Christians from one another, a separation that too often has been accompanied by violence. Ecumenically minded Christians believe that the universal church is always in need of renewal and is always led by the Holy Spirit. As such, they argue that gifts of the Spirit given to one community may be absent from another. Thus the full potential of the Christian people, united as the church, can be realized only as a whole.

Although many churches seek Christian unity, it is not easy to overcome theological divisions. Furthermore, some churches have no desire to participate in the ecumenical movement.

The ecumenical movement takes different forms. Sometimes churches undertake dialogues with several other denominations simultaneously. Churches may also enter into bilateral dialogues, in which leaders of two separate church communions convene to discuss issues and address historical grievances. Bilateral dialogues, for example, could take place between Catholics and Orthodox, or between Baptists and Lutherans. Multilateral dialogue opportunities can also occur in wider forums, such as the World Council of Churches (WCC), a fellowship of more than three hundred churches. In the WCC, church leaders and theologians convene yearly to discuss specific aspects of faith, worship, and Christian life. Often Christians join together through social justice and service acts. Though some in the ecumenical movement strive for full unification, others prefer smaller steps and modest goals for advancing ecumenical relations. Examples of such ecumenical activities include common prayer in nonsacramental worship, concelebration of weddings, and service programs.

Conclusion

Christian diversity is as old as Christianity itself. Within a single church, one will find differences of opinion. Among different church families, there are often prominent differences with deep historical roots. Major differences may be grasped first by asking whether a specific group is Eastern, Orthodox, Catholic, or Protestant. Second, by asking questions about the group's location, heritage, history, and connections to other Christian churches, one may gain insight into the nature of the belief and worship of the church. Third, by studying the statements of faith, leadership structures, and worship practices of the church, one can learn how it lives out its Christian identity.

Diversity forces Christians to ask how one determines the boundaries of the Christian community. Is belief in Jesus as God and savior according to the Bible sufficient, as it is for membership in the WCC? Must one have certain worship practices, such as the observance of specific sacraments? Must one have certain interpretations of scripture, such as the literal approach to the Bible taken by the holiness churches of Appalachia, who demonstrate their faith by handling serpents, as is mentioned in Mark 16:18? Must one recognize the supreme leadership of the pope, or, conversely, reject that leadership?

In the past, different answers to such questions sometimes led to bitter conflicts. Today the ecumenical movement gives reason to hope that a sense of charity and unity will prevail over historical differences. Despite diversity in doctrine, leadership, or readings of the Bible, Christians strive to find mutual ways to live their common values of service and justice.

Questions for Discussion and Review

1. Describe differences among the first Christian communities. What factors contributed to these differences?

2. On what grounds did early Christian theologians identify some beliefs as "orthodox" and others as "heretical"? What might Christianity look like today if these judgments were reversed?

3. Name the various branches of Eastern Christianity. What is the relationship of each to the Roman Catholic Church?

4. What are the two major schisms in the history of the Roman Catholic Church?

5. Describe distinctive elements of the Roman Catholic Church hierarchy. How do Roman Catholics understand the passage in Matthew, quoted in this chapter, in which Jesus singles out Peter as the "rock" on which he would build his church?

6. Why are there so many Protestant churches? What are some of the major points of disagreement between these churches?

7. What experience, if any, have you had of diverse Christian groups? What do you think were or are major points of contrast in belief or practice in those groups?

8. Describe the ecumenical movement. What are some of the obstacles to unity? What might be some effective strategies for advancing unity?

9. Briefly research two or more Christian communities cited in this chapter. Chart their origins, major points of contrast, and commonalities. Then consider what steps they might take to overcome their differences.

Resources

Books

Angold, Michael, ed. *The Cambridge History of Christianity*. Vol. 5, *Eastern Christianity*. Cambridge, MA: Cambridge University Press, 2006.

Kelly, Joseph F. *The Ecumenical Councils of the Catholic Church: A History*. Collegeville, MN: Liturgical Press, 2009.

McGrath, Alister. *Christianity's Dangerous Idea: The Protestant Revolution: A History from the Sixteenth Century to the Twenty-First*. New York: HarperCollins, 2007.

Murphy, Francesca Aran, and Christopher Asprey, eds. *Ecumenism Today*. Hampshire, UK, and Burlington, VT: Ashgate, 2008.

Parry, Ken, ed. *The Blackwell Companion to Eastern Christianity*. Oxford: Wiley-Blackwell, 2010.

Vidmar, John. *The Catholic Church Through the Ages: A History*. Mahwah, NJ: Paulist Press, 2005.

Websites

Confessions of Faith, at *http://confessionsoffaith.org.*, a site indexing Protestant confessions.

Fordham University; "Internet Medieval Sourcebook" (see "Selected Sources: Reformation"), at *legacy.fordham.edu/halsall/sbook1y.asp.*

The Lutheran Church Missouri Synod, at *www.lcms.org.*

New Advent; "The Catholic Encyclopedia," at *www.newadvent.org/cathen.*

Presbyterian Church (USA), at *www.pcusa.org.*

World Council of Churches, at *www.oikoumene.org/en.*

Films

Christianity: The First Two Thousand Years. A&E Home Video, 2001.

Empires: Martin Luther. PBS, 2002.

CHAPTER 7

Christian Worship and Spiritual Practice

What to Expect

This chapter introduces major aspects of Christian worship and spiritual practice through discussion of the following:

- Worship in Prayer
- Worship in Liturgy
- Liturgical Year and Christian Holidays
- The Virgin Mary, Saints, and Martyrs
- Social Service and Outreach
- Religious Orders

What Is Christian Spirituality?

The common phrase "I'm spiritual but not religious" suggests a distinction between organized approaches to religion and a more innate or personal, even if less defined, awareness of God or the divine. While religious experience can be unstructured and individualized, spirituality may also be structured and channeled within a religion and its theological system of belief. In this sense, spirituality may refer broadly to the global and encompassing way that people feel, experience, and live out their religious faith.

Religious spirituality is lived formally and informally, communally and individually, boldly and subtly throughout all aspects of life.

145

People may express their spirituality by participating in ritual services on special days, reciting statements of belief, or praying. They may structure their life and work, including their approach to marriage or career or volunteer work, according to the tenets of their religion. Or they may journey to places their religion holds significant or sacred. All ways that people live their religious beliefs may be examples of spirituality.

Christian spirituality refers to the breadth and depth of how faith is lived and experienced by Christian believers, in both historical and contemporary contexts, by individuals and within larger church communities. The range of Christian spiritual practices is wide and varied, but all genuinely Christian spirituality will be rooted in the person of Jesus, attending to the story and example of Jesus' life as recorded in the Bible. Genuine Christian spirituality also entails a life of service to others in imitation of Christ. And it involves living in community with others so as to join one's individual life with one's church community and, more broadly, with all Christians as one Body of Christ. The many forms of Christian spirituality share the *Christocentric* ("Christ-centered") elements of charity, gifts, and community.

Charity

The most important commonality in Christian spirituality is charity (Latin: *caritas*), the self-giving love Jesus shows in the New Testament. Because Christians see Jesus as the model for how people should live, they attempt to model their spiritual practice on Jesus' self-sacrificing service to others. The New Testament encourages Christians to follow Christ's example of offering service and gift without expectation of reward or compensation. Christians are instructed to meet one another's material needs as a sign of their love of God (see 1 John 3:16–18).

Early Christians believed it impossible to love the unseen God without loving the people who were right before their eyes. Moreover, they believed that loving people means more than having kind feelings toward one another; it means serving one another for the flourishing of the whole human family. At base, Christian charity requires Christians to meet one another's needs for food, clothing, shelter, and so on. This charity differs from romantic love or the love among family members and friends; it is the fundamental compassion for and active service to all human beings that is required of Christians. This concept of charity serves as the foundation for Christian ethics and social justice. Thus Christian faith emphasizes loving everyone, even one's enemy, through actions that promote the other's welfare.

Christian Charity

Christian charity entails concrete acts of service and gift. For example, consider the use of material wealth in the following two biblical examples:

> The way we came to know love was that he laid down his life for us; so we ought to lay down our lives for our brothers. If someone who has worldly means sees a brother in need and refuses him compassion, how can the love of God remain in him? Children, let us love not in word or speech but in deed and truth. (1 John 3:16–18)

> All who believed were together and had all things in common; they would sell their property and possessions and divide them among all according to each one's need. Every day they devoted themselves to meeting together in the temple area and to breaking bread in their homes. They ate their meals with exultation and sincerity of heart, praising God and enjoying favor with all the people. And every day the Lord added to their number those who were being saved. (Acts 2:44–47)

Gifts

Another key aspect of Christian spirituality is the notion of spiritual gifts, or charisms. From the beginning of Christianity, Christians have recognized that people are graced with different abilities and ways of serving one another, and thereby serving God. The Christian doctrine of creation holds that all people are created with an inherent purpose and dignity, and thus each person has unique gifts. One person might have a gift for science, another for singing, a third for teaching, and so on. Each gift is a blessing to be returned in service to others.

Christian spirituality recognizes the diversity of human gifts and sees in every gift the potential for charitable service to God and neighbor. All gifts, whether individual or shared, must be used according to the guiding principles of faith, hope, and love—the three "theological virtues"—lest they become distorted and lose value. When guided by these virtues, however, all gifts find expression in service to the human family.

Unity in Diversity

The Apostle Paul speaks of the diversity of spiritual gifts even as he emphasizes the unity of community that all such gifts serve:

> There are different kinds of spiritual gifts but the same Spirit; there are different forms of service but the same Lord; there are different workings but the same God who produces all of them in everyone. To each individual the manifestation of the Spirit is given for some benefit. To one is given through the Spirit the expression of wisdom; to another the expression of knowledge according to the same Spirit; to another faith by the same Spirit; to another gifts of healing by the one Spirit; to another mighty deeds; to another prophecy; to another discernment of spirits; to another varieties of tongues; to another interpretation of tongues. But one and the same Spirit produces all of these, distributing them individually to each person as he wishes. (1 Corinthians 12:4–11)

Community

A third common element of Christian spirituality is the principle of community. From the beginning of the Christian era, adherents saw themselves as having a corporate existence. They called themselves collectively the body of Christ and the people of God, and individually brothers and sisters. They recognized that through their baptism, they had joined a family of believers.

Christians as One Body

In several places in the New Testament, the authors use the metaphor of the body to describe what the Christian community is like. Just as body parts act together to form a whole, so Christians work together to form a church community. In 1 Corinthians (12:12–13:13), Paul notes that all body parts are needed for the good of the whole. The foot should not be displeased because it is not the eye or the ear. In the same way, he suggests, people should not be jealous or alienated from one another on account of station, talent, or gifts. Indeed, the particular gift that each member of the community has is less important than love, and all gifts are to be used in loving service to one another. This metaphor of the body is repeated in the Letter to the Ephesians (5:22–33), in which the author states that Christ is to the church as the head is to its body, and a man is to his wife as Christ is to the church.

Both scriptural uses of the metaphor of the body invite the reader to think about the integrative nature of community, of God and the church, and of spouses. However, both also suggest hierarchy in the body of Christ, and this is a source of some debate and even contention among Christians today. In 1 Corinthians, people are differentiated on account of their spiritual gifts; some therefore naturally have a higher station than others. In Ephesians, husbands have a higher station than wives, which is underlined by the comparison of the husband to Christ and the wife to the church. The integrative and holistic implications of the body metaphor may seem to be compromised by the hierarchical arrangement of persons based on talent or gender that it implies. Both passages soften such implications by suggesting that love is the guiding principle in applying spiritual gifts and in mutual service between spouses. While the body metaphor is widely used in describing the Christian community, it continues to pose a challenge to Christian interpreters today to think creatively about healthy relationship structures among members of the community, such as ecclesial relationships between clergy and laity and gender relationships in marriages and church practice.

The metaphor of the body was vital, symbolizing the idea that diverse persons, like different parts of the body, work together to form a whole. Early Christians placed the value of being a part of the family of believers even before their biological families. The family of believers was open to all people, regardless of race, social status, or gender. Moreover, it offered hope that through the life of Jesus, all people would one day unite and heal the rifts and conflicts that divided them.

Though Christians act as individuals in their lives and work, they also commonly see their work as an aspect of their service to the community as a whole. Especially within the church, Christians work together to maximize their gifts and efforts on behalf of others.

Worship in Prayer

Christian communities call their devotional acts and observances worship. *Worship* as a noun usually refers to communal acts of devotion, such as a church service or holiday observance. As a verb, *worship* typically means to honor or revere, such as to revere a divine being or supernatural power. *Worship* need not be in the form of overtly religious practices, but may also refer to what one does when praising God through a variety of more secular activities, as in, "I worship God through my work as a pediatrician." Two of the most important expressions of worship are prayer and liturgy.

Prayer derives from the Latin root *precari*, meaning "to beg or beseech." The Bible, in both the Old and New Testaments, mentions

© photogoiler / Shutterstock.com

The woman depicted in this third-century fresco from the Roman catacombs stands in the *orans* position, the traditional posture of prayer.

prayer frequently. It often refers to people praying publicly and includes many prayers. Indeed, the biblical book of Psalms is an ancient prayer book. In the New Testament, Christian prayer is modeled on Jesus' many acts of prayer; his best-known prayer is the Lord's Prayer, recorded in the Gospel of Matthew (6:9–13) and the Gospel of Luke (11:2–4). In the slightly longer Matthean version, Jesus also teaches that people should not make a grand show of devotions and good deeds, because their public performance then becomes its own reward. Rather, he instructs people to pray and do good quietly so that their reward will be in heaven, not on earth. Following this instruction, Jesus says:

> This is how you are to pray:
>> Our Father in heaven,
>>> hallowed be your name,
>>> your kingdom come,
>>> your will be done, on earth as in heaven.
>> Give us today our daily bread;
>> and forgive us our debts,
>>> as we forgive our debtors;
>> and do not subject us to the final test,
>>> but deliver us from the evil one. (Matthew 6:9–13)

The Lord's Prayer is a good starting place for a discussion of Christian prayer. The term *prayer* suggests supplication or entreaty before God, and Christians use many forms of prayer in worship. Prayer can be a way of praising God ("hallowed be your name"), as in the Lord's Prayer. Prayer can also be a petition to God to intercede on behalf of human affairs ("Give us this day our daily bread"). And prayer can be an expression of thanks to God for blessings, or of contrition for wrongs. The different intentions behind specific types of prayer inform when and how prayers are offered.

Prayer may be individual or communal. Individual prayer is private and may be formal or informal in nature. Examples of informal individual prayer include a student praying before an exam or a job applicant praying on the eve of an interview. An example of formal individual prayer would be a person praying the Lord's Prayer during an evening meditation. Communal prayer is public, shared by two or

Psalms: Poetry and Prayer

The Psalms is a book of poetry. Scholars believe the biblical Israelites used these psalms as sung prayers in worship. Predominant themes in Psalms include praise of God, lamentation, and priestly prayer. The Twenty-Third Psalm, below, attributed to King David, is among the most celebrated because of its comforting words and bucolic imagery reflecting the pastoral life of the ancient Israelites.

> The LORD is my shepherd;
>> there is nothing I lack.
> In green pastures he makes me lie down;
>> to still waters he leads me;
>> he restores my soul.
> He guides me along right paths
>> for the sake of his name.
> Even though I walk through the valley of the shadow of death,
>> I will fear no evil, for you are with me;
>> your rod and your staff comfort me.
> You set a table before me
>> in front of my enemies;
> You anoint my head with oil;
>> my cup overflows.
> Indeed, goodness and mercy will pursue me
>> all the days of my life;
> I will dwell in the house of the LORD
>> for endless days. (Psalm 23)

more, and it too may be formal or informal. An example of a communal, informal prayer would be a family saying grace before eating. An example of a communal, formal prayer would be the prayers of a church community during Sunday worship.

Sometimes prayer is spoken out loud or even sung, while other times it is wordless and experienced as a silent meditation or visualization. Prayer may involve meditation upon an icon (or religious image).

Sometimes prayer has content, using words, images, or passages from the Bible. Other times prayer is without content, as the one praying attempts to empty his or her mind in order merely to be in the presence of God. Some prayer, following in the tradition of Christian mysticism, attempts to elevate the one praying to union with God.

Christian Mysticism

Prayerful contemplation of the divine is part of the mystical tradition within Christian spirituality. *Mystical* refers to non-conceptual ways of preparing the prayerful person for experiencing the divine; the mystical tradition strives to bring the Christian into union with God or into the presence of God, even while it recognizes that God exceeds the human's ability to know or perceive or understand. Notable examples of Christian mystics include Francis of Assisi (1182–1226), Catherine of Sienna (1347–1380), Teresa of Ávila (1515–1582), John of the Cross (1542–1591), Thérèse of Lisieux (1873–1897), and Thomas Merton (1915–1968). The following passage from a work called *The Mystical Theology*, by the fifth- or sixth-century writer known as Pseudo-Dionysius, captures the essence of this Christian writer's effort to put into words that which is unfathomable:[1]

Werner Forman Archive / Bridgeman Images

Hildegard of Bingen (1098–1179) was a prominent Christian mystic who wrote descriptions of her visionary experiences. The miniature reproduced here is from an illustrated manuscript of her visionary accounts, prepared about the time of her death.

---

1. *Pseudo-Dionysius: The Complete Works* (New York and Mahwah, NJ: Paulist Press, 1987), 141.

Christian Mysticism (continued)

Again, as we climb higher we say this. It is not soul or mind, nor does it possess imagination, conviction, speech, or understanding. Nor is it speech per se, understanding per se. It cannot be spoken of and it cannot be grasped by understanding. It is not number or order, greatness or smallness, equality or inequality, similarity or dissimilarity. It is not immovable, moving, or at rest. It has no power, it is not power, nor is it light. It does not live nor is it life. It is not a substance, nor is it eternity or time. It cannot be grasped by the understanding since it is neither knowledge nor truth. It is not kingship. It is not wisdom. It is neither one nor oneness, divinity nor goodness. Nor is it a spirit, in the sense in which we understand that term. It is not sonship or fatherhood and it is nothing known to us or to any other being. It falls neither within the predicate of nonbeing nor of being. Existing beings do not know it as it actually is and it does not know them as they are. There is no speaking of it, nor name nor knowledge of it. Darkness and light, error and truth—it is none of these. It is beyond assertion and denial. We make assertions and denials of what is next to it, but never of it, for it is beyond every assertion, being the perfect and unique cause of all things, and by virtue of its preeminently simple and absolute nature, free of every limitation, beyond every limitation, it is also beyond denial.

In all these ways, Christians attempt to place themselves in proper relationship to God through praise, lament, petition, contemplation, adoration, and thanksgiving. Christians use prayer as a way to receive the Holy Spirit and also to entreat God to be more fully present in their lives. Whether offered individually or communally, prayer is a regular and important part of any Christian spirituality.

Worship in Liturgy

One of the most important ways Christians pray is through formal worship, often called liturgy. Liturgies, also called services, are public acts of worship enacted by Christian church communities. Liturgies take place in the churches or sacred spaces where Christian communities meet, and may include the following components:

Rites. Ritualized and structured actions, usually accompanied by prescribed words, that the church community performs and recites for specific reasons at specific times of the year.

Repetition. Rites are typically orderly and follow prescribed behaviors that are always repeated in the same order as the ritual is performed. Many rites are practiced regularly throughout the year. Others are practiced only on special holy days. Still others are reserved for special events in the life cycle, such as marriage, baptism, or death.

Clergy. Most Christian communities have ordained priests, deacons, presbyters, or ministers who lead worship. These individuals are distinguished from the rest of the congregation, sometimes called the laity, by virtue of their ordination, the process by which one becomes an official minister in the church. This process usually follows some scholarly and ministerial education and preparation and also typically involves the laying on of hands of other church leaders as a sign of blessing and God's calling the newly ordained to service. Different church communions vary as to whether they ordain both women and men as clergy.

Vestments. Persons conducting or celebrating liturgies often wear ceremonial clothing, whose colors, shapes, and patterns signify and communicate spiritual messages. For example, the alb (a full-length white robe signifying the purity of baptism) is often worn by Christian ministers and priests leading worship services. Christian ministers will also often wear a stole, which is a long strip of cloth several inches wide that drapes across the celebrant's shoulders and hangs down the front of the alb, signifying authority to lead the community in worship. The colors, embroidery, and design of the stole signify different festivals, celebrations, or holidays.

Sacraments. For those churches that observe them, sacraments are the highest moments of Christian worship (see chapter 4), with the single most important among them being the celebration of the Eucharist.

Sacramentals. Some Christian communities also make use of sacramentals, objects (e.g., candles, incense burners, rosary beads) or actions (e.g., making the sign of the cross, blessing) that serve to enhance the sacred quality of worship or personal devotions.

Liturgical Year. Christian rituals follow a yearly calendar, organized around holy days (holidays), that guides what rituals are performed. Some denominations observe only a basic liturgical year, centered on Christmas and Easter. Others observe a fully-developed liturgical year, with the different liturgical seasons distinguished by different vestments, colors, readings, and practices.

Lectionary. Many Christian communities use a book of readings that follow the liturgical year. Readings or lections from the Bible often play an important role in rituals. Denominations that do not observe a liturgical calendar do not prescribe specific readings for specific days or seasons.

Music. Christian rituals are frequently accompanied by music, such as the singing of psalms, hymns, and prayers. Hymnals are books of music, commonly made available so everyone can join in the music of the worship service.

Altar. Many Christian churches have a large table, or altar, which serves as the central place for the celebration of the Eucharist.

Host and Chalice. Bread and wine (sometimes grape juice) are the foods used during the celebration of the Lord's Supper (or the Eucharist). Christian communities that understand the Eucharist as a sacrament believe that Christ becomes symbolically or truly present in the bread and wine during the celebration. Roman Catholics believe that through consecration the bread and wine are transformed into Christ's body and blood, and that Christ becomes wholly and entirely present under the appearance of the bread and wine. In Catholic practice, the bread, called the host, is typically a round, unleavened wafer made of wheat flour; the wine is frequently presented in a goblet, called a chalice.

Though many Christian communities include all of these elements in their official worship services, others incorporate only some, and some use none. Traditional Quaker worship, for example, does not take place in a consecrated church. While communal gathering is important, the goal of such meetings is to support one's sense of worship and spiritual investment in daily life rather than to set aside or establish sacred times, spaces, and sacramental observances. "Holiness" churches, rooted in the Pentecostal tradition, also have largely unstructured gatherings, intended to be open to the movement of the Holy Spirit, expressed in the unplanned singing, speech, and physical movements of the congregation.

Liturgical Year and Holidays

Throughout the liturgical year, Christians pay special attention both to the seasons and to holidays or feast days. In both the Eastern and Western traditions, the dates of some major seasons of the liturgical calendar are moveable, which means they vary from year to year. This is the case, for example, with Lent and Easter. On the civil calendar, the dates of these holidays are determined by the lunisolar calendar (based on the position of the moon relative to the sun from month to month). Various church communions may celebrate major Christian holidays on different days, depending on which calendar system is used to determine the dates of major holidays, but they generally agree on the order and basic time of year of key events and liturgical seasons. In the most developed systems, practiced among Roman Catholics, Orthodox, Anglicans, and Lutherans, these include Advent, Christmas, Ordinary Time (following Epiphany), Lent, Triduum, Easter, and Ordinary Time (after Pentecost).

Advent. The first season of the liturgical year, Advent begins four Sundays before Christmas. This period of waiting, leading up to the celebration of the coming of Christ, is often symbolized by somber colors, especially purple or blue.

Christmas. This season celebrates the birth of Jesus. It begins on the evening of December 24 and lasts through Epiphany on January 6 (celebrating the visit of the Magi to see the infant Jesus) or through the Sunday after Epiphany (celebrating Jesus' baptism). White vestments are commonly worn during Christmas. In Western practice, Christmas Day is December 25.

Ordinary Time. The first period of Ordinary Time in the liturgical year follows Epiphany. *Ordinary* derives from the Latin word *ordo*, which simply refers to "a series or a line." *Ordinary* here, as in *ordinal*, means the counting of the weeks until Lent begins. The colors green and gold are frequently used in ordinary time.

Lent. This is the season of fasting (a restricted diet, with abstinence from certain foods), almsgiving (giving money, goods, time, and services to those in need), and penance (acts of contrition). Lent stretches from Ash Wednesday to the Triduum (discussed next). The season of Lent lasts roughly forty days (not including Sundays) before Easter. On Ash Wednesday, which follows the often exuberant Mardi Gras festivities of the Tuesday before, many persons have their foreheads marked with ash to symbolize human mortality and the need for repentance. Lent concludes on the Thursday evening before Easter, which starts the Triduum. Though the season of Lent is penitential, Sundays are still considered days of celebration. This is especially true for Palm Sunday (the Sunday before Easter), which celebrates Jesus' triumphal arrival in Jerusalem, but also anticipates his crucifixion. Purple is associated with Lent, while red is often used in Palm Sunday worship.

Triduum. This refers to the three-day period (from *tri*, meaning "three," and *dies*, meaning "day") before Easter Sunday. The Thursday, called Maundy Thursday (from *mandatum*, meaning "command"), recalls Jesus' command to his disciples: "I give you a new commandment: love one another. As I have loved you, so you also should love one another" (John 13:34). Maundy Thursday commemorates Jesus' Last Supper with his disciples. The following day, Good Friday, represents the day of Jesus' crucifixion; it is the most solemn day of the Christian liturgical calendar. The Saturday, referred to as Holy Saturday, marks the period of anticipation of Jesus' Resurrection. From

Thursday through Saturday of the Triduum, the days are marked by major liturgies, as well as morning prayers (called matins) and evening prayers (called vespers). White, red, and black are colors often associated with the Triduum.

Easter. This is the high season of celebration in the Christian liturgical calendar because it remembers Jesus' Resurrection. In the oldest Christian traditions, the first celebration of Easter is the Easter Vigil, which occurs after sundown on Saturday.[2] Many Christian communities choose instead to begin their celebration of Easter on Sunday morning. Easter season also includes a celebration of the ascension of Jesus into heaven after his Resurrection, and concludes fifty days after Easter at Pentecost. Pentecost celebrates the descent of the Holy Spirit on Jesus' followers and the birth of the Christian church. The color white usually signifies the Easter season.

Ordinary Time. The second period of Ordinary Time follows Pentecost and lasts for the rest of the year until the start of Advent.

Embedded in the liturgical seasons are the major Christian holidays of Christmas (also called the Nativity) and Easter (also called Pascha). In addition to these holidays, other major observances may occur throughout the year. Among Catholics, for example, important observances include celebrations of Mary's Annunciation, when Mary conceived Jesus by the Holy Spirit, on March 25; Mary's Assumption into heaven, when Mary's earthly life ended, on August 15; and All Saints' Day, when the deceased are remembered, on November 1. Others are minor holidays and feast days (for example, days dedicated to certain saints), on which little or no special observance by the community is required.

Sunday is the most common and regular day of Christian worship. Every Sunday Christians gather in their places of worship to remember, study, and celebrate the life of Jesus. Sunday is the customary day of worship for many Christians because it represents the day of Jesus' Resurrection. Some Christian communities, however, prefer to worship on Saturdays. Such communities frequently align

---

2. This follows from ancient Jewish reckoning, in which a day ends at sundown; consequently, Easter Sunday begins at sundown on Holy Saturday.

their worship with the Jewish Sabbath, which lasts from sundown on Friday to sundown on Saturday. This practice is maintained in accordance with the Old Testament commandment to "remember the Sabbath day—keep it holy" (Exodus 20:8).

The Virgin Mary, Saints, and Martyrs

Throughout Christian history, the extraordinary lives and faith witness of key figures have inspired Christians. Many of these figures lived in the early Christian centuries, and some appear in the Bible. Though Christians worship only the Trinity (God the Father, God the Son, God the Holy Spirit), inspirational figures may become the focus of special devotion—for example, by naming a church in that person's honor. Certain Christian figures are associated with unique ministries or needs because of things they are believed to have done or incurred in their lives. For example, Saint Peregrine is associated with recovery from cancer, reportedly having been cured of cancer himself after a night of prayer.

Some Christian communities believe that persons who have departed this life are still able to intercede on their behalf. This belief is held because, in a Christian worldview, the deceased have not utterly ceased to exist but rather enjoy, or will someday enjoy, ongoing existence with God. Just as Jesus was resurrected, Christians hope for an eschatological, or future, resurrection for themselves. Thus all Christians—deceased, still living, and yet to be born—are in communion with one another. The term for this linkage of Christians across time is the *communion of saints*. Consequently, many Christians feel close to, inspired by, and even aided by remarkable figures from Christian history.

When Christians, particularly Catholics and Orthodox, feel a special devotion for a particular person, either personally or as a church, they might devote spiritual activities to honoring that person. These may include celebrating the saint's feast day, praying for the intercession of the saint, making a pilgrimage to a place associated with the person, meditating on visual representations of the saint, saying special prayers associated with the saint, doing work or service in the community in accordance with memorable actions of the saint, or naming a child, a church, or an organization after the saint.

Figures for whom Christians may feel special devotion include the Virgin Mary, figures from the Bible, and nonbiblical saints and martyrs.

The Virgin Mary. Jesus' mother, Mary, is particularly important for many Christian communities. The New Testament provides little information about Mary, and there is not much more from the early Christian era. Most of the devotion to Mary, therefore, has developed for spiritual and theological reasons.

Christians argued, for example, that Mary had special intercessory powers because of her close relationship to Jesus. They also argued that Mary must have been sinless to carry Jesus, who was himself the exemplar of sinlessness, in her womb. Others argued that Mary was co-responsible for human salvation, because she bore God Incarnate as Jesus in her womb. Responding to the Nestorian controversy, Christian theologians at the Council of Ephesus (431) concluded that Mary not only bore Jesus as human but Jesus as God. In this sense, it was deemed appropriate to call Mary the *theotokos* ("God bearer," or Mother of God).

Especially from the fifth century on, Christians found in Mary a special advocate and a feminine element to help balance the many masculine images of God in Christianity. Popular devotion to Mary as the Mother of God over the centuries led to the development in modern times of two Marian (related to Mary) doctrines in Roman Catholicism. The first was the 1854 pronouncement by Pope Pius IX of the Immaculate Conception as a dogma of the faith. This doctrine held that Mary, like Jesus, was born sinless, or conceived immaculately. The second, Pius XII's 1950 definition of the Assumption, taught that Mary was assumed into heaven at the end of her life, rather than dying and having her body decay.

From the early centuries through the present day, prayers and hymns, important feast days, and countless private devotions have been dedicated to Mary. One common example is the rosary, a spoken or silent series of prayers reflecting on the lives of Jesus and Mary, done while holding a string of special beads. Although Mary is not considered divine, she is seen as the first of the saints and the foremost follower of her son Jesus. Because of the possible error of divinizing Mary, some Christian communities eschew devotion to Mary. Protestants in particular tend to reject practices that involve veneration of Mary or other saints.

Biblical Figures. Biblical figures who hold special significance for Christians include prophets from the Old Testament, such as Jeremiah, Isaiah, and Elijah; angels, such as the archangel Gabriel, who announced to Mary that she would conceive Jesus; and major figures in Jesus' ministry or family life, such as John the Baptist (who baptized Jesus) or Joseph (Mary's husband and Jesus' earthly father). Many such figures are recognized as saints.

Some of the most important biblical figures for Christians include Jesus' disciples, the twelve men that the Gospels say Jesus called to be his innermost circle of followers: Simon Peter, Andrew, Jude (also called Thaddeus), James of Zebedee, James of Alphaeus, Thomas, Matthew, Phillip, John, Bartholomew, Simon the Zealot, and Judas (to be replaced by Matthias after his betrayal of Jesus). A number of women were also central to Jesus' earthly ministry, including Mary Magdalene and the two friends of Jesus, Mary and Martha. Apostles were the first Christian missionaries. The disciples of Jesus overlap this group, which also includes men like Paul (the "Apostle to the Gentiles"), who did not know Jesus during Jesus' life.

Feast days in the liturgical calendar are dedicated to many of these figures, and churches and people have been named in their honor. Prayers and practices are associated with them, and particular locations, especially burial places, serve as important sites for Christians to visit.

Saints and Martyrs. Between the mid-first century and early fourth century, Christians were a minority population in the Roman Empire. Because of their beliefs, refusal to worship the emperor, and poorly understood religious practices (after all, they were then a new religious movement), Christians were sometimes persecuted by the Roman officials. Persecutions under the emperors Diocletian and Galerius (fourth century) were particularly brutal. Although the number is uncertain, a great many Christians died as *martyrs* (Greek for "witnesses") to their faith during Roman persecutions.

Stories of martyrs' courage and heroism spread far and quickly. Rather than deter people from becoming Christians, these stories inspired people to have courage and faith even in the worst circumstances. Many apostles died as martyrs. Far more martyrs died in the postbiblical era. Many Christians express devotion for these figures, who include Ignatius of Antioch, Justin Martyr, Apollonia, Perpetua, and Felicity.

While some Christian communities consider all believers to be saints, many Christians restrict the term to persons who have died and are with God. Christians do not agree on the nature of the state of being that exists between human death and the final events of resurrection and judgment. Some view heaven as a present state of being for the deceased; others view it as a future reality. Some view the dead as merely sleeping, awaiting resurrection at the time of Christ's second coming; others view the deceased as somehow with God, yet absent the spiritual body they will inherit at the time of resurrection. Christians, moreover, represent a broad spectrum in understanding the scope of salvation—who is with God or who is or will be in heaven. Some Christian communities believe that everyone will be saved, others believe only Christians will be saved, and others believe only certain Christians will be saved. Much of the ambiguity comes from the breadth of possible interpretations of Bible passages dealing with the resurrection, such as 1 Corinthians 15:44b and 15:50–55:

> If there is a natural body, there is also a spiritual one. . . .
>
> This I declare, brothers: flesh and blood cannot inherit the kingdom of God, nor does corruption inherit incorruption. Behold, I tell you a mystery. We shall not all fall asleep, but we will all be changed, in an instant, in the blink of an eye, at the last trumpet. For the trumpet will sound, the dead will be raised incorruptible, and we shall be changed. For that which is corruptible must clothe itself with incorruptibility, and that which is mortal must clothe itself with immortality. And when this which is corruptible clothes itself with incorruptibility and this which is mortal clothes itself with immortality, then the word that is written shall come about:

"Death is swallowed up in victory.
Where, O death, is your victory?
Where, O death, is your sting?"

Canonization of Saints

The Roman Catholic Church has a formal process for recognizing a saint, called *canonization*; the life of the person is measured (*canon* means a "measuring rod") or assessed for its holiness. The process, which can take hundreds of years to complete, entails several official reviews of the person's life, confirmation of two miracles associated with the deceased figure, and pronouncement of sainthood by the pope. Persons even from modern times are still being canonized as saints.

The Roman Catholic Church has a formal process whereby a person's life may be officially reviewed, and upon meeting certain criteria, the individual is pronounced a saint.

Christian practices associated with devotion to saints include the following:

Pilgrimages. Journeys that Christians make to holy places, places where miracles are believed to occur, or places associated with a Christian saint. Popular pilgrimage destinations include Jerusalem; Rome; Fatima, Portugal; Lourdes, France; and Guadalupe, Mexico.

Shrines. Sacred spaces within churches, cemeteries, and even homes dedicated to a specific saint. Christians visit shrines for special prayer, meditation, and devotion.

Relics. Artifacts from saints, often body parts (especially bones) or personal possessions. Often shrines or churches will be built in honor of a relic. Because a relic represents a tangible, material connection with a holy person, many Christians treat relics with respect and veneration.

Icons. A piece of religious artwork depicting a saint or spiritual event of great significance. Christians sometimes use icons as a point of reference for meditation, centering, or prayer, enabling them to enter into a deeply religious state of mind.

Social Service and Outreach

Because of their commitment to charity and community, Christians frequently make social service and humanitarian outreach a major part of their spiritual practice. They do this as individuals and families through work and volunteer service, and as church communities by running ministries and engaging in mission activities. Many Christians also see political activism as part of their spirituality.

© blackboard1965 / Dollar Photo Club

The veneration of icons, such as this icon of Christ, plays an important role in Eastern Orthodox spirituality. Some, however, have opposed the practice: the term *iconoclast* (literally, "image breaker") comes from controversy over the use of icons in the eighth and ninth centuries.

Christians provide service in countless types of ministries. A short list of Christian ministries includes outreach to the homeless, youth gangs, substance addicts, prison inmates, persons suffering from disease, vulnerable women and children, human trafficking victims, and victims of natural disaster. Ministries also include educational institutions, from early childhood programs through professional preparation, as well as interfaith and peace-making projects, services for orphans, foster care and adoption programs, and ecojustice projects.

Christians also engage in missionary activities. Missionary activities include outreach efforts to non-Christians or to people suffering humanitarian crises. Frequently, missionaries have the dual purpose of meeting basic humanitarian needs of a community while also evangelizing (or spreading the doctrine of the Christian faith). In past centuries, Christian missionaries were often disrespectful of the native customs and beliefs of peoples they evangelized. Today, however, missionaries generally attempt to respect local culture while simultaneously providing services and education about the Christian faith.

Christians may also be politically active concerning social justice issues about which they feel strongly. Christians, of course, do not agree upon a single or correct Christian political platform. They range from liberal to conservative, but they bring their beliefs about morality and justice to the broader public dialogue. Some larger issues that engage Christian political activity include social services, military actions, medical ethics, family legislation, immigration, freedom of speech, freedom of religion, the judicial and penal systems, public education, science and research, and environmental concerns. Often church communities will suggest codes of conduct or guiding principles for their congregations to follow in matters of faith and morality. Catholic social teaching articulates one such set of principles. The U.S. Conference of Catholic Bishops summarizes this teaching in seven principles of social justice derived from the core belief that every human life is created with inalienable dignity. These principles include respect for the life and dignity of every human person, the call to participate in family and community life, respect for human rights and responsibilities, a focus on the poor as a gauge of society's adequacy, the right to dignified and fair employment, a commitment to human solidarity, and care for the environment and the natural world.

Religious Orders

Some Christians, particularly Catholic and Orthodox Christians, choose to live their call to service and justice through membership in a religious community (or congregation). In this context, the term *religious community* refers to an organization of people who adopt, and often make vows to follow, a special way of life oriented around a particular devotional practice, charism, or ministry. A religious community is usually founded or marked by the inspiration of a person who lived a remarkable Christian life and who galvanized others to follow his or her way—for example, Saint Francis of Assisi. There are Protestant, Orthodox, and Catholic religious communities.

Catholic religious communities have a diverse array of structures, rules, levels of participation, levels of engagement with society at large, and definitions of charisms. Some communities are composed of members of the ordained clergy, while others are composed of nonordained persons. Some religious communities are monastic or contemplative and stress minimal or no contact with the outside world, while others are apostolic and stress ministerial service in the world. Some religious communities require all members to take vows of poverty, obedience, and chastity, while others allow members to participate as second- and third-order members (which means they take fewer vows, no vows, or vows for a limited amount of time). When members of religious communities are cloistered (living exclusively within the confines of a monastery), they are called monks and nuns. When members live and work in active ministry outside monasteries, they are called brothers and sisters. Church authorities typically govern religious communities, but each congregation also has its own rules for daily life. Rules govern, for example, the times of day for prayer, mealtimes, and allowable work.

Christian religious communities provide extensive social services throughout the world. In the United States, religious communities (especially women's congregations) historically played a leading role in the health care system and in education from elementary school through college. Religious communities today are often at the cutting edge in meeting social needs and among the first responders to natural disasters and humanitarian crises worldwide.

Conclusion

Christian spirituality refers broadly to how Christians put their faith into practice. Christian spirituality is always rooted in the life of Jesus, and it is generally characterized by the attempt to bring love and service to the whole human community through the special gifts of grace that each Christian individually bears.

Questions for Discussion and Review

1. What does it mean to say Christian spirituality is rooted in the life of Jesus?
2. What do Christians mean by charity?
3. Describe the different types of personal and communal prayer.
4. What would you identify as the three most important aspects of Christian liturgy? Which Christian communities would you say are most focused on these aspects? Are there Christian communities that do not focus on these aspects?
5. Describe the flow of the liturgical year. Why are some holy days moveable?
6. What are the three major categories of historical figures for whom many Christians feel special devotion. Why do some Christians engage in devotional practices involving such figures, while others do not?
7. What sorts of practices, customs, and objects are entailed in special Christian devotions? How do these elements differ from formal worship of God?
8. Give some examples of Christian social service and outreach.
9. What is a religious order? What is the distinction between a nun and a sister, or a monk and a brother?

Resources

Books

Day, Katie. *Faith on the Avenue: Religion on a City Street*. New York: Oxford University Press, 2014.

Holder, Arthur. *Christian Spirituality: The Classics*. New York: Routledge, 2009.

Howard, Evan B. *The Brazos Introduction to Christian Spirituality*. Grand Rapids, MI: Brazos, 2008.

Jenkins, Willis (author, ed.), and Jennifer McBride (ed.). *Bonhoeffer and the King: Their Legacies and Import for Christian Social Thought*. Minneapolis: Fortress, 2010.

McGrath, Alister. *Christian Spirituality: An Introduction.* Malden, MA; Oxford, UK; and Victoria, Australia: Blackwell, 1999.

Tradigo, Alfredo. *Icons and Saints of the Eastern Orthodox Church.* Los Angeles: J. P. Getty Museum, 2006.

Tyson, John R. *Invitation to Christian Spirituality: An Ecumenical Anthology.* New York: Oxford University Press, 1999.

Websites

Center for Student Missions, at *www.csm.org.* Includes information about planning urban mission trips.

The Lutheran Church Missouri Synod, at *www.lcms.org.* Includes order of liturgy.

Mission Finder, at *www.missionfinder.org.* This site provides information about hundreds of short-term, medical, domestic, and international mission trips.

The (Online) Book of Common Prayer, at *www.bcponline.org.* Includes the order for the Liturgy of the Eucharist of the Episcopal Church, and other services.

"An Order for Holy Communion (1966)," at *http://justus.anglican.org/resources/bcp/Wales/HE_English1966.htm.* Celebration of communion in the Church of Wales.

Quaker Information Center; "Traditional Quaker Worship," at *www.quakerinfo.org/quakerism/worship.*

Seventh-Day Adventist Church Manual; "Ordinance of Foot-Washing," at *www.adventist.org/fileadmin/adventist.org/files/articles/information/ChurchManual_2010.pdf,* p. 119. Order for the celebration of foot washing and communion in the Seventh-Day Adventist Church.

United States Conference of Catholic Bishops; "Order of Mass," at *www.usccb.org/prayer-and-worship/the-mass/order-of-mass.* See also explanation of the new Catholic Roman Missal at *http://usccb.org/prayer-and-worship/the-mass/roman-missal/.*

"What to Expect at an Anglican Church," at *www.anglicansonline.org/basics/expect.html.*

Films

Hildegard of Bingen and the Living Light. Alto, MI: Alto Productions, 2012.

Mary's Dowry Productions, a Catholic film company that produces features on the lives of the saints. For a list of titles see *www.marys dowryproductions.org/shop/index.php?main_page=products_all.*

Mission: God at Work, Faith in Action. Produced by Dianne Becker (2004). Filmed at Indigenous People's Technology and Education Center in Florida.

CHAPTER 8

Christianity and Non-Christian Religions

What to Expect

This chapter introduces the relationship between Christian theology and non-Christian religious or spiritual traditions. Christian dialogue with the following belief systems is discussed:

- Judaism
- Islam
- Hinduism
- Buddhism

Defining a Religion

Religion in general might be described as a collection of beliefs, held by a community, communicated through symbols, rituals, traditions, and sacred texts, that establishes a worldview and moral code for adherents. This book, which explores many of these aspects of Christian religion, demonstrates how difficult it is to succinctly describe exactly what Christianity is.

All religions, in fact, are difficult to summarize in a few sentences. People of every faith are as varied as Christians. All faith traditions develop diverse expressions, spiritualities, and worship practices over time. People participate in them to varying degrees, from casually to rigorously, from everyday practice to religious vocation or employment. One cannot assume something is true of all Christians, nor can one assume something is true of all members of any other religious tradition. Any discussion of religion must be guided by the awareness that a survey can never capture the totality of religious beliefs in lived practice.

Furthermore, people disagree over what actually constitutes a religious tradition. Some define religion as any faith-based belief system to which people commit, as opposed to a belief system based only on observation and experience. Some see belief in God, gods, or a higher power as essential to religion. Still others view religion as culturally derived myths that help believers to explain or make sense of the shared reality that humans struggle to fully understand. More skeptical minds view religions as wishful fantasies born of the desire for justice or fulfillment in the face of death, loss, socioeconomic or other inequities, and the general hardships of life.[1]

However one defines *religion*, clearly many worldwide use the term to describe their most essential beliefs and practices. All such adherents must address the fact that multiple religious traditions coexist in the world. From the beginning, the early Christians interacted with many religious traditions, including Judaism, the ancient religions of Greece and Rome, and the diverse, competing expressions of Christian faith.

Engagement among faith traditions is sometimes difficult. As throughout history, recent decades have witnessed violent conflict among different religious groups; consider the range of contemporary, aggressive religious expressions, from violent cults, to religious terrorism, to "Islamaphobia," to anti-Catholicism. One reason for such conflicts is that religions typically hold ultimate worldviews—ways people think about and understand the world—and when two or more competing worldviews are present, people often feel threatened and can become defensive. Conflict between religions is rarely *only* theological—factors such as politics, money, and land access often play a larger role—but a close examination of theological differences can help in understanding and respecting the integrity, beliefs, and humanity of all people. For religious faiths to coexist peacefully and

---

1. Consider, for example, Sigmund Freud's appraisal of religion in his 1927 book *The Future of an Illusion*.

responsibly, religious people need to think carefully about how they interact with other traditions both practically and ideologically.

Christianity and Diversity

Christian theology offers several ways to consider relationships with other religions. Three such approaches are *exclusivism, inclusivism,* and *pluralism.*

Exclusivism. Christian exclusivism rejects the possibility that God's revelation could exist outside the Christian faith and consequently does not see a need for theological dialogue with other faith traditions. This point of view is uncomplicated in that it simply does not acknowledge other traditions in the discernment of its own truth claims, and as such it does not engage questions of revelation or salvation in diverse religious perspectives.

Inclusivism. An inclusivist view would claim that Christ is the only means of salvation, but explicit faith in Christ is not necessary; sincere faith in God, in accord with any religious tradition, is sufficient in the eyes of God. In fact, other faith traditions may have insights or practices that could be meaningfully incorporated within Christian faith. This view accommodates other religions but assumes Christianity has a fullness of truth superior to others. Such a belief may inhibit meaningful dialogue between Christian theology and the religions it would engage.

Pluralism. A pluralistic view would contend that no single religion is completely adequate for explaining God's being and relationship to the world. All religions can coexist, just as different languages coexist. The existence of Spanish, for example, does not invalidate or compromise the existence of French or German. In a pluralistic model, multiple religions, like multiple languages, may be studied and used to explore and explain the world. The difficulty with this perspective is that it may create a problem of *epistemology* (how one knows something is true) in which no religion can be determined as more nearly true or more accurate than another. This situation arises because this approach has no external standards for evaluating or comparing beliefs.

Part of the task of interreligious dialogue is to determine the nature of the dialogue, as well as the expected or desired outcomes. The degree to which people perceive differences among belief systems will largely shape how their dialogue will negotiate those differences. For example, virtually all religions try to make sense of human suffering and loss. In many ways, beliefs among different faith systems are similar regarding essential human experiences, such as birth, marriage, death, and other key moments in the human life cycle. Some maintain that all religions attempt to explain these basic human experiences, but each does so using different vocabulary. On the other hand, many argue that differences among religious belief systems are distinct. Polytheism and monotheism, for example, offer dramatically different models for thinking about God. As a result, some people hold that religions are trivialized by identifying ultimately inconsequential points of similarity between profoundly diverse beliefs and practices.

In considering religious diversity, Christians must negotiate relationships that are both *intra*religious (within Christianity) and *inter*religious (with non-Christian faith traditions). Intrareligious relationships are considered in chapter 5. This chapter surveys Christianity's interreligious relationships with the other Abrahamic traditions (Judaism and Islam) and with the Eastern traditions of Hinduism and Buddhism. The following discussion is written from an essentially pluralist perspective.

Judaism

Christianity is rooted in the same traditions that gave rise to modern Judaism and shares with Judaism the sacred writings of the Hebrew scriptures (or Tanakh). From the beginning, Christians have affirmed their continuity with the God proclaimed by Israel, the God of Abraham, Isaac, and Jacob. In spite of Christian roots in Judaism, Christianity has not always maintained a peaceful sibling relationship with it. A discussion of Christianity and Judaism requires consideration of historical tensions as well as present advances in interreligious dialogue.

Like Jesus himself, the majority of the first Christians were Jewish, and understood Jesus as the fulfillment of the ancestral hope for a Messiah. The New Testament holds that Jesus came not to abolish but to fulfill the requirements of Jewish law (see Matthew 5:17–18). The earliest Christians continued to follow the Jewish law, but its status as supremely binding was challenged by Jesus' interpretation. The question of how rigorously the law should be followed factors heavily in New Testament letters, particularly Paul's. As Gentile converts to Christianity began to transform the Hebraic character of the early Jesus movement, Christians no longer saw the Jewish law as a requirement.

JUDAISM An Overview	Location of Origin	Key Historical Figures	Founding Dates
	Mesopotamia and the Fertile Crescent	Abraham, Isaac, Jacob, Moses	1800–1300 BCE (ancient Israelite religion) 200 CE (Judaism)
Important Literature	**Key Beliefs or Practices**	**Major Holidays**	**Status and Location Today**
Torah, Tanakh, and Talmud	Belief in one God—YHWH Human life was created for covenant with God and observance of the law; afterlife is undefined Worship at synagogue or temple Worship on Sabbath	Rosh Hashanah (New Year) Yom Kippur (Day of Atonement) Sukkoth (Feast of Booths) Hanukkah (Festival of Lights) Purim (Festival of deliverance from occupation) Passover (Festival commemorating the Exodus) Shavuot (Pentecost)	14 million adherents Worldwide presence, esp. in Israel, Europe, and United States Major sects: Orthodox, Conservative, and Reform

Even though the Jesus movement was increasingly influenced by Greek culture, Christians continued to claim the Israelite religion as their legacy. Conflict arose as Christians and Jews disputed key interpretations of this legacy. The most important conflict concerned the identity and nature of the Messiah. For Christians, Jesus was the Messiah; for Jews who expected a Messiah (not all Jews did), the Messiah would deliver the Jewish people from colonial occupation and assume political control of the nation. As the two groups debated, the gap between them grew. Sociopolitical matters also came into play. For example, in the first Jewish revolt against Roman authorities in 66–70 CE, Christians sought to distance themselves politically from Jews for their own protection.

As Roman persecution of Jews intensified following the failed revolt, and as the Jesus movement took on an increasingly Hellenistic character, many Christians saw Christianity as having superseded Judaism—as having fulfilled its commandments and replaced Jewish law with worship of Jesus. This claim, known as *supersessionism*, was compounded by the misguided notion that Jews were responsible for Jesus' death (in fact, only Roman governors could inflict capital punishment at the time). As a result, later generations of Christians often engaged in coercive and violent treatment of Jewish people.

Anti-Semitism is a term used to describe violent actions and attitudes toward Jews as Jews. Anti-Semitism continues today. Some of its most brutal historical expressions include the Catholic Inquisitions in the Middle Ages and the Holocaust (also known as the Shoah) in the twentieth century. Responsible Christian theology today rejects and repudiates anti-Semitism, along with claims that Christianity supersedes Judaism or that Jews were responsible for Jesus' death.

Today Christian and Jewish scholars and religious leaders recognize the benefits of engaging in genuine theological dialogue. In recent decades, Christian theologians have renewed their interest in the persistent and pervasive threads of Hebraic thought and culture in Christian scriptural tradition. Members of both religions recognize that engaging one another, even in debate, is a valid expression of vital and dynamic faith. The biblical tradition each shares is not one of easy answers but rather one of searching, questioning, and even challenging God. The practice of vigorous dialogue with God is increasingly seen as essential in both Christian and Jewish faith. Fruitful areas for Christian–Jewish dialogue include the Jewishness of Jesus, the Hebrew scriptures, nonsupersessionism, and eschatological hopes and tensions.

Jesus: A Jewish Man. Focusing on the Jewish character and heritage of Jesus is important for Christians interested in the roots of Christianity. Christian doctrine that too quickly focuses on complex Christological concerns and terms may overlook the need to ground Christ in the historical person of Jesus. Appreciation of the Hebraic context in which Jesus emerged, especially the prophetic tradition he embodied, may move Christians toward richer dialogue with Jews.

The Hebrew Scriptures. Historically, Christians have erred in reading the Hebrew Bible as if it were exclusively oriented toward the foretelling of Jesus' life and death. Excessive emphasis on the Christocentric element in Hebrew prophecy can interfere with a rich reading of the Hebrew scriptures as an inherently integrated and

Although both Christians and Jews accept the Hebrew scriptures as sacred, the two groups view them very differently. Christians tend to regard the Torah (the Law of Moses) as a collection of difficult and onerous commandments, whereas for Jews, it is a source of delight, as in the annual celebration of *Simchat Torah* ("Rejoicing of the Torah"), shown here.

meaningful set of texts. Although Christians may see continuity with the Christ events in the Hebrew scriptures, Christian theologians advance interreligious dialogue with Judaism by developing skill in reading the texts in their own right, apart from a rigid Christocentric interpretation.

Nonsupersessionism. Christian theologians aid interreligious dialogue with Judaism by articulating alternatives to supersessionist theology. This involves a renewed understanding of both Christian conceptions of God's covenant through Jesus and Jewish conceptions of God's covenant through the law.

Eschatological Hopes and Tensions. Christianity and Judaism may also share political interests, driven by overlapping eschatological perspectives. Christians often speak in the language of hope for the return of Christ, although they differ considerably in regard to what, precisely, they expect will happen. Some Jews speak of hope for the restoration of the Temple in Jerusalem. Some Christians believe that rebuilding the Jerusalem Temple will usher in the era of Christ's return to earth. Rebuilding the Temple on the Temple Mount in Jerusalem, where two Muslim mosques currently sit, however, would have global political ramifications. The politicization and political consequences of faith can produce extreme social tension. As Jews, Christians, and Muslims attempt to negotiate the volatile realities of life in the Middle East, especially in the State of Israel, subscribers to all faiths are tasked with engaging responsibly and genuinely to achieve peaceful coexistence.

Islam

Like Christianity and Judaism, Islam claims Abraham as its founding father. Whereas Christians and Jews establish their lineage through Abraham's younger son, Isaac, Muslims trace their lineage through Abraham's elder son, Ishmael. Islam teaches that Abraham, with the help of Ishmael, built the Kaaba, the most sacred building in the Islamic tradition. This shared connection to Abraham places the three traditions in a sibling relationship. Additionally, all three religions believe in the monotheistic deity revealed by the prophets of Israel. All three have sacred locations throughout Palestine.

All three share overlapping accounts of revelation in scripture and the information contained therein concerning God's relationship to humanity.

ISLAM An Overview	Location of Origin	Key Historical Figures	Founding Date
	Mecca in Saudi Arabia	Muhammad	622 CE
Important Literature	**Key Beliefs or Practices**	**Major Holidays**	**Status and Location Today**
Qur'an Sunnah and Hadith collections	Belief in one God—Allah Goal for life is submission to God in the hope of resurrection after death and paradise after the Day of Judgment Worship in mosque Observance of the Five Pillars of Islam: 1. Profession of the creed (shahadah) 2. Recitation of daily prayers (salat) 3. Almsgiving (zakah) 4. Fasting during Ramadan 5. Pilgrimage to Mecca (Hajj)	Muharram (New Year) Ashura (Day of mourning) Mawlid al-Nabi (Muhammad's birthday) Ramadan (month of fasting) Eid al-Fitr (celebration ending the fasting of Ramadan) Eid al-Adha (celebration ending the Hajj)	1.5 billion adherents Worldwide presence, esp. in Middle East, Africa, North America, Europe, and Southeast Asia Major sects: Sunni, Shia, and Sufi

Historically, the relationship between these three religions has been tense and often violent. Any discussion of the dialogue among them, especially between Christians and Muslims, must recognize this history of tension, ranging from the Crusades of the Middle Ages to contemporary Mideast conflicts, wars, and acts of terrorism. Today the reality of these conflicts makes a committed effort at interreligious dialogue between Christians and Muslims all the more urgent.

The major theological differences between Christianity and Islam have to do with the understanding of God, the prophet Muhammad, revelation in the Qur'an, and engagement with the world.

Understanding of God. Islam and Christianity both embrace monotheism. Indeed, both religions acknowledge the same God professed in the biblical tradition of Israel. Islam derives from the same tradition that produced Judaism and Christianity but sees itself as the completion of and correction to its predecessors.

Islam's chief dispute with the Christian understanding of God lies in the latter's Trinitarian and Christological claims. For Christians, God interacts with humanity in a personal way, expressed through the persons of the Trinity and the Incarnation of Christ. Christians identify Jesus as part of or one with the One God; Jesus thus brings salvation in an immediate, direct, and personal encounter between God and humanity. For Muslims, God's oneness is utterly transcendent, and human claims to personal intimacy with God are judged to be presumptuous, even dangerous. In Islam, God's will is revealed not through a personal incarnation but through the succession of prophets begun in the time of the Old Testament and concluded in the final revelation of the prophet Muhammad. Both groups have at times oversimplified or exaggerated the claims of the other regarding, respectively, the Islamic insistence on God's transcendence and the Christian insistence on God's personal encounter.

The Prophet Muhammad. As noted earlier, Christianity historically has struggled to understand its relationship with its older sibling, Judaism—specifically in regard to the Jewish law and covenant. With Islam, Christianity must reenvision its relationship with its younger sibling.

The prophet Muhammad was born in Mecca in 570 CE and died in 632. According to Muslim belief, the prophet received revelation from God nearly six hundred years after the life of Jesus. In the last twenty-three years of his life, revelations granted to Muhammad were recorded scrupulously in the Book of God, known as the Qur'an. The revelation, along with the life and deeds of the prophet as recorded in the Sunnah provides the basis for Islamic practice and belief.

Muslims do not see Muhammad as the incarnation of God, as Christians see Jesus. Rather, Islam teaches that Muhammad is God's final prophet, who fulfills the revelation begun with Abraham and carried through the biblical prophets, including Jesus. Muhammad's prophetic revelation teaches about God's purpose in creating and commands humans to live ethical lives, create just communities, and submit rightfully to God. Although Muhammad is not worshipped as a deity, Muslims consider his role to be inestimable because he transmits God's final and definitive revelation, to which humans would otherwise have no access.

Christianity has not historically recognized Muhammad as a prophet, let alone as God's ultimate prophet. This represents one of the greatest theological tensions between the two religions. One reason for the traditional Christian rejection of Muhammad is that Islam postdates the events of Christ. For Christians, God's final and complete saving work was affected by Jesus; all subsequent prophets would therefore be secondary or even superfluous. A further problem for some Christians stems from the hostile conditions in which early Islam spread under the prophet. Whatever the explanation, Christian theologians, such as Hans Kung,[2] engaged in Islamic interreligious dialogue now take seriously the claim that Muhammad is a prophet and attempt (with varying levels of success) to understand him meaningfully in the tradition of the biblical prophets such as Isaiah and Jeremiah.

Revelation in the Qur'an. Islam teaches that God's revelation to Muhammad was fully and perfectly recorded in the Arabic text of the Qur'an, which represents the very Word of God. According to Muslims, its sacred character cannot be overstated, and because of

2. Hans Küng, Josef von Ess, Heinrich von Steitencron, and Heinz Bechert, *Christianity and World Religions: Paths of Dialogue with Islam, Hinduism, and Buddhism* (Maryknoll, NY: Orbis, 1993).

the unique nature of the Qur'an, it cannot be treated the same as other written texts. For example, it cannot be properly translated; the Arabic text is the only true expression of the revelation. In addition, the Qur'an is not subject to historical or developmental analysis.

In the last two centuries, many Christian communions have adopted methods of biblical scholarship that allow them to see the Bible as human-authored but divinely inspired, a compilation of writings produced over several centuries and reflecting different time periods, and redacted (or edited) to reflect worldviews pertinent to a range of sociopolitical contexts throughout that history. By contrast, the very idea of historical-critical analysis of the Qur'an militates against the notion of the unique and total revelation made to Muhammad. As such, Christians and Muslims dispute the value and appropriateness of bringing such analytic techniques to sacred literature.

Engagement with the World. Both Christianity and Islam are missionizing religions, meaning they seek to bring their message and beliefs to persons all over the world. Muslims and Christians sometimes see each other as groups that need to be missionized or converted. This missionizing attitude has historically been a keen source of tension between the two faiths. Mission practice today generally strives to be mindful of the integrity of all people and to pursue a noncoercive and politically neutral course.

Similar tensions often arise over ethical questions that straddle civil and religious laws in societies where Muslims and Christians coexist. One major contemporary question involves women's rights and social roles.

The ways that contemporary Christians approach Muslim-Christian dialogue, and the success they achieve, vary tremendously. The exclusivist, inclusivist, and pluralistic views suggest the possible directions this dialogue may take. Christian and Muslim mutual exclusivism negates genuine and constructive dialogue. Christian and Muslim inclusivist approaches offer more possibilities, but risk mutual appropriating, diminishing, distorting, or subverting of each other's original and essential claims, leading to a false or superficial sense of agreement. The most successful Christian theological attempts to dialogue seriously with Islam to date have taken a pluralistic approach, wherein both partners try first and foremost to enter into the religious beliefs of the other—first to understand as a native believer would and then to analyze as a point of comparison.

Holy War?

War is principally played out in the realm of the polis, conducted by soldiers or citizens, and its outcomes affect politics, economics, and geographical boundaries. What does religion have to do with war? One aspect of modern-day interreligious conflict that garners great popular attention is the idea of holy war. But how can war be holy? How can God, or the gods, of any religion justify or mandate the violence of war?

It is sometimes surprising to discover that the history of religions is integrally related to political history and therefore to war. This is because religion does not exist in a vacuum; it exists as the operating worldview that fundamentally drives and motivates people who are inescapably immersed in their social contexts. Religion can be invoked in justification for war for a number of reasons:

- The sacred texts of the religion speak of, mandate, or justify war, as happens in parts of the sacred books of Judaism, Christianity, and Islam.
- Religious leaders call believers to war, as happened in the Crusades or in modern-day religious terrorism.
- People believe God has called them as "soldiers" to enforce a certain moral code or social ethos, for example in contemporary, religiously-motivated abortion clinic bombings.
- People feel God wants them to reclaim sacred locations, as occurs in the contemporary Hindu-Muslim clashes in Kashmir, India.
- People of different religions or sects within a religion vie for the same land or resources, each believing that God is on their side and opposed to the other.
- People feel God wants them to go to war to stop an injustice or to liberate a people from oppression.

Holy War? (continued)

Islamic jihad is often defined as holy war, but that is a distortion of the concept. The term *jihad* means "struggle," and refers broadly to the multifaceted Islamic struggle to maintain one's faith, to live in rightful submission to God, to improve the conditions of society, and to defend the Islamic faith; it is a religious duty of Muslims. Islam accordingly speaks of jihad of the heart, jihad of the tongue, and jihad of the hand, as well as jihad of the sword.

Like Islam, Christianity has a long tradition of thought about holy war. As soon as Christianity became the leading religion of the Roman Empire (fourth century), Christian theologians began to consider what conditions merited use of force in the interests of the empire. "Just war theory" emerged with arguments from Augustine, and later Thomas Aquinas, that force could be used when certain conditions were met, including when war was initiated by a proper authority, was conducted for a just cause, was conducted by ethical means, had a chance for victory in combat, and was motivated by right intent.

The Crusades of the Middle Ages exemplify the terrible violence that can come from holy war rationale. Even a superficial study of the Crusades reveals that much more than religious debate was at stake among combating Eastern Christians, Western Christians, Muslims, and Jews. This dangerous historical epic is a useful talking point for comparison when one evaluates all modern-day warfare that is supported by religious claims. In considering modern war it is helpful to ask: Under what conditions is war just? What elements in religions justify or even mandate the use of violence?

Christianity and Two Eastern Traditions

In the interest of brevity, this chapter cannot consider all of Christianity's dialogue partners, such as Sikhism, Jainism, the Baha'i faith, Taoism, Confucianism, neo-paganism (or modern revisiting of pagan religions of the past), Wicca, and Scientology, as well as Native American, African, and other indigenous religions. This section discusses two key Eastern religious traditions that Christians encounter: Hinduism and Buddhism. These religions, perhaps better thought of as spiritual traditions, are sometimes lumped together as "Eastern religions" but in fact are distinct systems that warrant individual attention.

Hinduism

Christianity and Hinduism have widely differing accounts of revelation, theological anthropology, salvation, and afterlife. For example, Christians believe that human beings were made in the image of God but in their free will succumbed to sin. This resulted in a fall from grace and a need for salvation. Jesus uniquely offers salvation and restores his followers to a state of grace. At the end of life, human beings await resurrection and heavenly existence.

HINDUISM An Overview	Location of Origin	Key Historical Figures	Founding Date
	India	No specific founder	1500 BCE
Important Literature	**Key Beliefs or Practices**	**Major Holidays**	**Status and Location Today**
Vedas, Upanishads, Sutras, Puranas, Epics: Bhagavad Gita, Ramayana, and Mahabharata	Brahman is the ultimate reality Goal for life is to attain liberation from the cycle of reincarnation through following the dharma and understanding the nature of the self Worship in temples or domestic shrines	Diwali (Festival of Lights) Holi (Festival of Colors) Festivals of deities' birthdays and seasonal festivals	900 million adherents Worldwide presence, esp. India, United Kingdom, United States Major sects: Saivism, Vaisnavism, Saktism, and Smartism

By contrast, Hinduism holds that each human being carries the spark of the divine within. Humans have forgotten their true nature, however, and need to recall it. Human life is understood as a series of incarnations that leads ultimately to realization of one's true nature and liberation from the cycles of incarnation. The Advaita school of thought in Hinduism is "nondualistic" and holds that the self is liberated when it realizes itself as in no way separated or essentially distinct from the ultimate reality of Brahman. The Dvaita school of thought, in contrast, holds that souls are eternal and retain their distinctness within the ultimate reality of Brahman.

Any effort to encapsulate Hinduism as a discreet set of religious beliefs or practices falls vastly short of the cultural and historical complexities of Indian religious life to which the term "Hindu" is ascribed. It is therefore difficult to provide an adequate context for a Hindu-Christian dialogue in limited space. One possible direction for dialogue is the Hindu conception of God, which, like the Christian one, may be helpfully understood in Trinitarian language. Hinduism conceives of God as manifesting in the three principal aspects of Brahma, Vishnu, and Shiva, which may be compared with the Trinitarian Christian categories of Father, Son, and Spirit. In addition, the Hindu concept of liberation (called *moksha*) from the cycle of reincarnation (called *samsara*) may also be compared with the Christian concept of liberation from sin and eschatological salvation. Hindu and Christian spiritual and contemplative practices, such as yoga and meditation, may also be explored and compared. Both traditions contemplate the Divine Being and the Divine Presence in human beings, suggesting the possibility of interior illumination, divine intercession in human affairs, and revelatory insight.

Hindus and Christians share a relatively peaceful history, but Christian missionizing in India has sometimes led to violence and political conflict. Westerners have become increasingly aware of Hinduism, especially as an alternative to traditional conceptions of "church" and an enriching option for spiritual practice and development. The Hindu-Christian dialogue is producing a growing body of comparative theological study aimed at sharing information, mutual understanding, and collaboration.

Buddhism

Many Westerners are attracted to the spiritual, meditative practices of Buddhism, which is itself a reform movement of Hinduism. As with Hinduism, Christianity has increasingly engaged Buddhism in recent times. The Buddhist–Christian dialogue has become so sophisticated as to produce professional journals, partnerships, and academic centers of study.

As with any religious tradition, a good way of approaching Buddhism is to grasp its understanding of human life. A central tenet of Buddhism is the idea that human life, indeed all life, is transitory. Although people perceive themselves and others as distinct individuals, Buddhism teaches that people do not have fixed, eternal souls. This idea is termed *an-atman*, or no-soul. Suffering marks human experience because people misunderstand the basic fluidity of all nature and try to attach themselves permanently to that which is impermanent—especially to one's life, one's material goods, and

Christian mystics have found much of value in Buddhist meditative practices. The monk and mystic Thomas Merton, shown here with the Dalai Lama (1968), was among the first Christian authors to engage in fruitful dialogue with Buddhism.

one's relationships with others. Liberation from suffering comes in the form of enlightenment about the true nature of reality. Lifestyle and meditative practice, guided by the Buddha's teachings of the Four Noble Truths and Eightfold Path, can help Buddhists achieve enlightenment and freedom from suffering and to live joyfully and compassionately to help eliminate suffering in the world.

There is significant overlap between Buddhism and Christianity on the issue of human suffering and how that suffering may be overcome. Moreover, both Buddhism and Christianity have a central, liberating, historical figure: the Buddha and Jesus, respectively. Both traditions study the lives of the key historical figures at their origins, providing fruitful opportunities for comparison. Both traditions also teach faith-based practices aimed at compassion and liberation from suffering. Christian–Buddhist dialogue that focuses on doctrine, therefore, may consider categories of suffering, ethical and meditative teachings, selfhood, no-selfhood, and divine illumination.

An interesting aspect of Buddhist teachings is that they are often expressed in negative terms. This means that Buddhist teaching inclines more toward telling what something is *not* like than by asserting what it *is* like. In Christian theology, there is a comparable tradition called the *via negativa* (the way of the negative), whereby God is contemplated by negative analogies; for example, "God is not limited," "God is not alterable," and so on. Buddhism does not assert specific dogmas about the interior life or being of the Divine (as do the Christian doctrines of Trinity or Incarnation). Thus Christian theologians taking an inclusivist approach have been particularly open to Buddhist teaching, adopting aspects of Buddhist spirituality without having to accommodate competing assertions about God.

Christians and Buddhists in dialogue mutually engage questions of social ethics and personal conduct. Both traditions recognize the reality of suffering and seek to alleviate it through a compassionate, human response. Moreover, both seek human response as the result of transcendent insight. Both further stress the need for right personal conduct and prescribe meditative practices aimed at developing a mature spirituality. A number of Christian and Buddhist thinkers have found that Christian-Buddhist dialogue can mutually enrich each religion's sense of social participation and personal spirituality as a corrective response to suffering.

BUDDHISM An Overview	Location of Origin	Key Historical Figures	Founding Date
	India	Siddhartha Gautama (also called the Buddha)	520 BCE
Important Literature	Key Beliefs or Practices	Major Holidays	Status and Location Today
Pali Canon	Everything is impermanent Attainment of enlightenment (Nirvana) through observance of the Four Noble Truths: 1. All life is suffering. 2. Suffering is caused by desire. 3. Suffering can be eliminated . . . 4. . . . by following the Noble Eightfold Path: • right view • right intention • right speech • right conduct • right livelihood • right effort • right mindfulness • right concentration Meditation in a temple	The Buddha's birthday The Buddha's enlightenment	360 million Worldwide presence, esp. in Japan, China, Korea, and Southeast Asia Major sects: Theravada, Mahayana, and Vajrayana

Conclusion

Christianity is but one of many faith traditions in the world. The reality of multiple religious traditions calls on Christians to think constructively and dialogically about their relationship to others. The potential for misunderstanding, conflict, and even violence is too great to ignore.

The closest traditions to Christianity are Judaism and Islam. These religions stem from the same historical lineage and share closely overlapping themes in their sacred literatures and doctrines of God. It is also with these religions that Christianity has had the most historical conflict. Negotiating present-day political tensions requires an elevated care and commitment to interreligious dialogue among these faiths.

The Eastern faiths of Hinduism and Buddhism also constitute important dialogue partners for Christians. These dialogues have increasing relevance today as Hinduism and Buddhism more broadly permeate the spiritual practice and popular imagination of people in the West. Christian interreligious dialogues with traditions not mentioned in this chapter are extensive and also involve the study of Christian missionary practices.

There are, finally, many different Christian communities, each with its own understanding of the purpose of interreligious dialogue. For some, such dialogue is unnecessary and unwanted. For others, it is the most burning issue the community faces. Typically, Christian attitudes toward interreligious dialogue are exclusive, inclusive, or pluralistic. Each approach has theological strengths and drawbacks, but the inclusive and pluralist approaches tend to be best suited for continued mutual theological engagement.

Questions for Discussion and Review

1. What is the difference between interreligious and intrareligious dialogue?
2. Distinguish among inclusive, exclusive, and pluralistic approaches to interreligious dialogue.
3. Why are Judaism, Christianity, and Islam considered "Abrahamic faiths"?

4. If you were asked to identify the one religious tradition with which Christians most desperately need to develop a fruitful dialogue, which religious tradition would you pick? Explain your choice.

5. What are the principal areas of dialogue between Christian and Jewish thought? Where do the two faiths connect most closely? Where do they diverge most widely?

6. What are the principal areas of dialogue between Christian and Islamic thought? Where do the two faiths connect most closely? Where do they diverge most widely?

7. What are some theological similarities and differences between Hindu and Christian thought?

8. What are some theological similarities and differences between Buddhist and Christian thought?

9. Is interreligious dialogue necessary in the world today? Explain.

10. How would you respond to the statement, "Christians don't need to dialogue with that group because they only espouse a philosophy, not a religion."

Resources

Books

Chittister, Joan, Murshid Shaadi Shakur Chishti, and Arthur Waskow. *The Tent of Abraham: Stories of Hope and Peace for Jews, Christians, and Muslims.* Boston: Beacon, 2006.

Küng, Hans, Josef von Ess, Heinrich von Steitencron, and Heinz Bechert. *Christianity and World Religions: Paths of Dialogue with Islam, Hinduism, and Buddhism.* Maryknoll, NY: Orbis, 1999.

Robert, Dana L. *Christian Mission: How Christianity Became a World Religion.* Oxford: Wiley-Blackwell, 2009.

Smith, Huston. *The World's Religions.* New York: HarperOne, 2009.

Smock, David R., ed. *Interfaith Dialogue and Peacebuilding.* Washington, DC: U.S. Institute of Peace Press, 2002.

Websites

BBC; "Religions," at *www.bbc.co.uk/religion/religions.*

PBS; "Religion & Beliefs," at *www.pbs.org/topics/culture-society /religion-spirituality.*

Films

Moyers, Bill. *The Wisdom of Faith with Huston Smith.* Acorn Media, 1996.

On the Trails of World Religions. Princeton, NJ: Films for the Humanities and Sciences, 2001.

CHAPTER 9

Christianity and Ethics

What to Expect

This chapter examines Christianity and its relationship to the secular world through its engagement with ethics. Topics to be explored include:

- Christianity and the "Secular" World
- Moral Thought and Theology
- Christianity and the Polis
- Christianity and Justice
- Christianity and War
- Christianity and the Environment

Christianity and the "Secular" World

Everything that human beings do—including things religious—must occur in the world. This inevitable worldliness is a fact of human existence, which raises questions about how Christian thought and practice should be lived out in concrete ways. In its entirety, Christian thought establishes a worldview (one's all-encompassing perspective on the world) that systematically attempts to account for both epistemology (what can be known) and morality (what ought to be done and how). These areas necessarily intersect the world at large.

Sometimes a Christian worldview and a secular (or non-religious) one meet harmoniously. For example, there are secular reasons for supporting conservationism (ecologically based practices bolster a

193

local economy) and Christian reasons for supporting conservation-ism (all of God's creation should be stewarded responsibly). These two justifications for conservationism, although essentially different, complement each other.

Sometimes, however, a Christian and a secular worldview might conflict in a way that is dissonant or even intolerable. For example, corporate interests often run contrary to more environmentally sound business practices. A Christian ethic of environmental stewardship may be neglected or disregarded in favor of a company's focus on profit. Medical issues are another area of conflict. Christian ethics, emphasizing individual human dignity and worth, the value of life at all stages of development, and the importance of a broad under-standing of human flourishing, can clash with positions that empha-size values of convenience or financial profit. The outcome may be conflict in the lives and practices of Christians navigating health care issues in the real world, both as consumers and as health care providers. Moreover, whether business or medical ethics are involved, there can be any number of complications: What influence or voting power do Christians have in shaping business or medical practices? How much should a Christian perspective steer laws guiding these practices? And what happens when different Christian groups dis-agree with regard to questions of medical or business ethics?

As noted in previous chapters, Christians are required to nego-tiate plurality among themselves as well as among people of other religions. Christians must also engage the socio-political realities of the world in which they live. How should Christians think about the discoveries of modern science, especially at points where they appear to run contrary to established Christian doctrine? How should Christians respond to claims that religion is an outmoded and even dangerous way of thinking? How and to what degree should Christians publicly voice their opinions in legislation? How should Christians resolve intrareligious disputes on gay marriage, abortion, evolution, health care coverage, and other contentious mat-ters? In both harmonious and contentious situations, Christians face the challenge of living out their beliefs in meaningful ways in daily practice. This includes every aspect of life—from where Christians work, to where they invest their money, to where they shop, to how they vote.

The relationship between Christian belief and daily practice encompasses a vast range of topics, matched by an equally great variety of Christian approaches at the communal and individual levels. This brief survey in no way exhausts the many possibilities for Christian engagement or the diverse worldviews various Christian people and communions bring to each of these forums.

Moral Thought and Theology

The area of thought that specifically speaks to the Christian engagement with the world is Christian ethics. Christian ethics involves study of the broad principles and commitments that underlie moral decision-making as well as the application of those principles to ethical practice in the world. Christian ethics thus fosters engagement between Christian thought and practice, examining what it looks like when a Christian person or community concretely lives out beliefs.

The study of ethics as an academic discipline can be a technically sophisticated endeavor, involving careful analysis of different ethical points of view, methodologies, and situations—often in a case-study fashion. In general, depending on how they understand the nature of the world and the operation of human reason within it, ethicists adopt varying frameworks for thinking about human behavior. Some argue that behavior is ethical if it follows certain rules (the "deontological" perspective), while others argue that behavior is ethical if it maximizes good and minimizes suffering (the "utilitarian" or "consequentialist" perspective).

A relevant question is whether a distinctly Christian ethics differs from any other rational approach to moral thought and action, or is Christian living merely an expression of ethics generally? One distinction is that Christian thinkers (from professional theologians to ordinary believers) invoke elements from scripture, tradition, and church teachings, along with their rational discernment, in making decisions about how to act personally and politically. In short, Christians use not only reason but also the revealed and established Christian tradition, as well as dialogue with their faith communities, as ethical guides and standards.

One approach to the study of Christian ethics is to consider topically some of the major categories of concern that Christians face when making decisions about how to think and act. Here we will consider a few such subdivisions of ethics: Christianity and the polis, Christianity and justice, Christianity and conflict, and Christianity and the environment.

Christianity and the Polis

Although some Christian communions are sectarian, or withdrawn from society, the relationship between many Christians and the polis (the political entity in which one lives) is more often one of active engagement and participation. Christians sometimes distinguish between being "of the world" and "in the world" to explain their sense of involvement. Christians do not see themselves as ultimately *of* the world, for the church is not generated by and destined for secular life, but Christians do recognize that they are *in* the world and must live out their faith amid secular society. This dynamic invites Christians to participate in their communities—neighborhoods, cities, counties, states, nations—as citizens and political persons, even though they may not always be satisfied with the current state of the society. Some of the ways that Christians participate in the polis include: citizenship, economic participation, media presence, and education.

Citizenship

As citizens who vote, make decisions, hold jobs, serve, and lead, Christians help shape the communities in which they live. Often, specific pieces of legislation will touch on deeply held morals and values. Propositions concerning relief for the poor and underprivileged, the legalization of drugs, definition of marriage, or penalties for hate crimes are examples of legislation that reflect the moral values of the culture. When Christian voters come to the polls, their sense of faith and morals often guides them. In addition, when Christian citizens run for office, their platforms often reflect their deepest convictions about what is best for the flourishing of individuals and society. Like candidates of every stripe, they seek to bring their vision of a good society to the polis.

Economics and Consumption

Christians also participate in the polis through economics, including how they earn income and how they use or invest their money. The notion of household management is deeply rooted in the Christian conception of God as Trinity, insofar as the theological tradition often speaks of Trinitarian participation in human history as "economic" (from *oikonomia*, Greek for "household management"). The language of the "economics" of salvation sets the cosmic precedent for the idea that Christians have an obligation to manage their homes and their communities in a responsible and charitable fashion. The New Testament, moreover, is rife with mention of economic concerns and expresses wariness over the acquisition and preservation of material wealth.[1] Economics continue to be one of Christians' most pressing ethical concerns. This consideration ranges from the places where Christians work, to how they invest, shop, donate to charities, and vote on economic initiatives at all levels of government. In affluent nations, these questions take on a special character in light of the culture of consumerism, excessive waste production, and the pursuit of prestige through brand purchasing and the desire to have the newest version of a given product. In impoverished nations, these questions take on a life-and-death character as people—often with inadequate work options—seek to meet the basic survival needs of themselves and their families.

Media and Social Communications

Christians use many forms of modern media as conveyors of faith-based content, including TV and radio broadcasting, the Internet and social networking, and Christian publishing in all forms.

---

1. The biblical tradition strongly critiques the pursuit of monetary gain. In Matthew 6:24, the author quotes Jesus observing a fundamental conflict between the love of God and the love of money. One cannot be simultaneously devoted to God and worldly gain. As such, the New Testament community seems to have viewed money as a means to meet basic needs rather than as an end to be celebrated in itself. Among other biblical passages, similar sentiments on the value of money can be found in Luke 3:14; Luke 16:13–15; 1 Timothy 6:10; and Hebrews 13:5. Perhaps the greatest indicator of the community's assessment of money is found in Acts 2, which indicates that the early Christians lived communally, holding all their property in common. The traditions of living in common and valuing elective poverty in pursuit of spiritual illumination have persisted throughout Christian history, especially in religious orders like the Franciscans and the Poor Clares.

Modern forms of media, however, raise a variety of questions for Christians. Can liturgical celebrations be held online? How should pastors and ministers use media in their pastoral efforts? How can Christian content be responsibly and effectively communicated through media channels?

Perhaps a larger concern for Christians is the constructive use of social media. It is an ongoing challenge for Christian individuals and communities today to use social media responsibly in the service of the Christian community, while at the same time safeguarding people from the potentially depersonalizing effects of social interaction that occurs virtually instead of in the flesh. Though it is certainly possible to experience community electronically, in the Christian view, it is nevertheless critical to preserve the human qualities of compassion and presence as electronic media shape societies and the church communities within them.

The dialogue between Christianity and modern media is a two-way street. The content of modern media helps to frame and inform how all media consumers, including Christian consumers, perceive the world. For example, one might argue that the shifting public perspective from a negative to a more positive evaluation of same-sex marriages is due in part to favorable media presentations of same-sex couples.[2] On the other hand, Christian values or ideas may be expressed in media in ways that also influence popular attitudes or trends. As another example, the use of sexual abstinence or purity pledges by some Christian teenagers and their families, symbolically represented by the wearing of a "purity ring," is now a referenced phenomenon in some popular media and may be a factor in changing attitudes toward premarital sex among teens.[3]

Education

Christians may participate in the larger community by trying to influence public school curricula. As taxpayers who support school

2. See Seth Goldman, "Framing Effects, Elite Competition, and the Debate about Gay Marriage," paper presented at the annual meeting of the International Communication Association, Dresden, Germany, June 2006.

3. See Jimmie Manning, "Exploring Family Discourses about Purity Pledges: Connecting Relationships and Popular Culture," in *Qualitative Research Reports in Communication* 15, no. 2, 2014 (Philadelphia: Routledge, 2014), 92–99.

districts, Christians sometimes raise their voices in support of or in opposition to certain aspects of a curriculum. The teaching of both the theory of evolution and sex education in schools, for example, has generated significant public debate in recent decades. More recently the teaching of the history of the American gay rights movement has prompted debate. Other education-related issues include educational vouchers and school choice, and the question of whether taxpayer dollars ought to supplement the cost of private education, including Christian education. Some argue that Christian history and religious education in general are precluded from school curricula, even when taught from a sociological (rather than confessional) point of view. All these issues raise policy questions about the intersection between education and Christian religion.

Christianity and Justice

Christians have been concerned with social justice since biblical times. The prophets of the Old Testament were not so much predictors of future events as social critics who called the political class to be accountable to God's law. The prophets' concern for the poor led them to condemn rigged scales in the marketplace, oppressive handling of debt, unfair transmission of inheritance, unjust handling of property rights and land ownership, and the oppression of orphans and widows. Although the prophets each had their own, unique perspective, they all agreed that God cares more about fairness and justice in the ordinary activities of life than about religious rituals.

In the New Testament, Jesus summarized the law of God in two rules: love God, and love neighbor (Luke 10:25–28). God cannot be loved apart from one's neighbor, and by loving one's neighbor, one shows love for God. This principle means that Christians must actively meet the needs of other human beings, beginning with the basic needs for food and clothing. This form of active Christian charity, established in the Bible, continues to underlie Christians' attitude toward charity today.[4] Part of Christian evangelism involves meeting the basic needs of people all over the world. Dilemmas often emerge as Christians strive to live justly and meet the needs of their

---

4. See, for example: Acts 4:34; 1 Timothy 6:17–19; and 1 John 3:17.

"neighbors." Some key areas where this occurs include health care and medical technology, family legislation and social outreach, dialogue against discrimination, and criminal justice.

Health Care and Medical Technology

Health care is a key area for Christian moral theology. Christians are typically concerned with ensuring people's fair access to health care. Most Christians are critically aware, however, that medical technologies invariably raise ethical questions. Should technologies be used to alter a fetus in utero or terminate a pregnancy when the developing baby has a known congenital defect? Should technologies be employed to prolong life when an individual is in a permanently vegetative condition? If so, for how long? Who should decide when enough is enough? Who should pay? Should technologies be used or invented to clone humans, to grow or harvest organs, to produce pregnancies, or to alter or select the characteristics of a baby? Should medical technologies be used to hasten death for persons who are

Wellcome Library, London

Christians have a long tradition of caring for the sick and needy. Medieval hospitals, like the one in Paris shown here, were typically run by the church and staffed by monks and nuns.

terminally ill and suffering? Although different Christian groups do not all agree as to what constitutes the appropriate Christian understanding of these issues, they all recognize their duty as Christians to strive for the responsible, respectful, and ethical use of medical technologies.

Family Legislation and Social Outreach

Family life is a core concern of Christian ethics, for families are the first place children encounter Christian faith and morals. Christians frequently provide charity for families, and especially children, in need. Christians recognize that family life needs the protection and support of society at large and often undertake service work to protect vulnerable persons and families, single-parent families, families dealing with long-term illness, and families with elder care responsibilities. Some Christians also actively engage legislators about laws that affect social outreach, including health insurance coverage and programs that affect the poor, and laws that affect family life, including laws regarding marriage, abortion, adoption, custody of children, divorce, child support, and inheritance rights.

Gay Marriage?

A recent example of the heated dialogue on family issues that intersects with Christian religious values is legislation concerning the definition of marriage in the United States. The U.S. government passed a federal law in 1996, known as the Defense of Marriage Act, which defined marriage as a legal union between one man and one woman. This law was overturned by a divided (5-4) United States Supreme Court in 2013. In 2015 the U.S. Supreme Court further ruled that same-sex marriage is legal in all fifty states. At the time of the decision, gay marriage was legal in thirty-seven states. In that same year, beyond the United States, ten countries worldwide recognized same-sex marriage, while in dozens of others, homosexual activity was considered a crime. In at least seven countries, homosexual acts were punishable by death.

Gay Marriage? (continued)

Many Christians feel that God intended marriage to be between one man and one woman, for the procreation of children. These Christians support their argument from such biblical passages as the creation stories in Genesis, the prohibitions against homosexuality in the book of Leviticus and elsewhere, and teachings on marriage scattered throughout the Old and New Testaments. A number of church leaders of major denominations have endorsed this understanding of marriage, pointing to the millennia-long history in the West of heterosexual marriage. Other Christians support same-sex marriage, arguing variously that biblical passages on marriage and sexuality are ambiguous, that many aspects of the Bible do not speak to contemporary culture with authority, and that there are many biblical teachings that modern people reject as binding (for example, killing children as a penalty for disobedience as prescribed in Deuteronomy 21:18–21). These Christians often support their stance on the basis of the dignity, rights, and justice concerns of homosexual persons.

Contemporary Christian debate on same-sex marriage ranges from terse "bumper-sticker" assertions to sublime arguments that attempt to synthesize the theological tradition with the best modern understandings of gender, biology, brain chemistry, psychology, sociology, and even jurisprudence. Moreover, even if Christians could agree unanimously about marriage, should their understanding of morality be required of non-Christians? This ongoing discussion reveals the depth, range, and even tension that exists among Christians, as well as between Christians and the polis at large.

Dialogue against Discrimination

In the past century, antidiscrimination movements have profoundly influenced Christian thought. Minority populations and women increasingly have been able to articulate the social injustices they have historically suffered; in response, many Christians have become active in promoting the fair and equal treatment of all persons regardless of race or gender. The idea that members of the community become "one" in baptism, which dates back to the first years of Christianity, set the precedent for egalitarianism within the Christian churches. Unfortunately, Christians throughout the eras have fallen prey to the same tendencies of gender and racial discrimination that are manifested in society at large. Today, however, many Christian communities recognize past error in this regard and work for the full social enfranchisement of all people, despite ethnic, gender, and lifestyle differences. Many such communities today also strive to identify and to end discrimination against homosexual persons within their churches. Thriving African American, Hispanic, Asian American, and Native American communities have used the church as a prime location for organization, education, advocacy, and action in support of members of their ethnic demographics. Since the mid-nineteenth century, gender equality has become a major concern among many Christian communities. Though some Christian denominations admit women to positions of leadership, many still do not, citing theological or biblical reasons why women and men should retain separate, delineated roles in church as well as society and household. As women today gain legally protected access to more equal opportunities in society at large, the question of women' status in the church is an indelible part of an engaged, contemporary Christian dialogue.

Criminal Justice

Christians have a historical interest in the treatment of prisoners and persons accused of crime that stems from the biblical concern for vulnerable persons. In the Gospel accounts, Jesus expressed concern for the treatment of prisoners. The invitation to love one's neighbor is an invitation to love even "unlovable" individuals. Even if people disfigure the image of God within themselves, human beings must honor one another's value as creatures of God.

Christians believe that God offers opportunities for reconciliation in the face of moral failure. They see Jesus' death on the cross as the ultimate opportunity for reconciliation, to which all people are invited. Thus many Christians feel called to extend themselves generously to people in prison and lobby for prisoners' humane treatment as persons of value, who are capable of reconciliation and forgiveness. Many Christians reject the death penalty on these same grounds. In

204 | Christian Thought and Practice

recent years, especially, one can follow interesting stories of women religious who have prominently lobbied for the dignity, rights, and lives of convicted persons, such as in the example of Roman Catholic Sr. Helen Prejan, whose story was popularized in the 1995 film *Dead Man Walking*.

Christianity and War

The first Christian communities lacked the ability, resources, and motivation to wage war. Furthermore, they modeled their response to violence on Jesus, who willingly gave himself over to the authorities even though he faced an unjust death. Jesus' life and death established a precedent of pacifism in Christian thought, as well as a special appreciation for martyrdom for one's faith.

Yet the Bible depicts God as calling upon his people to wage war, and even participating in war on behalf of the Israelites.[5] Even Jesus is sometimes depicted as espousing violence in word and deed, as when he overturns the money changers' tables in the Temple (Matthew 21:12) and when he says, "Do not think that I have come to bring peace upon the earth. I have come to bring not peace but the sword" (Matthew 10:34). Christians have historically taken such militaristic language as metaphor for the spiritual battle between cosmic good and evil.

Since at least the time of Constantine in the fourth century, Christians have participated in war as part of the larger political bodies in which they live. Indeed Christians have at times embraced violence for the cause of Christianity, as in the Crusades of the Middle Ages. Christians have even urged violence against other Christians believed to be in the wrong, as in the religious wars in Europe in the sixteenth and seventeenth centuries, and the Catholic-Protestant conflict in Northern Ireland in the twentieth century.

As citizens of the political states in which they live, Christians often serve in the military, sometimes as noncombatants, although some Christian pacifist communities, like the Amish, refuse military service altogether. Most Christian communities accept that war is

---

5. See, for example, God's intervention at the battle of Jericho, causing the city walls to collapse before the invading Israelites (Joshua 1:1–6:25).

Modern nuclear warfare fails to meet the criteria of a just war on two counts: the response is not proportional (the destruction it causes is massive), and the destruction is not limited to combatants, but effects the entire civilian population and natural environment.

sometimes necessary, but seek to restrict it to only certain contexts deemed appropriate. The conditions for a just war include: when the cause is just, when war is initiated by one's proper governmental authority, when there is a reasonable chance of victory, when proportional methods are used, and when only enemy combatants are targeted. Critics of just war theory point out that, even under optimal conditions, the effects of war always extend beyond the death and injury of military personal. War also produces civilian casualties, widows, widowers, orphans, and collateral damage to persons, property, animal life, and the natural environment. Today, moreover, military technology and nuclear weaponry put the whole planet at risk.

Militarism and war occur not simply because people do not get along or because they have competing belief systems. Rather, conflict erupts most fundamentally over land access and resources, including human persons, whose bodies are resourced for labor, production, and reproduction. As the global population rises, people move about more rapidly through immigration and interact through cultural exchange, resulting in increased tensions over cultural identity, resource allocation, economic participation, and more. Today's warfare brings new considerations to the perennial discussion of whether, how, and when war can be justly waged. Terrorism, for example, blurs the lines between political states and self-appointed agents of war acting out of ideological interests. Terrorism also blurs the lines between military combatants and civilians, as does the use of child soldiers. The controversial application of "enhanced interrogation" techniques opens new dialogues over what constitutes "torture" and what punitive actions are licit in the service of perhaps life-saving information gathering. New weapons technologies allow for remote military strikes by drones, an evolution that radically reshapes the combat experience for drone pilots and targets. All these issues invite ethical scrutiny over whether and how combat is disclosed and reported accurately in media coverage. War and conflict thus remain basic creaturely concerns that demand critique from a Christian worldview, insofar as such a worldview affirms the goodness of creation, the divine image in all human persons, and the human requirement of earthly stewardship.

Christianity and the Environment

Christian interest in environmental issues has burgeoned in recent decades, especially in response to the ecological crises of the twentieth century that demonstrated how vulnerable we are as a species and how dependent we are on a healthy planet. The current ecological crisis stems from technological and industrial developments of traditionally Christian Western culture. Theologically, Christians have been accused of condoning the exploitation of the environment.[6] Christian faith places its ultimate hope in a world-yet-to-come, and this other-worldly or even apocalyptic perspective may justifiably be cited as one of the reasons people in Western-Christian cultural contexts have taken this present world for granted.[7] On the other hand, there is long precedent in the Hebraic and biblical traditions for ecological awareness and environmental care, rooted in the belief that God created the world and, according to the Bible, "It was good" (Genesis 1:12). The Bible commands human beings to be stewards

---

6. The biblical command to subdue and dominate the creation (Genesis 1:28) has been seen as encouraging such an attitude.

7. Catherine Keller makes this argument in her landmark work *Apocalypse Now and Then: A Feminist Guide to the End of the World* (Minneapolis: Augsburg Fortress Press, 2004).

of God's creation, and this stewardship includes care of other people, animals, and the land. Increasingly, Christian theologians have come to recognize water, land, and air pollution, soil erosion, exploitative industrial agriculture, endangerment of animal species, human overpopulation, and environmental damage resulting from military action as moral evils that require repudiation and correction on the part of Christians at the societal and individual levels.

Interesting new approaches to Christian ethics in recent decades have focused, for example, on such diverse issues as animal ethics, water access and drinkability, industrial farming and agriculture, waste management, environmental racism, recycling, stewardship of parks, lakes, and forests, and more. One finds in the emergent field of ecotheology a new appreciation of cosmology, earth-centeredness, the body as a location for salvation, and the continuity of the human with other animal species. These sorts of issues, which may not strike one as self-evidently theological in nature, become so within a Christian ethical framework that seeks to honor creation and the limits of finite, creaturely participation in the world.[8]

Contemporary Debate about Natural Theology

An interesting corollary to ecologically mindful theologies is the renewed modern debate concerning natural theology. Natural theology is the branch of theology that tries to demonstrate through reason alone the existence of God, as well as the divine purpose and design of creation. Natural theology therefore does not rely on revelation to prove God, but rather asserts that God can be known through the study of the natural world. From the time of the Greek philosophers and the beginning of the Christian era, people have

---

8. Demonstrating a heightened environmental consciousness, Pope Francis issued a landmark encyclical entitled *Laudato Si'* in May 2015. The encyclical focuses on the earth as humanity's common home, urging care and stewardship of God's creation. The full text of the document is available at *http://w2.vatican.va/content/francesco/en/ encyclicals/documents/papa-francesco_20150524_enciclica-laudato-si.html.*

Contemporary Debate about Natural Theology (continued)

attempted to know the divine purpose of the world through rational inquiry. The endeavor to know God apart from special revelation became a special point of interest during the Enlightenment of the seventeenth and eighteenth centuries, characterized by the turn toward reason. In 1802 the English theologian and moral philosopher William Paley published a work called *Natural Theology*, representing a classic distillation of the rational attempt to prove God.

Rational arguments for the existence of God and the purpose and design of nature have met with mixed success historically. Anselm of Canterbury (1033–1109) argued that God is "that than which nothing greater can be thought," and Thomas Aquinas argued that there were "five ways" (motion, causation, contingency/necessity, degree/perfection, and intelligent design) in which God was implied in the fabric of creation. Such arguments have been countered by critics like David Hume (1711–1776), who argued that nature does not prove inherent purpose or design and that deriving God from nature is speculative rather than conclusive.

In recent decades the natural theology dialogue has been taken up again by a panoply of scientists and theologians. Physicist and Anglican priest John Polkinghorne (b. 1930), for example, has argued for the complementarity of theology and physics. His work represents the contemporary trend in natural theology, which argues that theological and scientific models together provide a fuller and more coherent explanation of the natural world than either would independently. Conversely, staunch critics of natural theology, such as Richard Dawkins (b. 1941), look at the same evidence and conclude that God either does not exist or cannot be proven. As scientists continue to penetrate ever deeper into the universe's mysteries, the debate over whether God can be demonstrated or not, apart from revelation, will only intensify.

Conclusion

Christian dialogue with the world will always be in process, just as the issues to which Christians will need to respond will always be in flux. This is so because Christians of every era are of necessity people of their times. Their cultures, social backdrops, technologies, economies, and so on provide the context in which they encounter and live their religious beliefs.

Although basic elements of the religious tradition are handed down in a stable and careful transmission, the context in which that tradition is received always changes. A few decades ago, it would not have made sense to ask whether a liturgical service could be held online, but today that question is relevant. Just decades ago, it would have been inconceivable to ask whether stem cell research was morally licit, because stem cell research had not yet been invented. The lived context will always bring new questions for people living their faith. The Christian person will always face the task of relating contemporary questions to the historical tradition. People with an active and reflective faith will thus be challenged continually to play the role of translator-theologian as they seek to know and do right ever anew.

The Bible and the entire theological tradition that accompanies it encourage a basic belief in the dignity of the individual and the need for a good society, understood analogically as "love of neighbor." When love of neighbor is coupled with love of God, Christians have a powerful set of guidelines for understanding their faith and putting it into meaningful practice in every aspect of life.

Questions for Discussion and Review

1. Why is religion inevitably concerned with the world?
2. Can a poem or a song be "true"? If yes, in what way? Does something have to be scientifically or historically verifiable for it to be true?
3. Describe three ways some Christians engage in the political arena. Can you think of others, not stated in this text?

4. Do you think Christian taxpayers should help shape the curriculum of the public schools their children attend? Why or why not?

5. What are the benefits, losses, and general tensions of bringing one's religious sensibility to legislation?

6. Describe some aspects of social justice that engage Christians.

7. What are the biggest concerns, in your opinion, that Christians face in the world today? How do you think Christians should address those concerns?

8. How does love of God relate to love of neighbor in the Christian faith?

9. Christianity has been accused of encouraging the exploitation of the environment. Do you think that claim is justified historically? Do you think it is possible to develop a Christian environmentalism? Explain.

10. What is "natural theology"? Do you think there is value to such an approach? Explain.

Resources

Books

Deane-Drummond, Celia. *Eco-Theology*. Winona, MN: Saint Mary's Press, 2008.

Forster, Greg. *The Contested Public Square: The Crisis of Christianity and Politics*. Downers Grove, IL: InterVarsity Press, 2008.

Glanzer, Perry L., and Todd C. Ream. *Christianity and Moral Identity in Higher Education: Becoming Fully Human*. New York: Palgrave Macmillan, 2009.

Horsfield, Peter, Mary E. Hess, and Adán M. Medrano, eds. *Belief in Media: Cultural Perspectives on Media and Christianity*. Burlington, VT: Ashgate, 2004.

Hunt, Mary E., and Diann L. Neu. *New Feminist Christianity: Many Voices, Many Views*. Woodstock, VT: Skylight Paths, 2010.

McGrath, Alister. *Science and Religion: A New Introduction*. 2nd ed. Oxford, UK: Wiley-Blackwell, 2010.

Panicola, Michael R., David M. Belde, John Paul Slosar, and Mark
F. Repenshek. *Health Care Ethics: Theological Foundations, Con-
temporary Issues, and Controversial Cases.* Winona, MN: Anselm
Academic, 2007, 2011.

Websites

Center for Environmental Philosophy; "Ecotheology Book List," at
www.cep.unt.edu/ecotheo.html.

Just War Theory, at *http://www.justwartheory.com/.*

New Advent; "Moral Theology," at *www.newadvent.org/cathen
/14601a.htm.*

Valerie Brown. "The Rise of Ecotheology," at *www.columbia.edu
/cu/21stC/issue-3.4/brown.html.*

Films

God in America. Six part series. PBS, 2010.

What Would Jesus Buy? Virgil Films and Entertainment, 2007.

CHAPTER 10

Contemporary Spirituality and Christian Thought

What to Expect

This chapter will explore formative elements of contemporary spirituality in dialogue with traditional Christian thought and practice. Topics to be considered include:

- Spirituality in Popular Culture
- Cultural and Ethnic Diversity as a Cultural Value
- Environmental and Ecological Movements
- Liberation Movements

Spiritual but Not Religious

The Pew Research Religion and Public Life Project undertook extensive surveys of religion in the United States in 2007 and 2014. The data, collected on over 35,000 Americans over the age of eighteen, revealed a flexible and dynamic religious landscape. This was especially true for older millennials, those born in the years spanning from 1981 to 1989. They demonstrated a trend toward departure from the religious traditions of their childhoods. Most strikingly, in 2007 twenty-five percent of people in this group indicated no religious preference or affiliation at all, and in 2014 thirty-six percent of them indicated no religious affiliation. These data, combined with data that shows that older Americans are more religious, suggests that generational replacement will lead to a future for religion in America that may be as colorful and variegated as a patchwork quilt. Add a global perspective, and it becomes apparent that "religion" as traditionally understood faces dramatic new challenges as well as opportunities for growth, renewal, and meaningful application.[1]

Why are spiritual beliefs and practices shifting? One way to approach this question is to consider what kinds of things inform people's imaginations, worldviews, and concerns today, and then to evaluate the spiritual messages of those influences. Immediately, for example, one might recognize changes in social communication that enable people to connect almost instantaneously with not only friends and family but also with acquaintances, contacts, colleagues, and even like-minded strangers. Electronic media and social networking make it possible to experience global events in real-time, to research and share ideas immediately, and to participate virtually in academic, professional, and social experiences. But even as these technologies facilitate the scope and speed of human interactions, they also challenge the historical ways of communicating, relating, and learning. We may get information more quickly, but read less. We may have hundreds of virtual friends, but little face-to-face contact with them. We may communicate efficiently electronically, but struggle to express ourselves in spoken dialogue. Embedded in all these issues, one finds the foundational questions of relationship formation and participation, and the epistemological search for truth and meaning. Social media and electronic communication technologies, then, significantly inform the way people today learn to relate, to love, to know, and to value, all of which are characteristically (even if not exclusively) "spiritual" dimensions of the human experience.

Consider the role of entertainment media in the formation of cultural sensibilities, values, attitudes, and beliefs. Movies, such as the Star Wars and Harry Potter franchises, tap into, express, and even contribute to shifting attitudes toward traditional religious thought. Popular cultural options, like online role-playing games and fan-based discussion boards, offer consumers an opportunity to participate in grand mythic stories and communal activities that, for some,

---

1. *http://religions.pewforum.org/reports.*

may mimic and even satisfy elements of traditional worship communities. The broad incorporation of religiously-styled themes and heuristics within consumer entertainment products, often brilliantly enacted and musically scored, adds to their rhetorical significance and sense of truth or legitimacy. Role-playing games that involve ethical decision-making engage moral agency, affective response, and personal investment in ways that can become very real for the participant. The messages communicated in these stories have an impact upon contemporary religious sensibility.

In light of such insights, how does Christian thought and practice intersect with developments in cultural movements and popular spirituality? The following discussion approaches this question by looking at four critical areas in which modern spirituality and Christianity might meaningfully be brought into dialogue: spirituality in popular culture, cultural and ethnic diversity as a social value, environmental and ecological movements, and liberation movements.

Spirituality in Popular Culture

"Popular culture" is a vast and varied topic. For which demographics are we analyzing content and messages? Why consider these books, games, movies or songs and not others? Any conversation about spirituality and popular culture will attempt to participate in a larger, ongoing conversation about the overlapping realms of the secular and sacred in which human beings experience creativity, expression, and inspiration. Every such conversation will recognize its own limits and the vast opportunities for expansion and inclusion of more examples and ideas.

The overlap between secular and sacred realms may be framed in at least three ways. One way is to ask how the secular has had an impact upon religious thought and expression—for example, how "sacred" art may participate in, express, or reflect secular modes of expression. The church has a long history of adopting secular music for sacred purposes; many of the great choral settings of the Latin Mass are based upon secular songs,[2] and a number of

---

2. Examples include Guillaume Dufay's Mass, *L'homme Arme*, Josquin des Prez' Mass, *Dung Aultre Amer*, and John Taverner's Mass, *Westron Wynde*.

popular hymns began as secular songs.[3] Some contemporary religious music, such as that produced in the contemporary Christian music[4] movement, is styled after secular musical forms, such as today's Christian rap music that draws its textual content from biblical language.

The information revolution has also had an impact on religious thought, as people of faith are constantly reminded that different faith perspectives also exist. Similarly, awareness of the plight of the poor and oppressed in other parts of the world helps foster a global conscience. Some wonder, however, whether constant exposure to such problems may not have a numbing effect. Does the ability to see visually and in real time the devastation of war or natural disaster as recorded on someone's smart phone and posted on YouTube make a person more compassionate or more desensitized to the realities of suffering and violence of fellow human beings?

A second way in which the overlap between the sacred and the secular may be framed is by asking how religious ideas have an impact upon the secular—how secular things express or reflect the sacred, whether intentionally or unintentionally. The emergence of religiously or theologically themed material in such unexpected sources shows that popular culture is an important venue for exploring spirituality in ways that are liberated from the classical constraints of church authority. An example of this would be exploring the meaning and value of religious themes in contemporary music, which often expresses a deep theological discourse on the part of the artists. One striking example is the music of the folk singer Bob Dylan, which straddles and merges the breadth of secular and spiritual themes in such songs as "Forever Young" or "Blowin' in the Wind." More contemporary examples include Imagine Dragons' "Demons" and Death Cab for Cutie's "I Will Follow You into the Dark."

One also sees in various art media the perennial emergence of spiritual themes and types in human imagination and experience,

---

3. Examples include "O Sacred Head Now Wounded" ("*Mein G'müt Ist Mir Verwirret*"), "What Child Is This?" ("Greensleeves"), and the children's hymn "Jesus Loves the Little Children" ("Tramp, Tramp, Tramp, the Boys Are Marching").

4. For a resource that discusses multi-genre Christian music today, see *www.ccm magazine.com/magazines*.

called "archetypes" by psychoanalyst Carl Jung. Twentieth-century scholar and mythologist Joseph Campbell devoted his career to examining in comparative perspective these archetypes, evaluating the many masks or faces that spiritual themes assume in varied cultural and religious contexts. The great insight of work such as Campbell's and Jung's is the awareness that many elements and themes of the great world religions are the codified but common and persistent spiritual experiences that human beings have across time and culture. Redemptive figures, angelic beings, tricksters, healers, and so on may represent archetypes, whether really extant or contrived by the human imagination, that are commonly expressed in specifically religious venues or language but which may also be expressed in secular culture at large. An example of this would be the theme of salvation mediated by a Messianic or Jesus-like figure in the character of Neo from the Matrix movies and video games (Warner Bros. Pictures, 1999, 2003). Conversely, one finds the comparable opposite figure in the menacing lord of darkness, Darth Vader, of the Star Wars franchise.

A third way of framing the religious-secular overlap is by examining syncretism or the blending of religious and secular language, imagery, and behaviors. In religious studies, one way in which researchers study human behavior is to examine it by the common categories that surface in religious behavior. Such categories include: observance of sacred spaces, holidays, and ritualized meals; the donning of costumes or special types of clothing; making pledges or oaths; gathering at critical times in the week, month, or year; reading from or memorizing special books or texts, and more. These kinds of behaviors constitute the practical backbone of participation in a religious community. People often participate in such behaviors in nonreligious contexts as well as in religious ones. What is more, people may well achieve the same benefits of participating in nonreligious ritualized behaviors as they derive from classically religious ones. Examples here include participating in sororities or fraternities; participation in political organizations or parties, especially during election cycles; making secular "pilgrimages" to concerts; or participation in sports culture as fans, viewing games at home or in stadiums. It is an interesting exercise to consider how these and other activities mirror religious behavior in function and in the social and communal benefits of member participation.

All three frames point to an underlying tension that exists within the Christian theological tradition, which is the separation of the sacred from the secular; the revealed from the common; the supernatural from the natural. Theologians are beginning to recognize this tension in the assertion that God created the universe, which is in some sense to assert that God is not the universe. In this theological worldview, God can be known by what God has created, but only partially. Therefore, one needs special insight in order to learn about God, and this is where the ideas of sacred revelation, the Incarnation of God in the person of Jesus, and the sacramental character of the church come into play. This theological model, while embracing the personal quality of special divine revelation to the human being, also produces an epistemological ambiguity about what can be known in the world as a matter of course or by nature alone or through unaided human inquiry.

A cross in Baiona, Spain overlooks the coastline, raising the question: What constitutes sacred space versus natural space? Many indigenous religious traditions see no meaningful distinction between the two.

Researchers have observed that terms such as "religious," "sacred," and "spiritual" are often used to describe elements of monotheistic religions (Judaism, Christianity, Islam), but that these same terms do not comfortably fit with the behaviors, beliefs, and sacred traditions of natural or indigenous communities. The reason for this is that many indigenous traditions do not distinguish between what is sacred and what is secular. The secular, as it were, is infused with the sacred, and so everything is essentially spiritual. One could argue that the issue is not whether the secular can reveal the sacred or whether the sacred may participate in the secular but rather that the secular and the sacred have been falsely dichotomized. In this view, human spirituality infuses all of culture, whether the spiritual impulse emerges from popular culture or whether it comes from realms demarcated as "sacred."

This is not a new insight in Christian thought. Indeed, even early in Christianity's history, writers like St. Augustine were examining how and what resources from popular culture (plays, music, etc.) and from academic disciplines (language study, rhetoric, astronomy, etc.) could be used in the advance of Christian wisdom. Augustine's *On Christian Doctrine* and *Confessions* both demonstrate awareness of a (perhaps unnecessary?) tension between secular sources and culture and their application and suitability to Christian thought and practice.

Globalization, Diversity, and Spirituality

One major element that shapes contemporary attitudes toward spirituality is globalization. We are intricately connected to one another throughout the world in the exchange of our products, ideas, resources, and labor. If once it was possible to live in a context where most people shared common language, heritage, religion, and lifestyle, today life is marked by the reality of worldwide interchange and exchange. Immigration, economics, internal and foreign politics, conflict, war, revolutions, and bold contemporary religious expressions fill our news and imaginations in ways that dramatically color the spiritual arena.

The experience of globalization is an ambivalent one. We see ourselves as increasingly linked, and yet those linkages reveal an often uncomfortable interdependence. For example, conflict and war seldom remain localized because of multiple and competing political and economic interests. What is more, conflict cannot be ignored because of the media coverage that reports conflicts, both at home and abroad. The same is true for reportage on issues like weather events and natural disasters, which we experience personally through media even when the events we are observing happen far away from ourselves.

Perhaps no aspect of globalization has more shaped the spiritual experience of twenty-first century persons than the realities of terrorism and religious extremism, which have emerged in the wake of global politics and the cultural exchange of the past century. Both scholars and politicians have a difficult time defining "terrorism" because the causes, players, and motivations that drive such acts of violence evade easy quantification. Religious terrorism typically involves individuals who self-identify with a religious group or movement and use that identity to justify acts of violence against noncombatants or civilian populations in public, nonwar theater contexts or locations (such as cafes, malls, public modes of transportation, and places of worship). They choose "innocent" populations in unsuspecting circumstances precisely to invoke a sense of terror, vulnerability, unpredictability, and dread. Terrorists use the threat of repeat acts of violence as leverage to broadcast awareness of a religious or political message, or to make a statement about dissatisfaction with culture in general. Because those who enact violence in this way feel a sense of self-righteousness or of divine motivation, they often do not see themselves as "terrorists" but rather as soldiers of God, freedom fighters, or warriors performing the ugly but necessary tasks of war.

The reasons for such behavior can be highly idiosyncratic, such as when the cult group Aum Shinrikyo released toxic gas into the Tokyo subways in 1995, motivated by the highly syncretistic amalgamation of religious apocalypticism of the group's leader, Shoko Asahara. Religious terrorism, however, may also be motivated by more mainstream religious ideology, such as when individuals read their sacred texts as mandating violence against nonbelievers and apostates. Jack Nelson-Pallmeyer, in his book *Is Religion Killing Us?*[5] explores the potential for Jews, Christians, and Muslims to derive such violent messaging from their holy books, not as extremists but rather as readers of traditions that are inherently riddled with violent storylines. He cites Exodus and the crucifixion of Jesus, for example, as biblical stories in which God uses violence to accomplish God's ends. The implication here is that if God can use violence, so too might human beings legitimately use violence when they are acting as God's agents. Among Christians, this perspective at times led to religious warfare, such as during the Crusades and the wars of the sixteenth century.

In Western society, religious terrorism today is most often associated with conflicts in the Middle East following the rebirth of Israel as a nation in 1948 and the subsequent suffering of hundreds of thousands of Palestinian refugees. Among the various responses to the Palestinian plight have been a number of high-profile acts of terrorism that have changed the way contemporary people think of interreligious knowledge, dialogue, and coexistence. Such attacks include the Munich massacre of Israeli athletes in 1972; the 1985 hijacking of TWA flight 847 by Hezbollah hijackers who were seeking the release of Muslims in Israeli custody; and the September 11, 2001 attacks in the United States that were purportedly a response to United States support of Israel and the unwanted presence and influence of U.S. interests in the Middle East. Religious conflict that has emerged in the wake of globalization is not bilateral, not exclusively a Judeo-Christian-Islamic phenomenon, and does not always involve crossing national boarders. Violent or extreme religious ideology contributes to people's perceptions of the value and purpose of religious belief. For some, the threat of terrorism has galvanized religious fervor. For others, such acts have diminished confidence in faith systems generally.

Globalization is also characterized by the massive and increasingly easy movement of people around the planet through immigration (coming into an area) and emigration (departing from an

---

5. Jack Nelson-Pallmeyer, *Is Religion Killing Us? Violence in the Bible and Quran* (Harrisburg, PA: Trinity, 2003).

area). Immigration contributed to the shape of the U.S. religious experience in its foundation and development: for example, some Protestant groups immigrated to North America in the seventeenth century to avoid religious persecution in Europe, and Irish Catholics immigrated to the United States to escape famine. So too today the migration of people to and from many parts of the world shapes religious exposure and experience. One contemporary effect is increased western interest in Hinduism and Buddhism.

Globalization has heightened popular awareness of the impact of immigration on religion. For example, we are now more aware of the effect of European Christian immigrants on Native American religion and the impact of the expansion of the United States into what is now Hawaii and Alaska on the native spiritual traditions of peoples there. Globalization has encouraged appreciation for formerly suppressed traditions.

Within Christian dialogue, the turn to a greater appreciation of native religious traditions reflects the powerful influence of liberation theology, which pays particular attention to historical oppression and suffering. Liberationist thought draws attention to the damage done to native cultures in the wake of European colonization. From a liberationist perspective, reclaiming what was lost religiously and culturally becomes not only a matter of justice; this recovery also holds the potential for an illuminating exchange and cross-pollination of spiritual insights and knowledge. In particular, recovery of native traditions and myths, such as the repeating theme of the great circle of life, has led to new language for thinking about environmental responsibility, the interdependence of human beings with other living things, and the common destiny of all life forms on our planet. The syncretistic blending of spiritual ideas from a variety of religious traditions and the flexible approach people have to their own religious heritages represents the shifting of values in contemporary Christian thought toward more open attitudes. While Christians face the challenge of accepting responsibility for past expressions of Christian practice that may have been harmful or destructive, they also have the opportunity to embrace the wisdom that surfaces from consideration of non-Christian traditions and the nondominant yet rich cultural practices of ethnically and culturally plural Christian populations.

Kateri Tekakwitha: A Native American Saint

Kateri Tekakwitha was born in April 1656 to a Mohawk Indian chief and an Algonquin mother. At birth, Kateri was named *Iorágade* (meaning "sunshine"). She was born in the village of Ossernenon (modern-day Auriesville, New York).

Iorágade's early childhood was tragically interrupted by the onset of a smallpox epidemic that ravaged her village in 1659, taking the life of her parents and brother and leaving the girl badly maimed and nearly blind. As was customary after a great loss, the tribe moved and established a new village in Caughnawaga (modern-day Fonda, New York), where Iorágade lived with her uncle until she was eighteen. Sometime after the tribe's relocation, Iorágade traded her birth-name for her permanent name (usually bestowed upon a child at around seven years of age). She was called "Tekakwitha," meaning "she pushes with her hands."

At the age of eleven, Tekakwitha met three Jesuit missionaries to her Mohawk village: Jacques Fremin, Jacques Bruyas, and Jean Pierron. Her uncle opposed the Christian missionaries and severely restricted Tekakwitha's contact with the priests. Despite the disapproval of her family, on Easter Sunday of April 1676, Tekakwitha was baptized, taking the common European Christian name *Catherine*, rendered Kaiatanoran in Mohawk. It is uncertain whether in life she ever answered to the truncated form "Kateri." Only months after her baptism, Kateri fled covertly in the middle of the night to a Jesuit mission on the Saint Lawrence River, just outside of present-day Montreal, Quebec, in order to escape persecution from her tribe resulting from her religious conversion.

During her brief life in what was then "New France," Kateri practiced an extreme penitential asceticism and mutual flagellation, whereby she endured physical duress that likely shortened her life. In 1679 she became the first known vowed virgin among the Mohawk Indians. In the following year, on April 17, 1680 during Holy Week, Tekakwitha succumbed to her weakened physical state. As she died, her friend Father Claude Chauchetière recorded Kateri uttering, "Jesus, I love you."

Kateri Tekakwitha: A Native American Saint (continued)

Upon her death, remarkable things were reported. Her smallpox-marked face is said to have remarkably smoothed over. Her friends began reporting visions and visitations by Kateri. A chapel was built on

the mission in her honor, which began attracting pilgrims who had heard of the miraculous things associated with her death. Tekakwitha became a stirring figure for the French Canadians, especially of Montreal, representing an elegant synthesis of their Indian and Catholic heritages. Beloved in both the United States and Canada (due to her places of origin and burial), Kateri became the object of petitions for her canonization by Catholics of both nations in the late nineteenth century. Catherine Tekakwitha was beatified by Pope John Paul II on June 22, 1980, and she was canonized by Pope Benedict XVI on October 21, 2012, making Kateri Tekakwitha the first Native American Roman Catholic Saint.

This tapestry, based upon a European-style painting of Kateri Tekakwitha produced near the time of her death, is symbolic of the enigma that is Kateri: Does she truly represent a Native American perspective, or European culture?

From the moment of her death, Kateri's story was colored by religious biographers who processed her life through the lens of medieval European saints. Her identity became highly politicized, informed by the agendas of her biographers (including writers representing the interests of the American church, French Canadian church, Jesuits, Native Americans, feminists, and environmentalists). Today, Kateri stands at the crossroads of the Old World and the New World, of the United States and Canada, of European Christianity and indigenous conversions.

Riccardo De Luca/MCT /LANDOV

Environmental and Ecological Movements

Another factor in contemporary spirituality is the emergence of nature-centered religious beliefs and practices. The return to nature spirituality is at least in part an outgrowth of the ecological movement, spurred on by devastating environmental disasters of the twentieth and twenty-first centuries that have raised awareness of the precarious nature of human technological enterprises as well as human vulnerability. Events like the Chernobyl nuclear power plant disaster in 1986, the Exxon Valdez oil spill in 1989, and today's debate about the ecological risks and benefits of hydraulic fracturing ("fracking") have sensitized people to the natural world and our place within it.

In light of dangers of disease and natural disaster (such as droughts, earthquakes, hurricanes, and flooding) and environmental decay due to human activity (including the range of activities from residential building, to industrial agriculture, to militarism and warfare), many people today are looking to wed their spirituality with environmentally conscious practices and lifestyles. This raises a challenge for Christian thought because Christian theology classically envisions salvation as ultimately not of this world but rather as belonging to heaven or the world to come. That is, salvation is typically understood as something experienced after natural, creaturely life has come to its end. Such thinking can have the effect of downgrading the value of natural existence, since hope is shifted away from preserving or saving this world toward a vision of a heavenly world-yet-to-come.[6] When natural, creaturely life is downgraded, nature and the earth itself can be disregarded.

The inclination to regard nature as a merely physical body (and specifically as a female body) to be dominated, controlled, and exploited by the hand of man is a deeply rooted and dangerous legacy of the Western scientific and technological paradigm.[7] There is

---

6. Feminist Christian writers have explored this notion at length. Two excellent treatments of this theological trajectory may be found in Rosemary Radford Ruether's *Gaia and God: An Ecofeminist Theology of Earth Healing* (San Francisco: HarperSanFrancisco, 1992) and Sallie McFague's *Models of God: Theology for an Ecological, Nuclear Age* (Philadelphia: Fortress Press, 1987).

7. See, for example, Carolyn Merchant, "'The Violence of Impediments': Francis Bacon and the Origins of Experimentation," at *http://nature.berkeley.edu/departments/espm/env-hist/articles/90.pdf.*

debate as to how much Christian belief in other-worldly salvation and human dominion over the earth (Genesis 1:28) are historically responsible for this problem. The question invites Christians to consider whether and in what ways their theologies may be ecologically irresponsible, detached, or isolationist. In response, one finds an emergent new trend in Christian spirituality that is intentionally striving for greater dialogue and action toward realizing the interconnection among all peoples (regardless of creed or ethnicity) and toward the achievement of environmentally responsible living. The renewal and recovery of theologically rich visions that bolster and encourage more holistic living include revisiting the theology of creation, incarnation, and sacraments, all of which are "embodied" (or physical, material) ways for thinking about encountering God and experiencing grace.

Liberation Movements

The rapidly changing conditions of human experience in the past century, especially the lifestyle boons that flowed from technological and economic advances, were not and are not experienced equally everywhere by everyone. Huge disparities in wealth, access, and opportunity reflected and continue to reflect systemic privilege and underprivilege between social sets: men and women; the dominant ethnic population and ethnic minorities; the physically able and disabled; heterosexual and LBGTQ+ persons; rich and poor; the political elite and the taxpayer; persons of the developed and of the developing worlds; the conglomerate and the individual. The dynamics of unrest between the privileged and underprivileged came to the revolutionary boiling point several times in the past century. These irruptions continue to reframe historical class biases, assumptions, and practices, both in their ideological as well as structural-political expressions.

A number of social "movements" or "revolutions" have contributed to the changing assumptions of people today, leading us to revisit our traditional beliefs about self, others, and institutions of power and leadership. In U.S. contexts, such movements include:

- Black civil rights movements, both of the 1950s–60s and ongoing
- Women's movements, beginning in the nineteenth century and persisting through the twenty-first

- Sexual revolution, beginning in the 1960s and persisting through today's changing legislation and medical practice surrounding human sexuality and child-bearing and rearing
- Gay rights revolution, beginning in the 1960s
- Mexican American and Chicano civil rights movement, beginning in the 1940s
- Asian American civil rights movement, beginning in the 1960s
- Birth of modern psychology and psychoanalysis, beginning in the late nineteenth century

Flowing out of the paradigm shifts wrought by these movements, changing assumptions have had an impact upon people's credibility, establishing a *zeitgeist* (a cultural mood or spirit of the day) that is frequently critical of past "truths." Today's zeitgeist, sometimes described as "postmodern," is characterized by a sense of insecurity, uncertainty, relativism, redefinition of "fact," and a flexible sense of reality. Even as today's younger generations express interest in grounded points of reference (classical Latin is a growing major among college students!), today's world is infused with a certain independence from tradition. This independence reshapes our sense of the spiritual, making us more autonomous, selective, and critical, not unlike "consumers" choosing from among spiritual options according to our preferences and experiences.

The Black liberation theology movement provides a case study of the transformation of the Christian thought tradition, driven by contextual concerns and open to new insights. Originating in the turbulent 1960s, this movement continues to seek to make Christianity applicable to African American experience by simultaneously pointing out Christian racism in the American context and exploring how the Gospel of Jesus can yet offer a viable response to that racism. Black theology examines the way the Christian message was used as an ideological support for slavery in the past, even while it perhaps unintentionally provided a message of hope and resistance for slaves. Black theology investigates the theological trajectories that can be meaningfully reclaimed in the present context to denounce the historical suffering of Black Americans in order to bolster a healthy racial climate in the present and to make more accountable the Christian theological program in general.

To cite one example, James H. Cone[8] studies the origin and use of gospel music in the African American worship community as a rhetoric of resistance. This music draws its inspiration for black liberation in part from the biblical Exodus of the Israelites, who also once were an enslaved population. By arguing that the Bible asserts God's persistent identification with and care for the oppressed, Cone concludes that God is on the side of the oppressed anywhere and everywhere that people suffer. In the American context, Black theology argues that a foremost biblical concern, and therefore a foremost Christian concern, is the elimination of racial tensions through the creation of a society that is truly just for all. The Christian message, then, must be primarily oriented toward social action in light of human suffering. This example shows how the liberationist theological turn represents a spiritually attuned and contemporarily relevant revisiting and reapplication of the tradition in context.

Conclusion

Contemporary spirituality is invariably formed in the dialogue between tradition and modern life. Today's world is a panorama of new ideas, blended experiences, technological developments, global vision, and change, all of which can lead to spiritual insight and illumination. The context raises questions that religious thought needs to address if faith is to be lived meaningfully in the present situation. Contemporary spirituality is informed by popular culture, a global ethic, an ecological foundation, and the human impulse toward liberation. As one of every four younger Americans disaffiliates from formal religious expression, Christian communities are called upon to explore what is forming and informing spirituality in lieu of traditional beliefs and practices. Perhaps the most effective way to engage this exploration is to ask values-based questions about the driving cultural forces, modes, technologies, and trends of the era. Why is this movie resonating so deeply with audiences? How does participation in this community, movement, or social group

---

8. James H. Cone, *God of the Oppressed* (New York: Seabury, 1975).

shape one's sense of friendship, loyalty, or service? How am I being formed or influenced in my self-concept, my perception of others, or in my sense of social responsibility for others locally and globally? By exploring these questions, the spiritual value of popular and contemporary source material and messaging comes into clearer focus, both in its alignments and departures from Christian thought and practice. Such investigations will help to clarify the values behind the confession, "I am spiritual but not religious."

Questions for Discussion and Review

1. What elements of pop culture strike you as overtly, covertly, or inadvertently communicating spiritual messages?

2. Do you derive spiritual value out of movies, songs, or games? If so, pick one example and discuss how and why it conveys spiritual content to you.

3. How do cultural sources for spirituality relate to traditional sources, such as reading the Bible or going to church? Are they complimentary? Are they mutually exclusive alternatives?

4. What effect do you think globalization has on spirituality in general? For example, is a global economy a spiritual concern? Why or why not?

5. What exposure do you have to people with different religious beliefs from your own? How does dialoging with others affect your own beliefs?

6. Is the environment a spiritual concern for you? Why or why not? Why might it be an important concern for Christian thinkers?

7. What liberation movements strike you as the most important today, both in your political context and in the political contexts of others? How might Christian theology respond to one or more of the liberation movements you have considered in this chapter?

8. How would you define contemporary spirituality? What does it mean to be spiritual but not religious?

Resources

Books

Cadorette, Curt, et al., eds. *Liberation Theology: An Introductory Reader*. Maryknoll, NY: Orbis Books, 1992.

Fisher, Mary Pat. *Living Religions*. 9th ed. Boston: Pearson Press, 2014.

Gottlieb, Roger S., ed. *This Sacred Earth: Religion, Nature, Environment*. 2nd ed. New York: Routledge, 2004.

Hessel, Dieter T., and Rosemary Radford Ruether, eds. *Christianity and Ecology: Seeking the Well-Being of Earth and Humans*. Cambridge: Harvard University Press, 2000.

Ruether, Rosemary Radford. *Integrating Ecofeminism, Globalization, and World Religions*. Lanham, MD: Rowman and Littlefield Publications, 2005.

Websites

Georgetown University Berkeley Center for Religion, Peace & World Affairs; "Globalization and the Growing Church," at *http://berkley center.georgetown.edu/essays/globalization-and-the-growing-church*.

Liberation Theologies, at *http://liberationtheology.org*

The Forum on Religion and Ecology at Yale, at *http://fore.research .yale.edu/religion/christianity/*.

The Society for the Study of Christian Spirituality, at *http://sscs.press .jhu.edu/about/index.html*.

Films

The Rise of Ecology: 10 Disasters That Changed the World. En compagnie des Lames Films. France, 2011.

Waste Land. Entertainment One Films. Ontario, Canada, 2011.

CHAPTER 11

Global Christianity

What to Expect

This chapter will explore aspects of Christianity in world context. Its goal will be to broaden the understanding of the scope, experience, and placement of Christian faith and practice through discussion of the following areas:

- Mission in Christian Tradition
- Colonialism and Post-Colonialism
- Christianity in the Global South: Africa, Latin America, Asia, and the Middle East
- Christianity in the Global North: North America and Europe

Mission in Christian Tradition

Christianity is a missioning religion. The word "mission" is derived from the Latin verb *mittere*, meaning, "to send." From the earliest days of the Christian movement, Christians believed themselves to be sent into the world as messengers of Jesus' story, teachings, and salvation. Especially in the letters of Paul in the New Testament, one sees early Christians concerned about not just living out their faith but also sharing it. Indeed, to live the faith was to share it. By the end of the first century, early Christians had carried the incipient faith from Jerusalem in Palestine to cities throughout Greece and Asia Minor and all the way to the heart of the empire in Rome.

The expansion of the Christian world through the work of apostles,[1] like Paul, brought culturally Jewish Christians into dialogue with converts drawn from Greek and Roman cultures. The result was a rich blending and borrowing of cultural cues, for becoming Christian did not (and could not) cancel out such cultural experiences as language, philosophical disposition, and social conventions. As Christianity spread, local culture persisted, sometimes in spite of the new faith, and sometimes as an inculturated aspect of it.

Once the Emperor Diocletian divided the ancient Roman Empire into Eastern and Western territories with capital cities in Constantinople and Rome in 285 CE, the respective Greek and Latin languages and cultures dominated the development of Christian thought and leadership in the two regions throughout the patristic era. Beginning in the third century, monastics were establishing communities and missions in Africa, Asia, Continental Europe, and the British Isles. These communities took on many of the cultural characteristics of those locations.

Sixth- to eighth-century ruins of the monastery on Skellig Michael, off the coast of Ireland. Monastic communities were often at the forefront of Christianity's advance into "pagan" Northern Europe.

---

1. Apostles were early followers of Jesus who went on missions to spread the message of Jesus after his death.

In a very important sense, Christian missionary activity could be interpreted as the foremost concern in the history of the church, from its beginning to the present. This is to say that the spread and growth of Christianity through its outreach constitutes the church's basic purpose. Yet missions constitute a discreet topic within church history, and its careful study would involve a vast cast of characters.[2]

Another way of studying Christian mission is to take a case study approach, examining how, when, why, and by whom Christianity was brought to specific geographic locations and population groups. Through studies like Henry Warner Bowden's *American Indians and Christian Missions: Studies in Cultural Conflict*,[3] one can analyze not only the broad course of Christian missionary history but also the specific outcomes of mission activity for particular peoples, both initially and over time.

Colonialism and Postcolonialism

Beginning in the fifteenth century, Europeans set out to expand their wealth and sovereignty in Africa, Asia, North America, and South America. This process, known as colonialism, involved the settlement or colonization of land and the acquisition of natural and human resources. European colonials benefited enormously from the wealth and power thus attained, while the conquered peoples lost their riches, resources, ways of life, traditional uses of land, and often their very lives. One of the farthest-reaching effects of European colonialism was the introduction of Christian belief and practice into lands previously unacquainted with Christianity. Colonizing missionaries, who accompanied or followed settlers and soldiers, saw themselves as furthering God's kingdom on earth. Tragically, the native beliefs and cultures of the missionized peoples were often held in low regard, with indigenous life being considered "uncivilized" and condemned as "pagan."

---

2. See, for example, Stephen Neill, *A History of Christian Missions*, 2nd ed. (New York: Penguin Books, 1991).

3. Henry Warner Bowden, *American Indians and Christian Missions: Studies in Cultural Conflict* (Chicago: University of Chicago Press, 1985).

The enlightenment philosopher Immanuel Kant exemplifies this attitude toward indigenous peoples. Kant argued for the compatibility of Christianity with rational morality, and attempted to prove that human nature requires the corrective cultivation of reason by offering up the example of native peoples' barbarity:

> That such a corrupt propensity must indeed be rooted in man need not be formally proved in view of the multitude of crying examples which experience of the actions of men puts before our eyes. If we wish to draw our examples from that state in which various philosophers hoped preeminently to discover the natural goodliness of human nature, namely, from the so-called state of nature, we need but compare with this hypothesis the scenes of unprovoked cruelty in the murder-dramas enacted in Tofoa, New Zealand, and in the Navigator Islands, and the unending cruelty (of which Captain Herne tells) in the wide wastes of northwestern America, cruelty from which, indeed, not a soul reaps the smallest benefit; and we have vices of barbarity more than sufficient to draw us from such an opinion.[4]

What is noteworthy about this passage is not so much that Kant identifies cruel or tortuous practices among tribal peoples but that he fails to identify similarly cruel or tortuous practices enacted in Christian nations and by Christian sovereigns. His example is typical of colonial era thinkers' skewed sense of Christian righteousness over and against non-Christian "paganism," an attitude that complicated and obscured the gospel message, vision, and action of Christian missionaries.

Although mission activity is a hallmark of the Christian faith, it raises critical moral questions about Christianity's placement in the world. Why should Christianity belong everywhere? What motives drove Christians of the past (and the present) to mission work? Do monetary gain or access to resources play a role? What political and governmental issues arise in world context? How might culture be preserved while also allowing for a syncretistic encounter with Christian faith?

---

4. Immanuel Kant, *Religion Within the Limits of Reason Alone* (New York: Harper Torchbooks, 1960), 28.

Postcolonialism is a term used to describe a contemporary approach to answering these questions.[5] It intends to provide a responsible lens for analysis, study, and action in the aftermath of imperialism, colonization, land usurpation, settlement, and the exploitation of human and natural resources in lands that bear a colonial legacy. Postcolonial analysis spans a variety of academic disciplines,[6] including theological studies. Here stakeholders attempt to move away from a Eurocentric vision of Christianity toward a new vision that is attentive to the complicated political, cultural, economic, and ethnic dimensions of peoples' lives. Particular attention is devoted to developments in the Global South, including Africa, Latin America, Asia, and the Middle East.

The Global South: Africa, Latin America, Asia, and the Middle East

Africa

Christianity initially came to Africa at the end of the first century of the Christian era, possibly brought by the evangelist Mark,[7] purported author of the Gospel of that name. Alexandria was a great hub city of the ancient world and the principle location of Christian immersion in Africa. In subsequent centuries, Christianity spread throughout cities in North, East, and West Africa. Africa produced some of the most influential contributors to patristic-era Christianity, including Origen of Alexandria, Tertullian of Carthage, Augustine of Hippo, Cyprian of Carthage, and Athanasius of Alexandria. Among the most notable developments of African Christianity was desert monasticism, a movement characterized by the hermit's reclusive life in the desert for the purpose of spiritual illumination. Monasticism,

---

5. See *www.postcolonialweb.org*, a website indexing a broad range of postcolonial authors and articles in world perspective, authored in English.

6. See also Rumina Sethi's *The Politics of Postcolonialism: Empire, Nation, and Resistance* (London and New York: Pluto Press, 2011).

7. This belief is derived from a letter of Clement of Alexandria "To Theodore," which suggests Mark visited Alexandria. See the *Dictionary of African Christian Biography* at *www.dacb.org/stories/egypt/markthe_evang.html*.

crystallized in the literary telling of Athanasius' *Life of Antony*, transformed the Christian spiritual experience. The legacies of the Coptic
Church (centered in Egypt), the Ethiopian Church, and the Eritrean
Church (in eastern Africa), moreover, are rooted in African Christianity of the first centuries. Islam halted the growth and persistence
of Christianity in Africa beginning in the seventh century, but these
three distinctive branches of early Christianity endure to this day.

In the colonial period, Christianity revisited Africa by way of
Dutch and Portuguese settlers. The Dutch settled in the seventeenth
century in Cape Town in southern Africa, forming the Dutch East
India Company. This settlement became an important rest stop for
ships sailing around Africa, and it also became a hub for the slave
trade of indigenous Africans to Europeans and American colonists.
By the eighteenth century, the British were coming to dominate
African colonization, leading to conflict over Dutch and English
land interests. In the nineteenth and twentieth centuries, such conflicts directly resulted in class division and racial segregation among
Africans and Europeans, political instability, and social crisis, such
as followed the independence movement of the Congo from Dutch
colonists in 1960. In the wake of colonial withdrawal, many African
nations experienced tremendous civil unrest as local principalities
vied for power. A prime example here is the British withdrawal from
the Sudan in the 1950s and the resultant Sudanese civil wars, which
ensued over the challenge of filling the British power gap.

Today, Christianity, represented by a variety of denominations,
is one of the two most-practiced religions in Africa, the other being
Islam. Between 1900 and 2000, Christianity garnered hundreds of
millions of new converts. The African countries with the largest
populations of Christians include Nigeria, D.R. Congo, Ethiopia,
South Africa, Kenya, Uganda, Tanzania, Ghana, Angola, and Mad-
agascar, totaling over five hundred million people.[8] Christianity's
expansion throughout Africa is largely attributable to Pentecostal
and spirit-driven (charismatic) evangelization, an approach that has
been far more successful than past models of Christian missionizing.
The unprecedented growth of Christianity in Africa, relative to the

---

8. Pew Research Center's "Religion & Public Life: Regional Distribution of
Christians," at *www.pewforum.org/2011/12/19/global-christianity-regions*.

slow growth of Christianity in Europe, indicates that the immediate future of Christianity is likely to be more African than European. As such, theologians anticipate a reverse model of mission practice, whereby Africans will be challenged to re-evangelize Europe and North America.

Latin America

Medieval Portuguese and Spanish monarchs colonized Latin America beginning in the fifteenth century, and with their settlers came Christian missions. In particular, the Spanish monarchs Isabel and Ferdinand enacted a program of stringent conquest over the indigenous peoples, imposing upon them not only feudal governance but also Christianity, and suppressing indigenous religious practices, such as those of the Aztec, Mayan, and Incan peoples. By the mid-sixteenth century, Christian convert Juan Diego, who became the first indigenous Catholic saint, famously began having visions of the Virgin Mary, which led to the founding of the Basilica of Guadalupe, now in Mexico City. Under colonial influence, native beliefs and customs were systematically eradicated or Christianized (such as the celebration of the Day of the Dead/Dia de los Muertos), and by the start of the nineteenth century, Latin America was largely Catholic, having been significantly missionized by Jesuits, Franciscans, Dominicans, and Augustinians.

Tradition asserts that the Virgin Mary miraculously left this image upon the cloak of a native Mexican peasant, Juan Diego, in 1531.

Colonialism in Latin America resulted in profound inequity, ongoing even to this day, in the distribution of wealth, land access, and resources, with the European-descended upper crust retaining the overwhelming preponderance of material comforts while indigenous Latin Americans experienced total impoverishment. Catholic Christianity, associated as it was with colonialism, at times rendered the Catholic Church complicit in this outcome. The nineteenth century was marked by extensive Protestant missions in Latin America. Successful Protestant missions found allies among those who wished to push back against colonialism and the ongoing vestiges of imperial power. In addition, Protestant Christianity has grown in Latin America due to nineteenth-century immigration from nations such as England and Scotland. In Brazil and Mexico, there are today hundreds of millions of Christians. In Columbia, Argentina, Peru, Venezuela, Chile, and Guatemala, there are tens of millions of Christians. Combined with Christian populations in North America (the United States and Canada), the Americas make up over eight hundred million Christians, the largest distribution of Christians in the world.[9]

Today, Christian thought coming from Latin America is characterized by its concerted effort at praxis-based evangelization, social justice, and service to the poor. Having taken stock of the radical poverty in Latin America, CELAM, the Latin American Episcopal Conference, convened two historic conferences in the mid-twentieth century (1968 in Medellin, Colombia and 1979 in Puebla, Mexico). They challenged the church to articulate a more just theology and ministry that would successfully attend to Jesus' basic mission of outreach to the poor, disenfranchised, and dispossessed. The Catholic hierarchy outside of CELAM, in particular, responded somewhat critically, fearful of the supposed Marxist leanings of the theology that the bishops were advocating. Nevertheless, the liberationist spirit of receiving and enacting the gospel message has found steady and, among many, enthusiastic support, including a new proponent in the person of Pope Francis, himself an Argentinian, whose apostolic exhortation *The Joy of the Gospel* beseeches renewed emphasis on action by Catholics (and indeed, all Christians) in response to world poverty.

---

9. Ibid.

Asia

Asia has experienced Christian missionary activity since the beginning of the Christian era. Thomas, identified in the New Testament as an apostle, is also the subject of a later Christian text called the *Acts of Thomas*, which tells the tale of Thomas' miraculous voyage to India. This apocryphal work may preserve some historical data, such as reference to a known Indian king of the era. The text suggests that Christianity reached Southern Asia in the first century; the persistence of Syriac Christian liturgical forms in India tends to support this claim. In any case, there is evidence of Christian presence in India from the time of the Council of Nicaea in the fourth century onward.[10] Christian presence in China is recorded from the seventh century onward.

In the nineteenth and twentieth centuries, India and China were attractive locations for missionary enterprises, fueled by Western commercial interests in Asia, such as the British opium trade of the nineteenth century. While mission activity in this era met with varying levels of success, the Christian populations of Asia have grown steadily over the past century, with Christians now constituting thirty-one percent of the region's religious makeup. Significant populations of Christians today are found in the Philippines, China, India, Indonesia, Australia, South Korea, Vietnam, Papua New Guinea, Kazakhstan, and Burma. In Papua New Guinea, the Philippines, and Australia, Christians constitute the religious majority.[11]

Christian experience in Asia is colored by location and context. For example, in China today, religious freedom is restricted to worship in spaces regulated and approved by the Chinese government. While millions of Chinese worship in government-registered churches, many millions more Christians worship each week in homes and nonchurch buildings. This situation complicates Chinese Christian experience and necessitates, among other things, a fluid ecumenical dialogue between Protestants and Catholics, who need to collaborate in the interest of tens of millions of Chinese Christians placed in a religiously challenging sociopolitical environment.

---

10. *www.newadvent.org/cathen/14658b.htm.*

11. Pew Research Center's "Religion & Public Life: Regional Distribution of Christians," at *www.pewforum.org/2011/12/19/global-christianity-regions.*

In his letter to Catholic Bishops, Protestant Pastor Aiming Ambrose Wang invites Catholics to collaborate with Beijing as well as with Protestant leaders to produce a truly ecumenical Chinese Christianity, founded on culturally sensitive translations of the Bible and rooted in shared doctrine. In the absence of this collaborative approach, the outcomes include idiosyncratic readings of scripture, the production of cult gurus, an elevation of personal authority in place of the historical church, weakened sacraments, and a diluted "kerygma" or Christian message. In this context, an ecumenical approach is necessary to serve the spiritual needs of Chinese Christians.[12]

This example illustrates how concretely Christian experience is changing. As Chinese Christians increasingly outnumber European or North American Christians, the need for an ecumenical Christianity becomes a central Christian concern as opposed to a marginal concern for missionaries. The once exotic missionary context is increasingly becoming the dominant context in which Christianity is experienced; this reality impels Christians today to reframe how they think about doctrine, including even the historical legacy of Christian divisions.

Middle East

It is ironic that the Middle East is a location for Christian growth and evangelization today, for it was Christianity's birthplace. Since then, however, the Middle East has undergone tectonic shifts in the religious makeup of the people.

From its rocky beginnings, Christianity came to dominate the late Roman Empire, but in the seventh century, Islam emerged. This new faith successfully spread from the Arabian Peninsula into the Holy Land and the territories of former Eastern Christianity, stretching all the way into Northern Africa. Islam became the religion of powerful and sophisticated rulers in these regions, and their kingdoms produced some of the greatest achievements of the medieval period. Medieval European Christians, however, saw Islam

---

12. Ambrose WANG Aiming, "Growth of Christianity in China: A Protestant Perspective of Ecumenical Challenges and Opportunities," at *www.yumpu.com/en /document/view/28974976/a-protestant-perspective-of-ecumenical-challenges-and-usccb*.

as a barrier to their economic and missionary interests. Christian efforts to "reclaim" the Holy Land from Islamic rulers, known as the Crusades, began in the late eleventh century and persisted in waves throughout the thirteenth century. These Crusades were marked by a savagery and violence that even today is not forgotten in Europe and the Middle East.[13] Islam remained dominant until the decline of the Turkish or Ottoman Empire in the late nineteenth and early twentieth centuries. By the beginning of World War I, the European interests of England, France, and Italy once again took root in Africa, paving the way for a renewal of Christian missionary activity in what had historically been Muslim lands.[14]

Today, Christians in the Middle East represent less than 1 percent of all the world's Christians. Egypt is home to roughly four million Christians. Sudan, Lebanon, Saudi Arabia, and Syria are each home to over one million Christians. The United Arab Emirates, Kuwait, Iraq, Qatar, and Bahrain each have populations of several hundreds of thousands of Christians.[15] Missionary activity in these regions today is largely oriented toward bolstering and supporting the already extant Christian communities. Due to foreign policies and political, military, and economic tensions, the history between contemporary Islamic states and Western nations is contentious. As a result, Islamic states today can provide a challenging and sometimes hostile environment for their minority Christian populations.

The Global North: Europe and North America

In the United States, there are over two hundred million Christians. In Canada, there are over twenty million Christians. Europe has a combined population of over five hundred million Christians, with

---

13. Consult the *Catholic Encyclopedia* for a summary of the Crusades at *www.newadvent.org/cathen/04543c.htm*. A brief history and interesting gallery of images of the Crusades in art may be found at the Metropolitan Museum of Art at *www.metmuseum.org/toah/hd/crus/hd_crus.htm*.

14. Justo L. González, *The Story of Christianity* (New York: Harper One, 2010), 2:431–36.

15. Pew Research Center's "Religion & Public Life: Regional Distribution of Christians," at *www.pewforum.org/2011/12/19/global-christianity-regions*.

the highest population centers in Russia, Germany, Italy, the United Kingdom, France, Ukraine, Spain, Poland, Romania, and Greece.[16] European Christians make up over 25 percent of the world's Christians; and it is European Christianity that has dominated the world Christian experience for most of the religion's history.

Under the Roman Empire, Christianity spread from Israel into much of Europe. Definitive aspects of Christian doctrine, liturgy, iconography, literature, and more were produced in Europe from the patristic era onward. Subsequently European Christians brought a European version of Christianity into Asia, North and South America, Africa, and the Middle East.

A question then emerges as to whether an elemental or fundamental Christianity can be discerned, or separated out from, or diversely embedded within a range of geopolitical contexts. A further question emerges concerning the growth or shrinkage rates of Christian populations in world context. What does it mean for a European-originated tradition to be on the decline in Europe while growing in Africa? Should Christians view this phenomenon as another form of colonial legacy, or as an authentic new experience of the good news of Jesus? Is the Christian message frozen in one cultural idiom, or can it be meaningfully reimagined in multiple cultural modes? Can the bread of communion be rice or tortillas, so to speak?

Conclusion

A postcolonial approach to thinking about global Christianity informs responsible scholarship about the historical, contemporary, and future ways in which Christians live in context. To apply this approach, students need to bear in mind several considerations that will help frame their analyses accountably and accurately, while minimizing bias and ideological preconceptions.

Christianity must be studied in light of its historical contexts. One must study Christian thought and practice of the past with a critical awareness of time and place, a sensitivity to the one who is

---

16. Ibid.

speaking, and an awareness of those whose voices and experiences have been omitted from consideration or participation.

Christianity must be evaluated in terms of its social position vis-à-vis governments and political powers. Students must attend to Christian experience relative to the dominant power structures in any given context. In Christian England in the thirteenth century, Christian kings held authority over all their subjects and thus could enforce Christian practice as a political goal. In contemporary Syria, the minority Christian population has recently experienced sporadic religious persecutions by hostile forces. The ecclesial-political relationship profoundly shapes the manner in which Christians have in the past or can today experience and express their beliefs in their daily lives.

Today, global voices challenge Christians everywhere to be open and dialogical with one another. As European dominance over Christian theological modes and expressions gives way to a global Christianity, voices of previously silenced people now are coming into the foreground. Those living with a colonial or neocolonial legacy, those marginalized by ethnic or social station, and women are now making their way into the mainstream of theological conversations. The insights they share about their historical experiences of oppression, violence, displacement, or depravation contribute valuable insight into the ways Christians might read anew and meaningfully apply the gospel in the world today.

Private Collection / Photo © Boltin Picture Library / Bridgeman Images

The anonymous Chinese artist of this Last Supper painting seems to be saying that the Christian faith need not be tied to European culture; Christianity can be thoroughly Chinese.

Likewise, gobal Christianity invites all Christians to be open to new models of church, interreligious and intrareligious dialogues, and religious syncretism. As the conversation broadens, Christians have increasingly become aware that they are not a hegemonic people, that is, they are not the dominant social or culture influence in the world. The breadth of social locations that are home for Christians invites Christians today to an experience of the faith that is much richer culturally. By incorporating and welcoming a vast range of local flavors and real-time relationships with others, both within and outside one's own ecclesial locality, Christians have an opportunity to envision a modern-day church that is truly universal even as it is a genuinely unified body of believers.

Questions for Discussion and Review

1. Describe the challenges of Christian missionary activity. Does mission work inherently involve conflicts of interest? Why or why not?

2. How might Christian ritual practice incorporate local customs and cultures while still retaining a universal character?

3. Globalization is a phenomenon that affects all aspects of modern life. What are some ways that the internationalization of economics or politics affect religion in general and Christianity in particular?

4. How is immigration changing Christian experience? Do you have a personal experience or example of meeting someone from another faith tradition or culture who has had an impact on your religious understanding?

5. Faith lived in context reflects not only the historical tradition but also the values and ideas of one's context. As such, the same phenomenon or idea could be received quite differently across a spectrum of cultural contexts—for example, women's leadership roles in church and society, or tolerance for a range of sexual lifestyles. Can you think of some areas of Christian thought and practice that might be contentious depending on location?

6. Is religion innately political? Why or why not?

7. Must Christian doctrine be tied to its cultures of origin? Why or why not?

8. What challenges and opportunities seem to be the most vital for global Christianity today?

Resources

Books

González, Justo L., and Ondina E. González. *Christianity in Latin America: A History.* New York: Cambridge University Press, 2008.

Isichei, Elizabeth. *A History of Christianity in Africa: From Antiquity to the Present.* Grand Rapids, MI: Eerdman's, 1995.

Jenkins, Philip. *The Next Christendom: The Coming of Global Christianity.* 3rd ed. Oxford: Oxford University Press, 2011.

Koschorke, Klaus, Frieder Ludwig, Mariano Delgado, eds., and Roland Spliesgart, contributor. *A History of Christianity in Asia, Africa, and Latin America, 1450–1990: A Documentary Sourcebook.* Grand Rapids, MI: Eerdman's, 2007.

Oden, Thomas C. *How Africa Shaped the Christian Mind: Rediscovering the African Seedbed of Western Christianity.* Downers Grove, IL: InterVarsity Press, 2007.

Pui-lan, Kwok. *Postcolonial Imagination and Feminist Theology.* Louisville, KY: Westminster John Knox Press, 2005.

Websites

Pew Research Center; "Religion & Public Life," at *www.pewforum.org.*

Pew Research Center; "Religion in Latin America," at *www.pewforum.org/2014/11/13/religion-in-latin-america.*

Pew Research Center; "The Global Catholic Population," at *www.pewforum.org/2013/02/13/the-global-catholic-population.*

Wayne A. Meeks. "Paul's Mission and Letters," at *www.pbs.org/wgbh/pages/frontline/shows/religion/first/missions.html.*

Films

Molokai: The Story of Father Damien. Vine International Pictures, Ltd., 1999.

The Mission. Warner Bros., 1986.

Glossary

Advent The opening season of the Christian liturgical calendar, consisting of the four Sundays preceding Christmas; also a term used to refer to the second coming of Jesus.

affective Nonverbal, noncognitive, emotional, or intuitive ways of knowing God.

agential An adverb used to describe freely elected action or one who has the capacity for acting as a moral agent.

alb A liturgical vestment that is worn by a minister, characteristically a white, ankle-length tunic with long, full sleeves.

Alexandria Prominent city in Ancient Egypt and one of the early, premier centers for Christian theological development.

altar The table in a Christian church used for the preparation and celebration of the Eucharist liturgical rites.

anabaptism A second baptism, undertaken during the Protestant Reformation, for adults who believed that their baptism as infants was invalid.

an-atman The Buddhist concept of no-soul, expressing the idea that human nature is fundamentally transient as opposed to permanent or eternal.

Antioch Ancient Greek city in modern-day Turkey and one of the early, premier centers for Christian theological development.

anti-Semitism Actions, postures, and beliefs that express hatred, violence, or discrimination against Jewish people, Jewish religion, or Jewish political identities.

apocalyptic A form of ancient Jewish and Christian literature involving special disclosure through revelation of that which is hidden, especially as it pertains to the end times.

Apocrypha Protestant term for a group of books written primarily by ancient Jews that were not included in the Hebrew Bible; Catholics term these books the deuterocanon.

apologia A defense of one's beliefs

apostles Early Christians commissioned to spread the gospel; the category overlaps the disciples of Jesus.

apostolic Connected to the apostles.

Ash Wednesday The Wednesday that marks the beginning of Lent.

Augustine Bishop of Hippo (395–430) whose writings have greatly influenced the development of Christian thought and belief.

autocephalous Self-headed, referring to church organizations in which their highest-ranking bishop does not report to any higher-ranking authority (such as the pope).

Babylonian exile Sixth-century-BCE exile of the biblical Israelites from their home in Jerusalem to Babylon.

baptism The Christian sacrament of initiation in which one is submerged in water or has water dribbled or poured over oneself in the name of the Father, Son, and Holy Spirit. Baptism may occur within a church (at a baptismal font or submersion tub) or in a natural body of water.

begetting The paternal term connotes the Father's eternal generation of the Son in the Christian Trinity.

begotten The filial term connotes the Son's eternal production by the Father in the Christian Trinity.

Bible For Christians, God's revelation and inspired word, comprised of the books of the Old (or First) and New (or Second) Testaments.

biblical studies Theology that studies God's revelation in history as it is recounted in the books of the Old and New Testaments.

Buddha Siddhartha Gautama from Nepal, born in the sixth century BCE, whose teachings led to the founding of the Buddhist religion.

canon The official list of books that comprise the Old and New Testaments of the Bible.

Cappadocian Fathers The fourth-century-BCE theologians Basil the Great, Gregory of Nyssa, and Gregory Nazianzus.

cardinal A high level bishop in the Roman Catholic Church who serves as a special aid to the pope. Together, the cardinals make up the College of Cardinals, which has the primary responsibility of electing a new pope.

caritas   Latin term for charity, a key theological virtue of Christian believers, expressing both love and charitable service and action.

Carthage   Ancient city in North Africa and one of the early, premier centers for Christian theological development.

Catholic Reformation   Sixteenth-century efforts on the part of the Roman Catholic Church to reform and refine its teachings and practices, culminating in the Council of Trent (1545–1563).

celibate   A person who rejects sexual activity as a sacrifice to God, often in the context of life in religious congregations as a monk or nun.

chalice   The cup of wine that is consecrated during the Eucharistic liturgy. In Catholic theology, the bread and wine become the body and blood of Christ.

Charism   A special gift or talent that God graciously bestows on a person to use in service to the church.

charismatic   Gifted by the Holy Spirit.

Charlemagne   Charles the Great, eighth-century French king who united western Europe and became its first Holy Roman Emperor in the year 800 CE.

chrismation   Term used by Eastern Orthodox churches for the sacrament of confirmation, which is performed by anointing with chrism oil and occurs simultaneously with baptism.

Christ   A title given to Jesus by the New Testament authors, deriving from the Greek word *Christos* ("anointed"), equivalent to the Hebrew word *Messiah*.

Christocentric   Centered on Christ.

Christological   Pertaining to the study of Christ.

church   The ecclesia or community of God's family, entered into usually through baptism.

Clement of Alexandria   Important second-century Christian theologian.

clergy   Ordained ecclesiastical leaders, termed "ministers" in most Protestant denominations, and "deacons," "priests," and "bishops" in the Roman Catholic and Orthodox Churches.

collegiality The relationship of equality among the bishops of the Roman Catholic Church.

colonialism Political act of conquest and control by one nation of another for the purposes of use and exploitation of natural and human resources.

communion A term to describe a community of Christian believers who are bound together by baptism, creed, and practice; also an alternate term for Eucharist or the Lord's Supper.

conclave The gathering of cardinals in the Roman Catholic Church for the purpose of electing a new pope.

Constantine Fourth-century Emperor of Rome who decriminalized Christianity, advocated for its imperial status, and convened the Council of Nicaea in 325 CE.

Council of Nicaea First ecumenical council of Christian bishops in Nicaea in the year 325 CE, noted most for producing the Nicene Creed and establishing the date for Easter in the liturgical calendar.

councils Assemblies of church leaders, historically convened to deal with issues or disputes about belief or practice.

creeds Formal, communal statements of belief.

Cyrus the Great Persian King who enabled the exiled Israelites to return to their homeland in Jerusalem beginning in the late sixth century BCE.

Dark Ages Negative term to describe the cultural decline that occurred in Europe after the fall of the Roman Empire, also known as the Middle Ages.

Darwin, Charles Nineteenth-century naturalist, known for authoring *On The Origin of Species* (1859) and popularizing the idea of evolution.

deacon In some denominations, an ordained minister of a lesser rank than a priest.

denominationalism The acceptance of many different Christian communions as legitimate expressions of God's church, despite differences in beliefs or practices.

diocese The territory pastored by a bishop, usually comprised of many parish churches.

disciple   One of the followers of Jesus.

doctrines   Official teachings or beliefs of the worship community.

Easter event   Jesus' Resurrection after his crucifixion.

Eastern Catholic   Autocephalous Eastern Rite Churches that remain in full communion with the Roman Catholic Church.

Eastern Orthodox   Also called the Orthodox Catholic Church, this is the communion of Christian churches originating largely from Eastern Europe, Russia, and the Middle East, whose ecclesiastical head is the Patriarch of Constantinople.

Eastern Religions   Any number of indigenous Asian religions, including Hinduism, Buddhism, Confucianism, Taoism, and Shinto.

Eastern Schism   Also called the Great Schism, the separation of Eastern Orthodox and Roman Catholic Christians, beginning in the eleventh century.

Easter Vigil   The first celebration of Easter, which takes place on the evening of Holy Saturday.

ecclesiology   Study of the church.

ecology   Biological study of organisms and their relationship to their environments.

economy   In Trinitarian theology, this term refers to God's action vis-à-vis creation, suggesting God's management of the "household" God made. Jesus' saving action is an integral part in God's economic plan.

ecumenical   Referring to unification efforts among Christian church communions who are separated from one another by historical circumstances or on account of ongoing theological or liturgical differences.

enlightenment   Buddhist notion of awakening to the fundamental truths of the universe, including the impermanence of human life.

epistemology   Branch of philosophy that deals with the discovery and study of truth.

eschatology   Study of the end times or the last days.

Eucharist   The sacrament of receiving the Body and Blood of Christ in Catholic theology. For many other Christian communions, Eucharist is alternatively referred to as Communion or the

Lord's Supper and symbolically represents Jesus' body or his sharing of bread and wine at the Last Supper.

evangelize To share and spread the good news or the gospel of Jesus.

exclusivism In interreligious dialogue, the perspective that one's own religious tradition is correct and other traditions are incorrect.

excommunicate To refuse participation within a church communion, including denial of the sacraments.

Exodus The second book of the Bible, which recounts the story of the Israelites delivery from slavery in Egypt.

first among equals A term that describes the ecclesiastical headship of the pope over other Roman Catholic bishops, which recognizes both the collegiality of all the bishops as well as the pope's supremacy as pastor over the entire Roman Catholic Church.

First Testament Another term for the Hebrew scriptures or Old Testament.

globalization Integration and interchange of services, goods, ideas, technologies, people, economies, and more across nations.

gnostic A term for many early Christian varieties that were eventually deemed heretical on account of irregular beliefs about either Jesus's humanity or divinity or both.

Good Friday The Friday before Easter Sunday and the day on which Christians solemnly remember the crucifixion of Jesus.

grace God's free offer of favor and forgiveness to sinners.

handmaid of theology Phrase describing the function of philosophy, popular in the Middle Ages.

heaven Christian conception of God's dwelling and the place where the blessed departed reside with God in eternity. Heaven may also be thought of as a state of being rather than a spatial-temporal location.

hell Christian conception of a location or state of being in the afterlife, characterized by the total absence of or alienation from God.

Hellenistic Referring to Greek culture or the influence of Greek culture.

heresy Religious beliefs contrary to or deviant from those normally or officially accepted as correct.

hermeneutics Term describing theories of interpretation, especially of biblical texts, that recognizes the complexity of the interface among readers, authors, and sacred texts, and seeks to understand the potential meaning and application of those texts.

historical theology The branch of Christian theology that explores the development of doctrine and practice over time.

homoousios Greek term meaning "same-substance," used at the Council of Nicaea in 325 to explain the oneness of the Father, Son, and Holy Spirit.

host The bread that is consecrated during the Eucharistic liturgy. In Catholic theology, the bread and wine become the Body and Blood of Christ.

humanism Intellectual movement during the European Renaissance that turned away from scholasticism and embraced new modes of human knowing, inspired especially by a return to classical source material.

icon A painted image of a holy personage, such as Mary or a saint, used for meditation, veneration, and prayer.

immanent In Trinitarian theology, refers to God's internal relationality.

Incarnation The embodiment of the Second Person of the Trinity in the fully human Jesus of Nazareth, through the miracle of Mary's virgin birth.

inclusivism In interreligious dialogue, the perspective that religious traditions other than one's own are also valid, such that one might benefit from the insights of those other traditions.

infallibility In Roman Catholicism, refers to the belief that the bishops in union with the pope are able to define without error doctrines of faith and morals; the pope is also believed to be infallible when proclaiming by definitive act a doctrine of faith and morals.

intertestamental The historical period between the writing of the Old and New Testaments.

Ishmael In the Bible and the Qur'an, Ishmael is the firstborn son of Abraham, born of Hagar, the handmaid of Sarah, Abraham's wife and eventual mother of Isaac. Ishmael is recognized as a lead patriarch in Islam.

Jesus movement Term used to describe the first followers of Jesus.

Jesus of faith Jesus as he is presented and reflected upon in the theological tradition; Jesus believed to be the Christ.

Jesus of history Jesus studied as a historical figure.

Judas Maccabeus Second-century Jewish leader who led the successful Jewish rebellion against the Seleucid king, Antiochus IV Epiphanes.

Judges Seventh book of the Bible, which recounts the period of Israel's history as a nation after the Exodus and before the period of the Israelite kingdom.

Kaaba Sacred mosque in Mecca, Saudi Arabia, believed by Muslims to have been built by Abraham. This building is the holiest physical location in Islam, known as the first human structure for the worship of God, and the destination of the Hajj pilgrimage, a journey undertaken by all able Muslims at least once in their lifetime.

laity Nonordained members of the church.

lectionary A book of readings from the Bible to be used in worship.

Lent In the Christian liturgical calendar, the forty-day period of fasting beginning on Ash Wednesday and concluding on Holy Saturday.

liberation theology The branch of theology that explores the sociopolitical implications of, for, and by Christian belief and practice on marginalized, impoverished, or suffering communities.

liturgical year The church calendar as observed in the more traditional denominations, marked by different seasons, including Advent, Christmas, Ordinary Time, Lent, Easter, and a second Ordinary Time.

Magisterium The teaching authority of the Roman Catholic Church.

mainstream Reformation Also called the magisterial Reformation, this term refers primarily to the reform movements of the Lutherans and Calvinists.

martyr A Greek term meaning "witness," applied to those who died for their faith, under persecution.

Maundy Thursday Also called Holy Thursday, the Thursday before Easter, when Christians remember Jesus' Last Supper on the eve of his crucifixion.

Messiah Hebrew term meaning "anointed one," used in reference to Israel's king and, in Christian and late Jewish thought, God's promised savior.

metaphysics The branch of philosophy that explores the nature of the world.

ministry A service activity carried out by Christian believers for the purposes of spreading Christian faith and the love of God.

missiology Theological study of the nature, meaning, purpose, and methods of Christian mission work.

mission In Christian perspective, the duty of every baptized Christian, who is sent out into the world to live, think, act, and share the good news of Christian faith.

missionary A person sent out to spread Christian faith through a variety of services, such as education, healthcare, or building projects, often in a foreign country.

moksha Hindu concept of liberation from the cycle of birth, life, death, and reincarnation.

monotheism Belief in a single God, as opposed to multiple deities.

morality Codes that direct one's behaviors in the discerning between good and bad actions, informed in Christian perspective by Jesus' example and church teaching.

Mother of God Equivalent of the Greek term *theotokos*, a title applied by many Christians to Mary, Jesus' mother.

Muhammad Prophet and founder of Islam in the seventh century of the common era.

Nag Hammadi City in Upper Egypt where a number of gnostic texts were discovered in 1945.

natural theology The branch of theology that investigates what can be discovered about God in nature alone, apart from special revelation.

Nestorian Term used to describe the theological perspective of the fifth-century bishop Nestorius, which emphasized the distinction and separateness of Jesus' divine and human natures.

nonsupersessionism Approach to Jewish-Christian relations that does not see Christianity as having displaced or replaced Judaism or the Jewish people but rather as coexistent responses to God's biblical revelation.

omnipotence A term used to describe God as all powerful.

omniscience A term used to describe God as all knowing.

Ordinary Time The times during the liturgical year that lie outside the seasons of Advent and Christmas and Lent and Easter. Ordinary time follows Christmas and precedes Lent; it also follows Lent and precedes Advent.

Origen Second- and third-century systematic theologian from Alexandria, noted for his speculative work *On First Principles*.

orthodoxy Beliefs or opinions that are held to be true or correct by the entire religious community.

orthopraxy Correct or faithful behaviors and applications of religious belief.

Palm Sunday The Sunday before Easter and the day in the liturgical year when Christians remember Jesus' arrival in Jerusalem in the week that he was crucified.

pastoral theology The branch of theology that explores the practical application of belief through the ministerial work of individual ministers and also the church as a community.

patristic era Post-biblical period of Christian doctrinal and ecclesial development (roughly 100–700 CE).

philosophy Literally the "love of wisdom," this is the effort to rationally understand the fundamental nature of the world, human knowledge and experience of the world, and the right manner of human action in light of that knowledge.

pilgrimage A spiritual or religious journey, often to a special location associated with a saint, sacred space, or location of historical significance.

pluralism In interreligious dialogue, the perspective that multiple religious traditions may mutually coexist, contain truth, and represent different experiences of revelation and paths to salvation.

polemical Refers to argumentative writings intended to dispute an opposing theological perspective.

pope The Bishop of Rome and the head of the Roman Catholic Church.

post-colonialism The ongoing but especially the immediate period following a period of colonialism, during which lands and peoples are controlled by an outside government or other foreign force.

processing A Trinitarian term used in the Nicene Creed to describe how the Holy Spirit is generated by the Father and the Son within the Trinity. In Easter Orthodox Christianity, the Holy Spirit processes only from the Father.

purgatory In Roman Catholicism, refers to an intermediate state between death and heavenly afterlife for those souls destined for heaven that are still in need of purgation of sin. Purgatory may be thought of as a state of being as well as a spatial-temporal location.

Qur'an The sacred, holy book of Islam, written in Arabic, believed to be God's divine revelation to the Prophet Muhammad through the angel Gabriel.

Reformed The tradition of Protestant theology originating in sixteenth-century Switzerland under John Calvin, and churches that follow that theological tradition.

relic An artifact or body part (usually a bone) from a deceased person noted for his or her spiritual qualities or significance to the religious community. In some forms of Christianity, relics are venerated as sacred objects and sought out by pilgrims.

religious order A community of like-minded Christians who live together under rules of common life.

Renaissance Period and movement of cultural rebirth in Europe beginning in the fourteenth century.

resurrection, general The Christian belief that the faithful will one day experience renewed life with Christ after their death.

Resurrection of Christ Belief that Jesus rose from the grave on the third day after his crucifixion.

revelation God's self-disclosure to humanity, especially revealing truths that cannot be discovered in nature or by reason and science alone.

rites Formal ritual practices or collections of practices; the standard practices or observances of a religious community.

rituals Formal, structured religious acts that are usually repeated according to a regular or customary pattern.

sacraments Ritual actions using physical materials like water, bread, and oil that are intended to both represent and confer grace on the recipient. Christian communions differ in regard to the number of sacraments they observe (if any) and how they believe the sacraments effectively communicate grace.

saint In some Christian communities, an exceptionally holy person or a person who dies in communion with a Christian church, having lived a life of Christian practice and belief.

samsara Hindu concept of the cycle of birth, life, death, and reincarnation until eventual liberation.

scholastic Type of highly systematized theology produced in the Middle Ages.

second coming In Christian belief, Jesus' expected return at the end of ordinary history to usher in the events of the last days and the full reign of God.

Second Testament Another term for the Christian scriptures or New Testament.

sectarian Refers to a faction or sect of believers that withdraws from interaction with other Christian groups.

sensus fidelium Latin for "sense of the faithful," expressing the idea that teachings have to be received as meaningful by the faithful in order to be genuinely authoritative.

Septuagint Ancient Greek translation of the Hebrew Bible, begun in the fourth and third centuries BCE.

Sermon on the Mount Jesus' famous teaching related in Matthew 5–7.

Shoah Preferred term among Jews for the Holocaust in Nazi controlled lands during World War II.

special revelation Revelation in the form of a special act of divine self-disclosure, such as a verbal message or a vision, as distinct from what can be inferred about God through nature (general revelation).

spirituality Personal appropriation of religious belief or subjective perceptions of divine presence, beauty, and truth as revealed in the natural world.

Sunnah Lifestyle and moral codes established by the Prophet Muhammad that Muslims should follow.

supersessionism The belief, now condemned by most Christian communities, that Christianity succeeds, fulfills, and replaces Judaism theologically and historically.

systematic theology The branch of theology that explores and articulates the internal coherence and rationale of the composite body of religious doctrines.

Tanakh Hebrew term for the Hebrew Bible, an acronym for the books of the *T*orah (Teaching of Moses), *N*evi'im (Prophets), and the *K*etuvim (Writings): TNK. The Christian Old Testament consists of the Tanakh, supplemented, in certain Christian denominations, with a few additional texts.

theological method The deliberate and self-conscious manner in which one undertakes theological investigation.

theological virtues Faith, hope, and charity.

Triduum The three-day period leading up to Easter Sunday, consisting of Holy (or Maundy) Thursday, Good Friday, and Holy Saturday.

universal pastor Another term for the pope.

Vernacular The ordinary or common language spoken in one's region or country, as opposed to ecclesial languages, such as Latin.

vestments Garments worn during the liturgy in some Christian denominations; colors and shapes often signify the status or rank of the minister as well as the liturgical season or special significance of the worship service.

Western Schism Period of contested papacy in Roman Catholicism between 1378 and 1417.

zeitgeist German term for the cultural sensibilities characteristic of a particular time and place.

Index

Note: The abbreviations *c*, *cap*, *f*, *i*, *m*, *s*, *t*, or *n* that follow page numbers indicate charts, captions, figures, illustrations, maps, sidebars, tables, or footnotes, respectively.

Nelson-Pallmeyer, Jack, 220
Neoplatonism, 126
Nestorianism, 83, 85, 131–32, 161
Netherlands, The, 137t
Nevi'im ("prophets"), 36n2, 37t
New Testament. *see also* Bible, the
  Anabaptists and, 91
  canons of, 41t, 83
  defined or described, 39–44
  diversity and, 19, 123
  economics and, 197
  Jewish law and, 175
  justice and, 199
  manuscripts, 46, 46i
  origins of, 19n1
  prayer and, 151
  theologizing and, 18
  timeline of, 43f
  unity and, 141
New Testament period, 72, 77–80
Nicene Creed, 85, 100, 101, 106–7
  Church and, 113–14
  Eastern Christianity and, 132
  Holy Spirit and, 108
  humanity of Jesus and, 113s
  salvation and, 116
Nineveh, 48, 73m
non-Christian religions, 95,
  171–74, 190, 202s, 221. *see also*
  indigenous religious traditions;
  missionaries
nonsupersessionism, 177
Normans, 87cap
North America, colonial, 92
nuclear missiles, 205i
nuns, 167, 199i. *see also* monasticism; Ursulines

O

Old Testament. *see also* Bible, the;
  Hebrew Bible; prophets
  canon, 38t, 74n4

  defined or described, 35–39
  early Christians and, 19n1
  God-talk and, 17–18
  Judaism and, 36, 37t–38t, 72n3
  New Testament and, 78–79
  overview, 33–38
  reason and, 60s–61s
  Sabbath and, 160
  timeline, 38t–39t
Old Testament period, 72–76,
  74–77
omnipotence, 102, 111
omniscience, 102–3
On Christian Doctrine (Augustine),
  218
one and uniquely divine, 102, 108,
  110–11, 180
orans, 150cap
Ordinary Time, 158, 159
Oriental Orthodox churches, 132
Origen of Alexandria, 82, 234
Orthodox Christianity. *see also*
  Eastern Orthodox Church
  liturgical year and, 157
  metaphors for church and, 114
  New Testament canons and, 41t
  Old Testament canon and, 36,
  37t–38t
  religious communities and, 167
  sacraments and, 115s–116s
  saints and, 160
Orthodox Judaism, 175t
orthodoxy, 26
orthopraxy, 26

P

paganism, 85
Palestine, 38t, 39t, 45m, 76, 104,
  125, 178
Paley, William, 208s
Palm Sunday, 158
papal banner, 87cap